# MAKING QUALITY CRITICAL

Recent years have seen an exponential growth in quality initiatives. In common with other management techniques and programmes, there has been a considerable hyping of their potency and effectiveness. Yet there is a marked dearth of critical studies of the area. Just how effective are these programmes? What are the challenges associated with their implementation?

This collection offers an exploration and assessment of the operation of quality initiatives. Leading contributors explore the assumptions and practicalities of approaches to quality, covering both public and private sectors. Providing a counterbalance to the largely prescriptive literature on quality, they look at a number of issues and problems associated with quality initiatives, including the tensions between policy and practice, the benefits and costs to employees and the role of training in the organization of quality programmes.

The studies presented in this book cover a wide range of contexts and initiatives. The critical nature of the essays provides an alternative to conventional wisdom in the field, which often tends to assume quality is universally beneficial. *Making Quality Critical* will therefore be invaluable for students, practitioners and teachers who currently lack access to more analytical cases of quality management.

**Adrian Wilkinson** is a Lecturer in Human Resource Management at Manchester School of Management, UMIST. **Hugh Willmott** is Reader in Organizational Studies, also at the Manchester School of Management, UMIST.

# CRITICAL PERSPECTIVES ON WORK AND ORGANIZATION

## General Editors: David Knights, Chris Smith, Paul Thompson and Hugh Willmott

Since the appearance of Braverman's *Labour and Monopoly Capital*, the impact of labour process analysis has been experienced in the fields of industrial sociology, organization theory, industrial relations, labour economics, politics and business studies. This series examines diverse aspects of the employment relationship across the range of productive and service industries. Some volumes explore further the established terrain of management control, the intensification of work, the deskilling of labour. Others are attentive to associated topics such as gender relations at work, new technology, workplace democracy and the international dimensions of the labour process.

### LABOUR IN TRANSITION
The Labour Process in Eastern Europe and China
*Edited by Chris Smith and Paul Thompson*

### SKILL AND CONSENT
Contemporary Studies in the Labour Process
*Edited by Andrew Sturdy, David Knights and Hugh Willmott*

### GLOBAL JAPANIZATION?
The Transnational Transformation of the Labour Process
*Edited by Tony Elger and Chris Smith*

### RESISTANCE AND POWER IN ORGANIZATIONS
*Edited by John Jermier, David Knights and Walter Nord*

# MAKING QUALITY CRITICAL

## New Perspectives on Organizational Change

*Edited by Adrian Wilkinson and*
*Hugh Willmott*

London and New York

First published 1995
by Routledge
11 New Fetter Lane, London EC4P 4EE

Simultaneously published in the USA and Canada
by Routledge
29 West 35th Street, New York, NY 10001

© 1995 Adrian Wilkinson and Hugh Willmott

Typeset in Garamond by J&L Composition Ltd, Filey, North Yorkshire
Printed and bound in Great Britain by
Mackays of Chatham PLC, Chatham, Kent

*British Library Cataloguing in Publication Data*
A catalogue record for this book is available from the British Library

ISBN 0–415–11569–8 (hbk)
ISBN 0–415–11754–2 (pbk)

*Library of Congress Cataloging in Publication Data*
Making quality critical: new perspectives on organizational change
edited by Adrian Wilkinson and Hugh Willmott.
p.  cm. — (Critical perspectives on work and organization)
Includes bibliographical references and index.
ISBN 0–415–11569–8. — ISBN 0–415–11754–2
1. Total quality management.  2. Organizational change.
3. Employee empowerment.  I. Wilkinson, Adrian, 1963–
II. Willmott, Hugh.  III. Series.
HD62.15.M348 1994
658.5′62—dc20      94–10912
CIP

# CONTENTS

*List of contributors*                                              vii
*Acknowledgements*                                                 xii

INTRODUCTION
*Adrian Wilkinson and Hugh Willmott*                                  1

1 FROM QUALITY CIRCLES TO TOTAL QUALITY
  MANAGEMENT
  *Stephen Hill*                                                    33

2 IDEOLOGY, QUALITY AND TQM
  *Alan Tuckman*                                                    54

3 QUALITY THROUGH MARKETS: THE NEW
  PUBLIC SERVICE MANAGEMENT
  *Kieron Walsh*                                                    82

4 QUALITY MANAGEMENT AND THE
  MANAGEMENT OF QUALITY
  *Janette Webb*                                                   105

5 GOVERNING THE NEW PROVINCE OF
  QUALITY: AUTONOMY, ACCOUNTING AND
  THE DISSEMINATION OF ACCOUNTABILITY
  *Rolland Munro*                                                  127

6 TOTAL QUALITY MANAGEMENT AND
  PARTICIPATION: EMPLOYEE EMPOWERMENT,
  OR THE ENHANCEMENT OF EXPLOITATION?
  *Louise McArdle, Michael Rowlinson, Stephen Procter,*
  *John Hassard and Paul Forrester*                                156

7 MANAGING QUALITY IN THE
  MULTI-CULTURAL WORKPLACE
  *Patrick Dawson*                                                 173

8 TQM, THE NEW TRAINING AND
INDUSTRIAL RELATIONS
*Ken Roberts and Yvonne Corcoran-Nantes*                    194


9 EMPOWERING THE 'QUALITY WORKER'?: THE
SEDUCTION AND CONTRADICTION OF THE
TOTAL QUALITY PHENOMENON
*Deborah Kerfoot and David Knights*                         219

*Index*                                                     240

# CONTRIBUTORS

**Yvonne Corcoran-Nantes** is a lecturer in Politics and Women's Studies at the Flinders University of South Australia. She has written on gender and work, employment training and skill formation in Britain and on gender and politics in Latin America and the Third World. She is currently working on a UN report on the changing status of women in Central Asia and a book on gender and grass-roots politics in Brazil.

**Patrick Dawson** is Senior Lecturer in Organization Studies at the University of Adelaide. The main areas in which he has conducted research comprise the financial strategies of low-income households; organizational culture; management strategy and industrial relations; new technology and management techniques; collaborative projects and the development of computer software; and the historical emergence and changing role of the industrial supervisor. His current research is on quality management, technology and workplace change. He is author of *Organizational Change: A Processual Approach* (Paul Chapman Publishing, 1994).

**Paul Forrester** is Lecturer in Production Management in the Department of Management at Keele University. His principal research interests lie in the areas of operations systems design and organization, and his research has been funded by the SERC and ESRC to investigate the management and organizational issues of flexible manufacturing and computer-integrated manufacturing. More recent work has focused on international comparisons in the management of technology and he is involved in EC and British Council funded work in Eastern Europe, China and South East Asia.

**John Hassard** is Professor of Organizational Behaviour in the Department of Management of Keele University. He previously taught at the London Business School and Cardiff University. His publications include *Time, Work and Organization* (Routledge, 1989, with others), *The Theory and Philosophy of Organizations* (Routledge, 1990, co-edited), *The Sociology of Time* (Macmillan, 1990, edited) and *Sociology and Organization Theory* (Cambridge University Press, 1993). His research interests lie in organization theory and industrial sociology.

**Stephen Hill** is Professor of Sociology at the LSE. He has published several papers on the organizational and social dimensions of quality management over the last decade. His current research interests include the sociology of management and employee relations, organizational restructuring and the management of new technology, and the development of new systems of industrial relations in the former socialist societies. He has written widely, including several books on ideology and the sociology of employment.

Having recently completed a doctorate at Manchester, **Deborah Kerfoot** is now Lecturer in Organizational Behaviour in the School of Business and Economic Studies at the University of Leeds. Her research interests and publications are in the fields of sociology and critical studies of management, work and organization; empirical research on management and managing practices; and gender and sexuality in organizations.

**David Knights** is Professor of Organizational Analysis in the Manchester School of Management at the University of Manchester Institute of Science and Technology. He has conducted research and published in the following areas: industrial relations, equal opportunity, labour process, management strategy, the management of information technology and regulation in financial services. His current research is on financial services and on inter-organizational relations and the use and development of IT. He is co-author of *Managing the Multi-Racial Workforce*, *Managing to Discriminate* and *Managers Divided* and co-editor of a number of books on the labour process.

**Louise McArdle** is Lecturer in Business Organization in the Department of Organization Studies at the University of Central

Lancashire. Research interests include total quality management and debates on human resource management and industrial relations.

**Rolland Munro** is Reader in Accountability at the Department of Management, University of Keele. Drawing on his ethnographies of large organizations, he has published a number of articles reworking notions of 'the social' in ways that avoid traditional dualisms, such as self and society or people and technology. His work challenges the 'partition' solution of teaching organization behaviour and accounting as separate management disciplines, and he is currently editing a book *Power, Ethos and Accountability* for Chapman and Hall, drawing together leading contributors to the emerging field of studies in accountability.

**Stephen J. Procter** is Lecturer in Organizational Behaviour in the School of Management and Finance, University of Nottingham. His research interests include the labour process, the flexibility debate and the organization of manufacturing production. He is at present writing a book on the recent performance of the UK economy.

**Ken Roberts** is Professor of Sociology at the University of Liverpool. Much of his research into employment and labour markets has focused upon young people. He directed the Liverpool-based enquiry in the Economic and Social Research Council's 16–19 Initiative, and is currently investigating the impact among young people of the reforms in Eastern Europe and parts of the former Soviet Union.

**Michael Rowlinson** is Lecturer in Organizational Behaviour in the School of Management and Finance at the University of Nottingham. His current research interests include organizational economics and organizational theory, the labour process debate, flexibility and the flexible firm. His publications include C. Smith, J. Child and M. Rowlinson, *Reshaping Work: the Cadbury Experience* (Cambridge University Press, 1990).

**Alan Tuckman** is Senior Lecturer in Sociology at the University of Humberside in Hull where, among other things, he teaches on the MSc in Quality Management. His research interests are currently on new management strategies and working practices in the chemical industry in the UK, and on foreign investment in the bicycle industry in China. He has published work on the subcontracting and construction industries, and on Thatcherism, as well as TQM. He is also a member of the Centre for Industrial Policy and Performance at the University of Leeds and is involved in writing a text, with others, on *Industrial Policy in Britain*.

**Kieron Walsh** is Professor of Public Sector Management at the University of Birmingham. His principal interest is the impact that the introduction of market principles will have upon the operation of the public services. He is conducting research into the use of contracts in health, social care and local government; management change in the public sector; and the operation of networks in local governance.

**Janette Webb** is Senior Lecturer in the Department of Sociology at the University of Edinburgh. She has conducted research and published in industrial relations, equal opportunity, gender and employment and the management of expertise. Her current research is on the sociology of management and she has recently co-authored a book, *Organisational Change and the Management of Expertise*.

**Adrian Wilkinson** is a Lecturer in Human Resource Management at Manchester School of Management, UMIST. He has written widely on industrial relations and human resource management. The main areas of his research interests are quality management, employee involvement and HRM in financial services. He is currently the principal investigator in a three-year project examining quality and the human resource dimension funded by the Engineering and Physical Sciences Research Council (EPSRC).

**Hugh Willmott** is Reader in the Manchester School of Management at UMIST. His research has been focused in the areas of organizational analysis and different aspects of the accounting industry. He is currently working on a number of conceptual and empirical projects whose common theme is the critical examination of the changing organization and management of work in modern society. His most recent books are *Labour Process Theory* (Macmillan, 1990 co-edited with David Knights), *Critical Management Studies*

(Sage, 1992, co-edited with Mats Alvesson) and *Skill and Consent* (Routledge, 1992, co-edited with Andrew Sturdy and David Knights). *Making Sense of Management* (Sage, co-authored with Mats Alvesson) is in press.

# ACKNOWLEDGEMENTS

We would like to acknowledge the ESRC for funding the project 'Managing Quality Strategically: Change Initiatives and HRM in the Financial Services' (R000234403) which has facilitated the preparation of this volume. We would also like to thank our collaborators on this project, David Knights, Deborah Kerfoot and Glenn Morgan, for their advice, encouragement and support. Finally, we thank the contributors to the volume for putting up with the pressures and deadlines we sought to impose upon them, and to Rosemary Nixon and Laura Large at Routledge for their assistance with the volume's speedy preparation. We would also like to thank Michelle Brierley and Mary O'Brien for their contribution in coordinating the communication with contributors and retyping our manuscripts.

# INTRODUCTION

*Adrian Wilkinson and Hugh Willmott*

'This word has no meaning. Use it as often as possible.' Ascribed to post-modernism, this counsel is also attributable to current management practices and to fashionable management gurus. 'Quality' has been attributed to all kinds of management techniques and initiatives. The appeal of the term is that it can be used to legitimize all sorts of measures and changes in the name of a self-evident good.

It will come as little surprise, therefore, to learn that quality initiatives are reportedly occurring in three-quarters of companies in the United States and the United Kingdom (*The Economist*, 1992; Wilkinson *et al.*, 1993), or to learn that such initiatives are supported enthusiastically by 90 per cent of chief executives who regard it as 'critical' for their organizations (McKinsey, 1989). The diverse and fluid meanings ascribed to quality initiatives and programmes make it a seductive and slippery philosophy of management (Pfeffer and Coote, 1991). They also make it an elusive topic of study.

This elusiveness partly explains why there are so many books that champion the cause of 'quality management' (e.g. Oakland, 1989; Drummond, 1992; Bank, 1992; Dale and Cooper, 1992), yet so few studies that address its actual meaning, or reflect upon its practical implementation or social significance (see Xu, 1993, and Rippin, 1993 for exceptions to this rule). As Rees (1993) has observed of the literature on total quality management (TQM),

> There is usually very little discussion of the problems that managers may experience in applying the techniques, and little or no information about how TQM is perceived by employees. Moreover, the principles of TQM are assumed to

1

be universally applicable, and one organization is assumed to be much like any other.

(Ibid.: 2)

To this complaint may be added the observation that leading advocates of quality management are disinclined to refer to previous management literature – or, indeed, to reference anything outside of the quality management field.[1] Critical of such failings, management academics who are not themselves busy promoting 'the quality revolution' (Oakland, 1989: x) have been inclined to be contemptuous of its triviality, dismissing ideas about quality as merely the latest in a long line of management fads or 'snake oils'. One consequence of this disdain has been that the quality gurus have enjoyed a virtual monopoly over the definition and discussion of this field. Studies that begin to offer a more detached and reflective consideration of its claims have been the exception, (e.g. Garvin, 1988; Wilkinson and Witcher, 1991; see also Webb in this volume for an overview).

Provoked both by the rapid growth and influence of quality initiatives and by the dearth of non-prescriptive studies in this expanding field, this volume is intended to provide a set of readings for students, managers and other employees with an interest in the nature and effects of quality initiatives.[2] In this introductory chapter, we present a general but critical orientation to the field before providing summaries of the other chapters.

## THE MEANING OF QUALITY MANAGEMENT

The word 'quality' conveys the suggestion of subtle and nebulous factors that are not readily quantifiable – that is, factors that are not easily concretized, measured or tied down. Arguably, its vague, but nonetheless positive, associations make the appeal of 'quality' immediate and extensive:

> Quality can be a compelling value in its own right. It is robust enough to pertain to products, innovations, service standards, and calibre of people. . . . Everyone at every level can do something about it and feel the satisfaction of having made a difference. Making products that work, or providing first-class service, is something we can identify with from our own experience.
>
> (Pascale, 1991: 248)

2

Perhaps the most obvious difficulty, and the principal source of confusion, in the field of quality management stems from a conflict of meaning between, on the one hand, an established, commonsensical association of quality with superior or exceptionally high standards of goods and services, and on the other hand, the quality gurus' conception of quality as meeting reliable and consistent standards – standards which may or may not be commonsensically identified as exceptionally high.

From the quality 'expert' perspective, any good or service can legitimately receive the seductive sobriquet of 'quality' so long as it consistently meets the standards – however 'inferior' these may be – that beat the competition within its market niche. Or, as Crosby (1980: 14–15), one of the leading quality gurus, puts this argument, 'The first erroneous assumption is that quality means goodness, or luxury, or shininess, or weight. . . . That is precisely the reason we must define quality as "conformance to requirements" if we are to manage it. . . . If a Cadillac conforms to all the requirements of a Cadillac, then it is a quality car. If a Pinto conforms to all the requirements of a Pinto, then it is a quality car.'

The same logic is applied to the method of organizing work. For quality management gurus, 'quality' does not necessarily mean the attainment of exceptionally high standards with regard to employees' terms and conditions of work. Instead, it means the development of 'uniform and dependable' work practices that are congruent with delivering products or services at low cost with a quality suited to the market (Deming, 1986). The objective of 'continuous improvement' does not necessarily mean the steady amelioration of working conditions in the direction of improved pay, fringe benefits, career prospects, quality of working life, etc., although these may be facilitated by the gains in productivity achieved by successful quality initiatives. Rather, for the quality gurus, quality means whatever methods of work and organization generate low cost, dependable products and services.

In pursuit of 'quality' methods of manufacture and service delivery, some advocates have tied the meaning of quality management closely to a particular approach or technique – for instance, quality control, quality assurance and quality circles (see Tuckman, in this volume; Hill, 1991 and in this volume). Others have sought to reserve 'quality' for the description of a more holistic programme, such as Total Quality Management (see Tuckman, in this volume). The meaning of quality has been associated with a range of philosophies and practices. Not infrequently, quality initiatives contend that internal and external customer requirements dictate such changes, and that failure to respond positively to such requirements will undermine job security and promotion prospects:

> the key to motivation *and* quality is for everyone in the organization to have well-defined customers – an expansion of the word, beyond the outsider that actually purchases or uses the ultimate product or service, to anyone to whom an individual gives a part, service or information.
>
> (Oakland, 1989: 4)

What quality initiatives broadly share is a concern to encourage each employee – the term includes managers as well as office or shopfloor workers – to take responsibility for the continuous improvement of production and delivery processes. In general, this emphasis upon responsibility is directly concerned with the elimination of waste and removing the duplication of effort through changes in job design and work process. It does not necessarily extend to the enhancement of working conditions or greater control over key decisions about investment, the fundamentally hierarchical division of labour, or the organization of work.

## THE HISTORY AND SIGNIFICANCE OF QUALITY

### The Japanese connection

Challenged and inspired by the success and speed of Japanese domination of major world markets, the management of quality has been widely identified as a key, and not infrequently as *the* key, to securing a market advantage in a highly competitive and rapidly changing global economy. The quality of goods and services, as well as their price, has increasingly been identified as a critical source of commercial success, the firm of Toyota being the icon of quality management.

Ironically, during the 1950s, 'Made in Japan' was synonymous in the West with cheap and shoddy consumer goods. This reputation was, of course, deceptive: it obscured the fact that Japanese industry was being reconstructed to compete, in terms of quality

4

for price, in the emergent global markets for high-value consumer goods such as cars and electronic equipment. The prowess of Japanese firms in major world markets only became fully apparent during the late 1970s and the 1980s. There is indeed a double irony in the recent quest by Western organizations to improve quality, largely in response to the Japanese challenge, for many of the basic techniques of quality management were originally brought to Japan by Western academics and consultants, who found that their ideas were better appreciated there than in the West. One of the quality gurus, Juran (1993), has suggested that the long-established Japanese tradition of fine craftsmanship and attention to detail through miniaturization, etc. meant that his ideas about how wastage rates could be substantially reduced and the reliability of manufacturing processes improved were well received (see also Deming, 1986: 2 *et seq.*). Subsequently in the West there was increasing interest in the 'secrets' of Japanese success and Peters and Waterman's best-selling *In Search of Excellence* (1982) sought to identify ways of responding to the Japanese challenge. While the contribution of a strong corporate culture was widely taken as Peters and Waterman's chief lesson, it is relevant to note that they also stressed the importance of quality, in a way that anticipated the writings of more recent champions of quality management:

> Cost and efficiency, over the long run, *follow from the emphasis on quality*, service, innovativeness, result sharing, participation, excitement, and an external problem-solving focus that is tailored to the customer.
>
> (Ibid.: 321; emphasis added)

## From mass production to continuous improvement

Many decades earlier, Henry Ford – seeking to maximize efficiencies derived from economies of scale – derived a recipe for commercial success which had involved paying production-line workers, who performed semi-skilled (boring, physically demanding and repetitive) tasks, an ostensibly generous five dollars a day. This deal dramatically celebrated a shift from craft production to mass consumption as a primary source of status and identity for working-class people. Considerations relating to the lived experience of working life – in terms of job security and/or the autonomous exercise of discretion – were subordinated to the goal of winning (through unionization, if necessary) a higher wage to spend on mass consumer goods, including Ford's cars – a pattern that was fuelled during the post-war boom and beyond.

During the 1970s and 1980s, the continuing emphasis upon volume production and value for money was complemented by 'quality' (and, most recently, mass customization – Boynton *et al.*, 1993) as a new means of gaining competitive advantage in mass markets. With this development, increased attention is currently being paid to the flexibility and continuous improvement of production processes, and to the careful selection and training of multi-skilled labour. Employees are not expected or even encouraged to derive a sense of purpose and esteem from the lived process of crafting goods of exceptionally high quality; but neither are they required mindlessly to comply with (Fordist) routines exclusively designed by others. Rather, quality initiatives seek and reward employees who maximize their contribution to the continuous improvement of methods for producing goods and providing services that are of a quality suited to the market. Although the requirements of the market have changed, work continues to be defined in terms of the marketability of what is produced.

## Rolling out the quality revolution

During the 1980s, the plausibility of quality initiatives was bolstered by a broader shift in political philosophy across the Western world that promoted the sovereignty of the individual as a consumer and championed the market as a means of securing and protecting this freedom (see Webb, in this volume). At the heart of this moral and cultural movement was an elevation of the 'virtues of self-reliance and initiative through participation in markets of various types' (Binns 1993: 5, see also Tuckman and Webb, both in this volume). In its wake, 'quality' has been ascribed to almost any initiative that aspires to reduce waste and delay, including reforms within the public sector where, in the UK, there has been a widespread move to create quasi-markets and 'internal customers' (see Walsh, in this volume). The difficulties of securing adequate resources for implementing quality initiatives have been compounded in the state sector, where a fiscal crisis in public expenditure has combined with a pro-market ideology that seeks to replace an ethic of public service with managerial disciplines derived from the private sector (Ezzamel and Willmott, 1993).

Commenting upon the continuing influence of quality ideas and initiatives in reforming the UK public sector, Pollitt (1993: 186) has observed that

> Quality might be the theme of the 1990s but it will have to be won through gains in efficiency, not large increases in spending. The increased prominence of competitive mechanisms in almost every public service appear to have at least as much to do with driving down costs as with promoting quality.

In common with earlier management gurus, such as Taylor, authorities on quality management attribute most of the blame for inefficiency and waste to management. In Deming's words (1986: ix), 'The basic cause of sickness in American industry and resulting unemployment is failure of top management to manage.' Since it is invariably possible to identify points at which the gurus' recipes are not faithfully followed or are insufficiently resourced, or when the leadership and support of senior managers falls well short of the gurus' ideals, failures of quality programmes are readily ascribed to the deficiencies of those responsible for their implementation (Economist Intelligence Unit, 1992). However, even the limited empirical evidence gathered by researchers does not, and perhaps cannot, resolve the question of the effectiveness of quality initiatives, let alone the issue of their desirability. For so much depends upon the type and level of expectations that are generated, as well as whether partial fulfilment of these expectations is deemed to fall well short or to be half-way there.

## Total quality management

The first gurus of quality management focused primarily upon the management of production (e.g. through processes of quality control and quality assurance). Their lessons have subsequently been extended to cover virtually every area of organization and management, including general management. As noted above, in this process, the meaning of 'quality' has been attached indiscriminately to a multitude of diverse practices. However, far from being viewed as a difficulty for the coherence and credibility of quality management, this promiscuity, and its attendant confusion, is embraced by some as a principal virtue.

> It sometimes seems unfortunate that there are so many different interpretations of quality. But by being amenable to

wide and differing interpretations it remains appropriate in widely differing situations and circumstances. Thus it has a unifying effect in that all genuine aspirations to improve quality are known to be moving in the same direction. . . . The total quality image is the sum of a set of attributes, each of which has its own quality criteria.

(Dale and Plunkett, 1989: 346)

TQM has become the most celebrated and widely adopted form of quality management, in part perhaps because it holds out the promise of 'a unified set of principles which can guide managers through the numerous choices [open to them] or might even make choosing unnecessary' (Huczynski, 1993: 289). As its name indicates, TQM aspires to build 'quality' into every conceivable aspect of organizational work. In principle, all systems and interactions are to be reformed so as to exemplify a commitment to a philosophy of continuous improvement. However, in reality, the theory and practice of TQM continue to be dominated and constrained by the disciplinary orientations and preoccupations of its major advocates (e.g. Deming, 1986; Juran, 1979; Ishikawa, 1985; Feigenbaum, 1983). With backgrounds in operational research and statistical methods of control, many of the leading gurus sought to develop and refine seemingly objective (e.g. statistical) means of gaining 'hard' information about processes of production and service delivery. Much attention and effort has been directed at the measurement and documentation of procedures and outcomes through the use of flow charts, scatter diagrams, control charts, etc. Comparatively less consideration is given to the 'softer' process of winning employee support for, and commitment to, the TQM philosophy of continuous improvement (Wilkinson et al., 1991; 1992).

There are signs that the balance between 'hard' and 'soft' formulations of TQM (Wilkinson, 1992, 1994) is beginning to shift, with the appearance of a new generation of gurus. Oakland (1989), for example, has been forthright in stressing the importance of developing an approach to TQM that makes employees more responsible and accountable (see Munro, in this volume). Getting employees to become 'committed to attaining quality in a highly motivated fashion', Oakland has argued, requires the development of an understanding on the part of management that 'people do not need to be coerced to perform well, and that people want to achieve, accomplish, influence activity and challenge their abilities' (Oakland, 1989: 26).

TQM's concern to increase employee involvement echoes the aspiration of neo-human relations thinking (e.g. McGregor's Theory Y) to replace a reliance upon 'external control' favoured by scientific management (Theory X) with a concern to tap intrinsic forms of motivation. However, whereas neo-human relations thinking identifies 'self-realization' as the key to human motivation, TQM is not directly concerned with designing work in ways that will fulfil the 'self' of the employee. Rather, its concern is to induce the employee to identify with the TQM mission of 'attaining quality' (Willmott, 1992, 1993). TQM requires employees to be responsible for managing the 'quality' of their individual contributions; and, relatedly, to accept and internalize forms of surveillance and control that monitor their activity and commitment (Sewell and Wilkinson, 1991, 1992). Although present in the writings of Deming in particular, this concern with employee involvement has been amplified by champions of TQM working with companies in the West, where commitment to the corporation cannot be assumed.

The abstract and universal character of TQM philosophy also differs from that of Theory Z (and 'excellence') prescriptions (Ouchi, 1981; Peters and Waterman, 1982). The latter seeks to tie individuals into the local values of particular corporate cultures, which are often found to be an impediment to continuous change and can also be an unintended source of employee collectivism and resistance (Ray, 1986). TQM, in contrast, seeks to focus employee attention upon the universal principle of continuous improvement rather than upon (pre)serving the specific, local norms and values of the corporate culture. However, TQM is increasingly coming under attack from those peddling new panaceas for reversing the decline of Western economies. Criticizing quality initiatives for preserving established structures and territories, advocates of Business Process Re-engineering (BPR) suggest that

> Despite the application of TQM principles [and, it might be added, because of its principles], most Western companies remain *highly bureaucratic*, with departments acting individually and 'throwing over the wall' to the next department designs, information, product, and most of all problems . . . barriers to overall business effectiveness are raised and turf is jealously guarded.
>
> (Johansson *et al.*, 1993: 7)

9

In many ways, the proponents of BPR are repackaging TQM ideas. In particular, they have emphasized the importance of developing cross-functional approaches to the design and delivery of goods and services. They argue that companies should

> be broken apart and rebuilt as a process-oriented business . . . where everyone regards working in cross-functional teams as the norm . . . and where everyone knows that the key goal is to produce a service or product that the marketplace perceives to be best.
>
> (Ibid.)

This sounds remarkably similar to the process emphasis in TQM.[3] It is therefore questionable whether favoured BPR recipes for surmounting what they identify as 'the barriers to overall business effectiveness' will be much more successful than TQM.[4] Indeed, it is possible that 'the rigid hierarchies which isolate top management, confine middle management to administrative roles and frustrate operational and supervisory management in their decision-making' (Thurley and Wirdenius, 1989: 91) will prove more potent than any of the diverse recipes for performance improvement currently being touted by management gurus.

## Promoting quality: faith and politics

Much hinges on faith and politics. A similar point has been made in relation to HRM:

> Belief in HRM is not based upon deconstructing theory or looking for proof, but on faith. The HRM prophets guide the way to business improvement, harmonious employee relations, customer care and societal well-being: the promised land for advanced industrial societies. Those who like the message and have faith, follow.
>
> (Noon, 1992: 29)

Strong believers in the ideals and potency of quality initiatives will tend to see the glass as half-full, and diagnose shortcomings in terms of failures of implementation (Witcher, 1993). Sceptics are inclined to see the glass, at best, as half-empty. They will tend to point to broader issues and problems – for example, over the strength of support for the prevailing structures of ownership and control – that remain largely unaddressed by quality initiatives because these structures are taken as given and are assumed to be legitimate. In contrast to the believers, the sceptics are inclined to suggest that problems of motivation associated with Taylorism – where employees are induced to comply with the programme of work determined by others – do not necessarily evaporate when TQM programmes are introduced, however skilfully they are implemented and with whatever level of management leadership and support[5] (Webster and Robins, 1993). As Wilkinson *et al.* (1992: 18) observe of the evidence they draw from a study of twenty-five companies, 'in the sense that quality methods of working emphasise monitoring and control (with the difference that workers do it themselves), TQM can also be used to reinforce a management style rooted in Taylorism'.

The argument is made even more forcefully by Dawson and Webb (1989: 236). On the basis of findings derived from an intensive study of change in the UK division of a multinational electronics company in which TQM programmes had become well established, they report that

> The changes reported are consistent with the view that new production arrangements serve capital in the search for more efficient exploitation of labour . . . the extent of discretion and autonomy introduced by the requirement to participate in incremental improvements in process and product engineering is consistent with attempts to incorporate the workforce in the projects of capital without extending to any substantive control over business strategy or the dispersal of profits.

From this more critical perspective, the 'quality revolution' can be seen as the most recent move in a developing process in which the organization of production is subordinated to the contradictory logics of capitalist labour processes. Means are now sought for securing an adequate return on capital in a situation where the basis of competition is quality and speed of innovation, not just price. To accommodate this shift, and thus to contribute to this change, quality initiatives are introduced that in many cases expand employee discretion and eliminate sources of frustration as they extend and reinforce processes of management control.

## SOME CONTRADICTIONS OF QUALITY MANAGEMENT

### The embeddedness of quality initiatives in social institutions

Earlier we noted how, from the standpoint of quality management, its 'revolutionizing' of work organization, bringing about the

11

increased involvement and empowerment of employees, is a self-evident, unequivocal good. The champions of quality management also assume that there will be willing cooperation from employees, so long as those who design and implement quality initiatives are experts who are adequately resourced and fully supported by senior management. Highly critical of 'management by fear', Deming (1986) argues that the principal remedy for poor organizational performance is effective leadership – by which he means the development of systems that empower the employee to give of his or her best: 'to do his job with pride of workmanship' (Ibid.: 54), however menial or repetitive the task may be. Poor performance, he argues, is symptomatic of systems that breed fear and thus fail to foster mutual trust. Poor performance is *not* a product of the forced or fragmented division of labour, but of management's failure to develop systems that enable each employee to perform his or her task at an optimum level.

It is taken for granted that employees will welcome, be committed to, and benefit from, an approach that minimizes unproductive activity and enables them to take a pride in the marketability of what they produce. Evidence of such benefits is acknowledged in a number of the following chapters (e.g. Hill, Dawson, McCardle *et al.*). Employees are seen to welcome the removal of irritants such as excessively close supervision, the unreliability of services received from other departments, the reluctance of management to lower needless barriers between themselves and the workforce, etc. For those released from such petty restrictions, these innovations are not trivialities to be dismissed as small beer. However, it is equally important to set such benefits in a wider context, so that their fragility and limits can also be appreciated.

As a number of the contributions to this volume show, the continuing hierarchical relationship between management and employees acts to restrict the scope and distribution of the benefits derived from quality initiatives. For example, Kerfoot and Knights (in this volume) note how, in the prescriptive literature on quality management, the significance of hierarchies is at once veiled and preserved (see also Elger, 1990). Quality management is represented by its advocates as a means of delivering universally beneficial gains in productivity. Little or no consideration is given to the possibility that the failings of existing systems are, at least in part, symptomatic of more fundamental divisions and contradictions in the organization of work within capitalist economies. And yet, as Scase and Goffee (1989: 188) have plausibly observed, 'authority relationships in larger organizations tend to reflect wider social divisions and militate against the imposition of shared values'.

'Involvement', 'participation', 'teamwork' and the promotion of 'empowerment' within hierarchies is unreservedly celebrated by the advocates of quality. They are regarded as innovations that serve to eliminate avoidable costs and needless waste. Such benefits may indeed flow from quality initiatives. But it is also relevant to place the current interest in such innovations in the wider context of pressures from shareholders upon managers to organize the work of employees in ways that are more profitable. When placed in this context, it can be appreciated how quality initiatives are often imposed upon an unprepared and hesitant, if not hostile, management by the intensity of (global) competitive pressures. However, in the prescriptive literature, the possibility that the development and implementation of quality initiatives are a response to the contradictory demands of capital, including pension fund managers, for profitable growth, is rarely recognized. As a consequence, it is not contemplated that failures of quality programmes may be attributable not only to managerial incompetence or lack of resources, but to resistance that stems from more fundamental conflicts of interest.

## The structure of employment relationships

Even if it is believed that capitalism is invincible or inevitable, and that quality management provides a more rational or 'participative' way of organizing productive activity, consideration of the politico-economic contexts of their conception and implementation may have relevance for understanding why many quality initiatives do not fulfil their expectations. Doubtless, problems and failures can be ascribed to 'human nature', which is resistant to change, to individual managers who have been inept in implementing quality initiatives, to conflicts within management over the relevance and appeal of quality initiatives for the future of their company and/or influence of their specialism etc. (Armstrong, 1986; Smith *et al.*, 1990). It is also relevant to recognize how capitalist employers seek to achieve levels of return (profit) through a variety of means (e.g. financial engineering, brand management) that are not reducible to the development of more effective means of management control over employee productivity, which encompasses the reduction of managerial overheads. But without denying that profits can be generated in diverse ways, that people frequently resist changes that are perceived to threaten their sense of well-being, and that managers are capable of ineptness as well as politicking for their specialism, it is relevant to take account of more systemic sources of failure.

Employees, including managers who neither own nor control the organization that employs them, are likely to be concerned primarily with securing or improving their wages and conditions of employment. They may therefore be responsive to initiatives that link their job security and prospects to changes in work organization, including changes that intensify their work. This interdependence means that there is considerable scope for gaining the cooperation of employees to implement quality initiatives. However, this rather obvious point – that the employment relationship is not 'zero-sum' – does not adequately address the argument that there are inherent conflicts over the costs and benefits of the employment relationship. Conflicts within the employment relationship are most evident in divergent views over the 'fairness' of wage increases, regardless of whether these are matched by productivity gains. But they are underpinned by structures of ownership and control that condition the focus and limits of employee 'involvement' within the employment relationship – including the willingness of managers, as suppliers of supervisory labour, to implement quality initiatives in disinterested ways (see Munro, in this volume).

## Constituting employees as internal customers

As we noted earlier, and as a number of the chapters in this volume illustrate, the language of the contemporary quality management gurus connects the rhetoric of enterprise with an appealing image of the employee as an autonomous, responsible individual. In Oakland's words (1989: 26) his concern is 'with moving the focus of control from outside the individual to within; the objective being to make everyone accountable for their own performance, and to get them committed to attaining quality in a highly motivated fashion'.

When constituted in this way, employees are expected to think of themselves as suppliers of the next person in the supply chain; and to take on the role of this person when performing their work so that they experience a sense of fulfilment when their 'customer' is satisfied. Relatedly, each employee is enjoined to watch and control the 'quality' of work that they receive from their suppliers (i.e. their fellow employees):

> it is a form of involvement in which the agenda is said to be dictated by customer requirements. Therefore, employees are immersed in the 'logic' of the market and are thus more likely to be convinced of the legitimacy of company decisions.
>
> (Wilkinson *et al.*, 1991: 30)

Or, at least, that is the hope and expectation of those who promote quality initiatives. Yet, paradoxically, the very promotion of 'participation', 'teamworking' and 'empowerment' by quality management itself may prompt questions about the extent to which employees are treated and rewarded as full members of the organizational 'team', the extent to which they participate in key decision-making, and the degree to which they are able to exercise control over their work.

## SOME QUESTIONS FOR QUALITY MANAGEMENT

We have suggested that the literature on managing quality, and on TQM in particular, is distinguished by a normative thrust that largely excludes consideration of ideas and evidence that might challenge or qualify its assumptions and prescriptions. In essence, this literature takes an evangelical line that excludes traditions and empirical data that fail to confirm its faith (Kerfoot and Knights, in this volume). Ideas and practices that deviate from the principles of quality management are interpreted as instances of irrationality that can be corrected through the proper and systematic application of quality principles. Where the introduction of quality management is found to be less than fully effective, there is a tendency to construe such evidence either as an instance of imperfect application or as symptomatic of an incomplete learning cycle that implies a need to redouble the efforts to apply it, rather than a symptom of more fundamental and intractable problems with its assumptions and prescriptions. To overcome this limitation, it is necessary to mobilize other traditions and perspectives, in order to acquire and develop a more measured and sceptical

15

assessment of the theory and practice of managing quality. In addition to contributions from mainstream sociology and organizational behaviour, ideas drawn from Marx, Foucault and other social theorists are shown by contributors to this volume to be of value in reflecting upon the coherence of the vision and the plausibility of the claims of quality management.

For many of the contributors, the *vision* of quality management is restricted by an exclusive concern with efficiency and effectiveness, to the exclusion of the rationality and defensibility of its values and priorities. Do advocates of quality management who emphasize the importance of employee involvement or urge respect for humanity (e.g. Ishikawa, 1985) regard such values and priorities as unassailable virtues, or are they viewed principally as a means of raising productivity? Do quality initiatives enable employees to develop a collective sense of purpose and identity at work, or do they act to intensify work and tie employees more closely to objectives that are defined by others? Unfortunately, such questions are either not examined, or are cursorily treated, within the quality management literature. It is simply taken for granted that quality management is benign and universally beneficial. In Dale and Plunkett's words (1989: 346), 'all genuine aspirations to improve quality . . . are known to be moving in the same direction'. But, revealingly, there is no attempt to specify or justify what counts as 'genuine', or why the 'direction' of movement is to be welcomed.

To move beyond the benign vision of the quality gurus, it is necessary to engage in radical questioning of the way quality is identified and pursued. As this shift is made, the meaning of quality is no longer restricted to the continuous improvement of existing means of achieving existing objectives. Rather, the concern to improve quality is linked directly with more fundamental questions about the rationality of the ends as well as the means of their attainment. When advancing an alternative vision of quality, it may be asked whether, for example, the widespread use of quality management significantly improves the quality of life for the majority of human beings. Or is a primary effect of quality initiatives to remove many people from productive activity and to intensify the pressures upon those who have the privilege of full-time employment? Is quality management part of the solution for improving the quality of human lives, or is its commitment to consumerism, including its constitution of producers as internal customers, part of the problem?

16

Again, it is widely assumed that, through a process of education and training, employees will come to equate notions of 'participation', 'teamworking' and 'empowerment' with the way these terms are evoked and applied by the gurus of quality management (see Roberts and Corcoran-Nantes, in this volume). And, indeed, this identification is likely to be facilitated by the capacity of quality initiatives to remove sources of frustration and to expand their discretion and sense of control. As we stressed earlier, these changes should not be dismissed as small beer, as their benefits to employees can make them more willing to cooperate with quality initiatives. And, yet, it is worth asking: are employees empowered to remove management, or even to reduce the effort made in exchange for a cut in wages? Or are they empowered only to take responsibility for activities that were previously undertaken by other employees (e.g. supervisors, quality controllers), without a commensurate improvement in their own wages and conditions? Does quality management facilitate the development of participation on key issues of resource allocation and accountability? Or does it use participation primarily as a stratagem for reducing managerial overheads and for promoting self-discipline, including the continuous identification and consenting introduction of efficiency gains at the point of production? As Binns (1993: 16–17) has noted, some of the ideas celebrated by the gurus of quality management are potential 'wild cards'. Talk of accountability and responsibility, for example, can inadvertently stimulate reflection upon issues of control; and once 'the genie of participation' is out of the bottle, it may prove 'difficult to recork'. Whether it is possible for the theory and practice of quality management to neutralize more radical–democratic meanings associated with concepts like 'participation' and 'empowerment' must remain an open question. But at the very least it may be doubted whether the celebration of 'participation' and 'empowerment' can be fully reconciled with the lived experience of employees if they simultaneously encounter a reduction in their job security and/or an intensification in the pace and pressures of their work.[6]

Further questions are begged. For instance, does quality management facilitate more appreciative and discriminating consumption of goods and services? Or does it take the priorities of capitalism for granted, and therefore fuel demand for an increased quantity of cheaper and more reliable goods? Do the teachings of quality management encourage a more careful and sustainable use of planetary resources? Or do they exemplify and reinforce a mentality that equates 'better' with 'more', paying scant regard to the social and ecological consequences? And if the answer to such questions is that ideas about quality, and their associated initiatives, are largely blind to these wider isues, is this because quality thinking is harnessed to capitalist objectives; or is it that a critical, reflective orientation is simply absent from the teachings of the quality gurus?

A more sceptical consideration of quality initiatives casts doubt upon the promise of quality management to expand employee autonomy, facilitate teamwork and promote participation. Their benefits must be balanced against their contribution to the undermining of collective efforts to improve the opportunities, terms and conditions of groups of employees, such as ethnic minorities, women and/or union members. While one visible and acclaimed outcome of quality management may be the removal of some practices that restrict productivity and limit flexibility, a less visible consequence may be the undermining, or even abolition, of institutions that have secured and defended rights and benefits which individual employees, acting alone, could not have achieved and cannot now sustain. Not only does quality management have a tendency to degrade, in Orwellian Newspeak fashion, the meaning of 'empowerment', 'participation', etc., so that, for example, 'involvement' becomes equated with the acceptance and resigned pursuit of managerial priorities, but, in doing so, it represents the politics of employment relations as an impersonal imperative of the market. Without denying that quality management can lower barriers between management and employees – for example, by removing layers of supervision and encouraging worker self-discipline – it may be asked how much the changes in work organization that depend upon 'participation' and promote 'empowerment' actually liberate hierarchies and managerial prerogatives, rather than serving to fortify them.

As the contributions to this volume show, there are no definitive or universally accepted answers to these questions. Some contributors tend to interpret the use of quality management as a new stage in the process of exerting control over employees for purposes of capital accumulation (e.g. McArdle *et al.*). Others see its increased control over employees more as an unintended consequence of efforts to deal with the contradictions of capitalism than as a primary objective of quality management techniques and

18

initiatives (e.g. Kerfoot and Knights). Yet others explore quality management in terms of its capacity to enable and constrain the work of managers rather than its effects upon their subordinates (e.g. Munro). What the majority of contributors share, nonetheless, is a concern to open up quality management to questions and perspectives that are absent from the received wisdom of the quality literature and textbooks.

## CONTRIBUTIONS

**Stephen Hill** argues a case for the effectiveness of TQM as a strategic means of realizing management objectives. When adequately resourced and properly implemented, he contends that TQM can produce significant and sustained gains in productivity, responsiveness and competitiveness. Based upon a study of four firms, three of which have been identified as 'model' TQM companies, Hill argues that TQM, like Heineken lager, is effective in reaching wider and deeper into organizations. In particular, it has the potential to overcome a number of limitations attributed to quality circles which seek to involve employees in making local improvements to working practices. The careful and effective implementation of TQM, Hill's findings suggest, results in increased employee involvement, self-discipline and commitment to quality, especially among middle managers, increased delegation of decision-making and gains in the efficiency of operations through reduced defects and wastage, 'delayering' and 'destaffing'.

A number of issues are raised by Hill's findings and analysis that are taken up by other contributors to this volume. First, as Hill acknowledges, the four companies he investigated are probably exceptional in their preparedness to devote considerable resources over a number of years to implement TQM. For many other companies, lack of resources restricts the extent to which comprehensive TQM initiatives can be adopted and sustained. Second, and relatedly, Hill makes little mention of the positioning of these companies within product, labour and capital markets. It is possible that they are unusual in enjoying a comparatively privileged (e.g. monopoly) position – a position that allows them the luxury of devoting resources to a TQM programme with a fairly long pay-back period. Third, it is also noted in passing that the TQM principle of introducing change through consensus rather than compulsion was breached in at least two of the companies. Here, established (instrumental and coercive) methods of gaining employee compliance were introduced 'in order to make TQM stick'. Fourth, the claim that surveys of employee attitudes indicated increased commitment to quality management needs to be seen in a broader context. This is not only because these were internal company surveys but because a key feature of TQM is the selection and training of employees to support and adopt values and positive attitudes that endorse quality management.

It is not necessary to deny that changes brought about by TQM can have benefits for employees – such as more control over their immediate working environment, greater pride in their work, and improved promotion opportunities – in order to appreciate that TQM can marginalize other frames of reference that offer alternative perspectives on the claimed benefits of TQM. So, when registering the generally positive responses of employees and managers to TQM, and accepting that people are not 'cultural dopes', it is also relevant to consider what access they have to other interpretations of reality that might enable them to reflect more critically upon ideas about 'quality' and 'participation' championed by TQM.

Finally, and most fundamentally, it is appropriate to ask whether TQM should be assessed purely in terms of its capacity to realize corporate objectives. What about the social effects of TQM? If, as Hill indicates, a widespread effect of TQM is 'destaffing', will its widespread adoption contribute to unemployment, or will its *non-*adoption lead to unemployment, as Deming (1986) argues? If it is as effective as Hill and others suggest, will TQM divide an elite of employees within 'world-class' TQM companies from a residue of employees in other companies that lack the resources required to implement full-blown TQM? Questions can also be raised about the extent and depth of the 'participation' promoted by TQM. It is striking that participation does not extend to key decisions relating to the ownership and control of companies. TQM may facilitate greater teamworking, cross-functional management and accountability, but its dominant effect may be to secure and reinforce hierarchical relationships in organizations, rather than to challenge or remove them. To develop a more rounded appreciation of TQM, and of quality initiatives more generally, it is appropriate to complement an assessment of claims about its instrumental efficacy in attaining comparatively narrow economic objectives with an evaluation of its contribution in terms of wider social and political criteria. In short, when evaluating TQM, it is (ironically) appropriate to develop a more comprehensive, 'totalizing' approach than has been commended either by its gurus or by the majority of academic commentators.

**Alan Tuckman's** contribution directly challenges the benign characteristics widely ascribed to TQM. He sees it as a central element of a wider project that serves to incorporate employees and citizens within the logic of a capitalist society: people are encouraged to understand themselves simply as buyers and sellers of commodities, including labour. Specifically, TQM is regarded as an integral part of an employer strategy that invites employees to identify themselves as elements of a customer/supplier chain in which human effort is exclusively directed to serving internal and external customers. This strategy is viewed as ideological or hegemonic, in the sense that it takes market relations as unproblematic and legitimate. Any working practice – however degrading or insecure – is then justified so long as it is deemed to contribute to the enhancement of 'quality'. In this process, Tuckman suggests, the very meaning of 'quality' is subtly (and not so subtly) redefined, distorted and debased to legitimize whatever terms and conditions of employment are deemed to produce sustained competitive advantage.

To illuminate and support this argument, Tuckman traces the historical development of TQM through quality assurance, statistical quality control and quality circles. He shows how an early attentiveness to 'hard' techniques for reducing product defects in mass manufacturing has been widened and extended to encompass 'softer', more holistic approaches to culture change. He also suggests that, in the West, the adoption and elaboration of TQM has proceeded through a number of stages – starting with experimentation with quality circles in manufacturing industry during the late 1970s and progressing to the application of its rhetoric and techniques within public sector organizations. For Tuckman, the spread of TQM rhetoric and techniques is not a benign process that serves to eliminate irrationality in the form of needless waste, restrictive practices and low levels of employee involvement and satisfaction. Rather, TQM is seen as part and parcel of a class offensive, one that is more or less consciously directed at making employees and citizens identify with the tenets of an ideology of employee-as-market-cipher that is conducive to the smooth functioning of capitalism. And yet, despite the potency and seductiveness of its hegemonic appeal, TQM does not provide a final cure for employee resistance – the Achilles' heel of management control. TQM continues to encounter difficulties in matching the rhetoric (e.g. of participation) with the experience of its effects in terms of 'destaffing' (the code for job losses) and intensification in the form of greater effort and pressures for little or no greater material or psychological reward (see also Kerfoot and Knights, in this volume). Precisely because employees are not 'cultural dopes', as Hill stresses, they are capable of developing alternative assessments of TQM.

**Kieron Walsh** discusses the application in the public sector of rhetorics and practices of quality management approaches that were initially developed in the private sector. According to Walsh, this move arose in response to criticisms of public services that have become increasingly vocal since the late 1970s: first, their alleged inefficiency and wastefulness and, second, their remoteness from those whom they are supposed to serve. 'Quality' in the UK public sector has comprised a variety of measures and initiatives, such as the closer specification of standards and the auditing of performance; the separation of purchaser and provider roles and the use of contracts and internal markets to regulate and discipline these relations; and the contracting out of services and the break-up of large structures into more autonomous, accountable units. Common to these initiatives is a concern to replace, or at least complement, direct employment by the State with the contracting out of services to private and public agencies which are formally required to meet tightly specified standards of service. The emergent transformation of public services is seen to involve a volatile combination of, on the one hand, market principles that emphasize the sovereignty of the individual consumer of public services (exemplified in the United Kingdom by the introduction of the community charge/'poll tax', which in principle levied the same amount of tax from each member of the local community, regardless of their income); and, on the other hand, democratic principles that stress the role of the community in controlling, and being accountable for, local activities (e.g. the decentralization of budget-holding for schools), often through the use of surveys that purport to monitor levels of customer satisfaction.

One difficulty encountered in the translation of quality management philosophy to the public sector, Walsh indicates, is the

comparatively intangible nature of many services and the associated difficulty of reaching agreement over what is to count as
'conformance to specification'. It may be widely agreed that
'customers' desire 'better quality services'. But it is not always
possible to specify what this means, or to develop an agreed
method for measuring improvements. A favoured solution to the
problem has been the centralized setting of precise standards and
associated audits that are intended to guarantee levels of provision.
Walsh notes how this move has enabled politicians to distance
themselves from responsibility for the management and delivery
of public services. However, whereas the acid test of 'success' in
the private sector is the continuing (profitable) sale of a company's
goods and services, public provision is not directly governed by
market forces. In this situation, there is considerable pressure to
demonstrate effectiveness in other ways – for example, through the
conspicuous adoption of other, surrogate measures of performance (seemingly regardless of cost), such as the accounting and
information provision of systems that have found favour in the
private sector.

Walsh concludes that a form of organization in the public sector
is emerging where, in Hill's terms, there is a growing dualism
between a highly paid core of staff responsible for the control of
contracts and procurement, and a mass of others who work for
organizations that service the contracts and upon whom market
pressures act to erode wages and conditions of employment, fringe
benefits and pay (see also Roberts and Corcoran-Nantes, in this
volume). If this is so then, on Hill's argument, it is to be expected
that the use of TQM-type techniques in the provision of public
sector services is likely to be quite selective and partial, and to
prove effective in economic terms only in the rare cases when
sufficient resources are made available to apply them consistently
and comprehensively. This would seem to be borne out in this
sector where, arguably, there is a heavier reliance upon the 'stick' of
contracting out than the 'carrot' of programmes of internal culture
change to accomplish 'the quality revolution'.

**Janette Webb** takes up the issues relating to the management of
quality and the role of managers. She suggests that when taken at
face value, TQM could be seen as an optimizing rather than
satisficing strategy; and that it acts to reverse the established
characteristic separation of conception and execution (planning

and doing) at work. Drawing on three cases from a project which examined the management of a section of a supply chain in the computer industry, Webb discusses the experience of these firms. Each of her cases pursued TQM-type initiatives with different objectives derived from the context in which they were operating and the aims of senior management. She found that TQM had a significant role in restructuring managerial roles and functions, with losses in lower and middle levels, and functional jobs replaced by more business-led ones. This had significant consequences for the informal status hierarchy and intra-managerial power relations. TQM changed the nature of managerial work, especially at middle management level, where they became less 'guardians' and more 'facilitators' of a function.

But TQM did not lead to salvation for ailing businesses and alienated workforces. Nor did it negate or transform the way that supply-chain relationships operate as power relationships. The idea of internal customers in a supply chain was meant to promote ideals of service, but the reproduction of exploitation, based on power, was found to be the other side of supply-chain relationships. Although prepared to accept that TQM could serve a useful purpose in overcoming some forms of British management authoritarianism, Webb concludes that it is hard to be optimistic about the participative scenario becoming reality, especially during an economic recession. Instead, such pressures make TQM into an object and medium of managerialist and immoral expediency.

**Rolland Munro** also focuses on managers, taking up Hill's findings that quality management is an activity largely carried out by middle managers. However, he takes issue with Hill's analysis that their autonomy increases, arguing that such claims must be grounded in a detailed analysis of changes in accountability. Lateral accountability in particular, Munro argues, may represent not so much a switch from hierarchical accountability as an attempt to extend it. He suggests that a redistribution of autonomy may represent power effects that are symptomatic of wider changes in the politics of managing. For Munro, the key issue is not 'who is for quality?', but 'how for quality?'; consequently he explores the issue of how people discover and shape their interests in the context of quality. In a case study of a car component manufacturer, middle managers are found to have promoted or enrolled 'quality' so as to secure and advance their own careers. The 'drive-on production' had been replaced by the emphasis on 'quality numbers'. Middle managers represented themselves as having the expertise over quality; within the new ethos of quality, they tried to act as spokespersons of the customer. At the same time, top managers took advantage of the collapse of faith in the surveillance properties of accounting. By rolling back budgets to restrict responsibility to a point in the line, delegation without surveillance was achieved by managing at a distance. In other words, while the language shifted from cost to quality, 'surveillance paths' were constructed around the concept of quality. The production territory cuts across traditional functions, thereby imposing lateral production paths which increased lateral accountability. The attractions of managing at a distance included dumping the 'burden' of conscience; what top managers didn't know about, they could not be held responsible for. As a discourse of control, 'quality' did not replace 'accounting'. Instead, accounting moved to a language game of pseudo-markets. The traditional approach of 'meet the numbers or we'll want to know why' was transposed to 'meet the numbers', with the language of pseudo-markets making the rider 'or else' unnecessary.

**Louise McArdle** and her co-authors explore the notion of participation and TQM. They point out that TQM writers such as Oakland and social scientists such as Hill (see this volume) have highlighted the importance of involvement by employees under TQM. Hill, in particular, has argued that such participation is likely to be more enduring than in the past because, in principle, it is introduced with changes in organizational design and management support. Some similarities between the 'soft' side of TQM and the quality of working life (QWL) movement are identified. QWL is largely seen as work humanization in response to failures of previous strategies to control the recalcitrance of labour. TQM, in contrast, is undertaken less as a response to labour pressure, and more as a response to market pressure to become more competitive.

McArdle *et al.* examine an electronics plant to explore issues relating to empowerment, involvement and control. Many workers reported that the introduction of TQM had led to harder work. However, they also regarded TQM as a better way of working, with workers taking on more responsibility for tasks, and with the factory being reorganized around a flexible manufacturing system.

Employees were 'empowered' to take decisions about the quality of work. In doing so they became more embroiled in the TQM production system. Employees' willingness to accept TQM, McArdle *et al.* argue, can be better understood in the context of a rationalization process carried out prior to the introduction of the initiative. This allowed management to shift responsibility for enhanced control away from themselves, and on to external forces. McArdle *et al.* also note how the nature of participation changed over a period of time. Power-centred participation was replaced by task-centred forms of involvement. 'Empowerment' intensified work, but it did not provide workers with input into the decision-making process. They conclude that TQM did not extend worker rights, but rather that it introduced management-by-stress and forced workers to engage in their own exploitation.

**Patrick Dawson** examines the issue of organizational culture in a comparative case study set in Australia. He first looks at how TQM ideas have been diffused throughout Australian industry via various quality gurus and associated consultants, and how the penetration of ideas eventually led to a government-sponsored quality campaign in 1984. In turn, this campaign stimulated a number of quality bodies to promote and coordinate the quality movement.

Dawson examines the introduction of TQM initiatives at two different plants within the same manufacturing complex of an international cables manufacturer. The adoption of such an initiative reflected a concern with the amount of wastage within the organization and the availability of TQM as a possible solution. Dawson notes that the issue of cultural change was not central to company thinking at this stage. However, as the programme evolved, it became apparent that a shift in employee attitudes was necessary if greater participation in problem-solving teams was to be achieved. Thus, TQM gradually became redefined as a programme of culture change aimed at securing greater employee involvement.

The shopfloor experience of employees varied quite widely between the two plants. This is associated by Dawson with the context of the plant operation, the local experience of TQM and gender composition. There were also similarities, however, in particular in relation to language and ethnicity, which constrained employee involvement. Dawson argues that, as a strategy for

26

cultural change, TQM raises major issues in relation to organiz-ational values. A key assumption of TQM is that developing a dominant organizational culture will improve commitment. How-ever, unlike in Japan, cultural pluralism is a feature of Australian society. Thus, to try to manage organizational culture towards a common approach is unrealistic. In Dawson's case studies, pre-existing cultural pluralism was reinforced by changing ethnic com-position. In such contexts, Dawson concludes, TQM is most unlikely to achieve its aim of total employee involvement, and may act to sustain or even create ethnic divisions.

**Ken Roberts** and **Yvonne Corcoran-Nantes** take up the issue of the 'new' training and industrial relations. The specific remit of their research was to explore skill shortages in the late 1980s. Seven of their nine case study companies were spending more on train-ing, employed more training staff and were providing more training days per employee. The growth of this training was seen as part of a broader set of interrelated changes, which was referred to by managers as part of a movement towards TQM. Roberts and Corcoran-Nantes report major changes in work organization which resulted in increasing workloads, flatter structures, greater work group and individual responsibility for guaranteeing work quality and quantity, and a trend towards multiskilling, with the number of recognized crafts reduced and operatives made responsible for routine maintenance.

In many respects the drive for quality is interpreted by the authors as laying a benign veneer over work regimes which required everyone to do more, and to have more responsibility. Training was an important factor in all this change. The aim was to produce a virtuous spiral whereby training produced quality employees who performed quality work, hence satisfying cus-tomers and producing profit. However, the authors suggest that much of the growth in training in the 1980s did not create a better-equipped workforce. Rather it simply organized and recognized what had previously been accomplished informally. Nor did the 'training culture' erode collective conflict. Trade unions had acquiesced in, rather than welcomed, change. Their relationships with plant management could not be seen as a partnership. So, whilst there was much change within the firms, the implementation of TQM did not dissolve existing divisions amongst interest groups, but rather (re)structured them.

**Deborah Kerfoot** and **David Knights** examine the 'rhetoric' of quality in relation to the conditions that make it attractive to practitioners, and the effects that it has within organizations. They argue that, while aspiring to flatten structures and empower workers, the reality is that it tends to renew the legitimacy of 'bureau-corporate capitalist organizations'. Quality is seen to appeal to management because it promises to fill a gap left by the erosion of collectivism (collective bargaining, unionism, etc.), and can thus be regarded as a new way of management getting to grips with the problems posed by fragmented workforces. In other respects it is seen as a possible alternative to flexible specialization in post-modern society, while at the same time reflecting the New Right philosophy in relation to the concept of the self-regulated worker.

Kerfoot and Knights also discuss the issue of 'empowerment' and examine contradictions which arise in the implementation of TQM. These are understood to arise from an engineering-like model of organizations and its simplistic assumptions about people. They argue that the TQM literature shows employees as obedient to the introduction of quality initiatives. Yet at the same time, they are expected to be creative. These simplistic and inconsistent assumptions about employee behaviour mean that TQM prescriptions tend to be 'impoverished, if not contradictory'. When contemplating the connection between quality initiatives and human resource management (HRM), they find a degree of convergence in their respective philosophies. However, in the context of contemporary changes in the financial services in the UK and elsewhere, there tends to be a contradiction between ideas of employee commitment and empowerment and the ongoing processes of rationalization and job loss. Their research suggests that the introduction of quality initiatives has no necessary connection with HRM, leading to possible charges of incoherence and duplicity on the part of senior management.

## NOTES

1 For example, Oakland (1989) refers only to Peters and Waterman's *In Search of Excellence*.
2 A number of papers were first presented in a specialist stream on quality management that we organized at the 1993 Labour Process Conference. One of the most provocative and penetrating of these was

presented by David Binns (1993). Although it proved impossible to include his paper in this volume, a number of its insights have been incorporated into this introduction. Additional contributions were subsequently solicited to shed light upon areas or issues not directly addressed at the conference.

3 Where Hammer's (1990) original formulation of BPR is different, arguably, is in its emphasis upon the role of information and communication technologies in transforming the organization of work – a consideration which is virtually absent from the quality management literature (see Willmott, 1993).

4 David Nadler, president of Delta Consulting Group, is reported to have said

'We have watched a number of re-engineering projects fail. They have involved huge promises of savings, but have either been stopped because they don't seem to be leading anywhere, or they have been completed but with none of the promised gains to show for it. Moreover, such projects generate payments to consultants of upward of $5 to $20 million. It's a nasty little secret.'

(Thackray, 1993: 41)

5 Wilson (1992) has remarked upon the extent to which the advocates of TQM rely upon 'effective leadership' as a substitute for other, more established forms of control. 'Such faith', he suggests 'would seem to be a little off-target, given the paucity of knowledge in the general field of leadership theories.'

6 In response to this effect, the Trades Union Congress has recently introduced the 'Quality Work Assured' servicemark which it is issuing to public services that demonstrate their commitment to 'quality staff, providing a quality service in a quality work environment' (TUC, 1992).

## REFERENCES

Armstrong, P. (1986) 'Management Control Strategies and Inter-Professional Competition: The Cases of Accountancy and Personnel Management', in D. Knights and H. Willmott (eds), *Managing the Labour Process*, Aldershot: Gower.

Bank, J. (1992) *The Essence of Total Quality Management*, Hemel Hempstead: Prentice-Hall.

Binns, D. (1993) 'Total Quality Management, Organization Theory and the New Right: A Contribution to the Critique of Bureaucratic Totalitarianism', paper presented at the 11th Annual Labour Process Conference, Blackpool.

Boynton, A.C., Victor, B. and Pine, B.J. (1993) 'New Competitive Strategies: Challenges to Organisations and Information Technology', *IBM Systems Journal*, 32 (1), 40–64.

Crosby, P.B. (1980) *Quality is Free*, London: Mentor.

Dale, B. and Cooper, C. (1992) *Total Quality Management and Human Resources: An Executive Guide*, Oxford: Blackwell.

Dale, B. and Plunkett, J.J. (1990) *Managing Quality*, London: Philip Alan.

Dawson, P. and Webb, J. (1989) 'New Production Arrangements: The Totally Flexible Cage?', *Work, Employment and Society*, 3 (2), 221–38.

Deming, W.C. (1986) *Out of the Crisis*, Cambridge, MA: MIT Centre for Advanced Engineering Study.

Drummond, H. (1992) *The Quality Movement: What Total Quality Management is Really All About!*, London: Kegan Page.

Economist Intelligence Unit (1992) *Making Quality Work: Lessons From Europe's Leading Companies*, London: EIU.

Elger, T. (1990) 'Technical Innovation and Work Reorganization in British Manufacturing in the 1980s: Continuity, Intensification or Transformation?', *Work, Employment and Society*, Special Issue, May, 5 (3), 397–415.

Ezzamel, M. and Willmott, H.C. (1993) 'Corporate Governance and Financial Accountability: Recent Reforms in the UK Public Sector', *Accounting, Auditing and Accountability*, 6 (3), 109–32.

Feigenbaum, A.V. (1983) *Total Quality Control* (3rd edn), New York: McGraw-Hill.

Garrahan, P. and Stewart, P. (1992) *The Nissan Enigma: Flexibility at Work in a Local Economy*, London: Mansell.

Garvin, D. (1988) *Managing Quality*, New York: Free Press.

Giles, E. and Starkey, K. (1988) 'The Japanization of Xerox', *New Technology, Work and Employment*, 3 (2), 125–33.

Hammer, M. (1990) 'Re-engineering Work: Don't Automate, Obliterate', *Harvard Business Review*, July–August, 104–12.

Hill, S. (1991) 'How Do You Manage a Flexible Firm? The Total Quality Model', *Work, Employment and Society*, December, 397–415.

Huczynski, A. (1993) *Management Gurus*, London: Routledge.

Ishikawa, K. (1985) *What is Total Quality Control? The Japanese Way*, Englewood-Cliffs, NJ: Prentice-Hall.

Johansson, H.J., McHugh, P., Pendlebury, A.J. and Wheeler, W.A. (1993) *Business Process Reengineering*, London: John Wiley.

Juran, J.M. (1979) *The Quality Control Handbook* (3rd edn), New York: McGraw-Hill.

Juran, J.M. (1989) *Juran on Leadership for Quality*, New York: Free Press.

Juran, J.M. (1993) 'Made in USA: A Renaissance of Quality', *Harvard Business Review*, July–August, 42–50.

McKinsey and Company (1989) *Management of Quality: The Single Most Important Challenge for Europe*, Montreux, Switzerland: European Quality Management Forum.

Noon, M. (1992) 'HRM: A Map, Model or Theory?', in P. Blyton and P. Turnbull (eds), *Reassessing Human Resource Management*, London: Sage.

Oakland, J. (1989) *Total Quality Management*, London: Heinemann.

Ouchi, W. (1981) *Theory Z: How American Business can Meet the Japanese Challenge*, New York: Addison Wesley.

Pascale, R. (1991) *Managing on the Edge*, Harmondsworth: Penguin.

Peters, T.J. and Waterman, R.H. (1982) *In Search of Excellence: Lessons From America's Best-Run Companies*, New York: Harper & Row.

Pfeffer, N. and Coote, A. (1991) *Is Quality Good For You?*, London: Institute of Public Policy Research.

Pollitt, C. (1993) *Managerialism and the Public Services*, Oxford: Blackwell.

Ray, C. (1986) 'Corporate Culture: The Last Frontier of Control', *Journal of Management Studies*, 23 (3), 287–97.

Rees, C. (1993) 'The Industrial Relations Implications of Total Quality Management', PhD research paper, Industrial Relations Research Unit, University of Warwick.

Rippin, A. (1993) 'From Factory Floor to Corporate Confessional: The New Meaning of Total Quality Management, *Notework*, 12 (1), 22–30.

Scase, R. and Goffee, R. (1989) *Reluctant Managers*, London: Unwin.

Sewell, G. and Wilkinson, B. (1991) 'Someone to Watch Over Me: Surveillance in a Total Quality Organisation' in P. Blyton and P. Turnbull (eds), *Reassessing Human Resource Management*, London: Sage.

Sewell, G. and Wilkinson, B. (1992) 'Empowerment or Emasculation: Shopfloor Surveillance in a Total Quality Organization', in P. Blyton and P. Turnbull (eds), *Reassessing Human Resource Management*, London: Sage.

Smith, C., Child, J. and Rowlinson, M. (1990) *Reshaping Work: The Cadbury Experience*, Cambridge: Cambridge University Press.

Thackray, J. (1993) 'Fads, Fixes and Fictions', *Management Today*, June, 40–2.

*The Economist* (1992) 'The Cracks in Quality', 18 April.

Thurley, K. and Wirdenius, H. (1989) *Towards European Management*, London: Pitman.

TUC (1992) *Quality Work Assured*, London: Trades Union Congress.

Webster, F. and Robins, K. (1993) 'I'll be Watching You: Comment on Sewell and Wilkinson', *Sociology* 27 (2), 243–52.

Wilkinson, A. (1992) 'The Other Side of Quality: Soft Issues and the Human Resource Dimension', *Total Quality Management*, 3 (3), 323–9.

Wilkinson, A. (1994) 'Managing Human Resources for Quality' in B.G. Dale (ed.) *Managing Quality* (2nd edn), Hemel Hempstead: Prentice-Hall.

Wilkinson, A. and Witcher, B. (1991) 'Fitness for Use? Barriers to Full TQM in the UK', paper presented at British Academy of Management Conference, Bath.

Wilkinson, A., Allen, P. and Snape, E. (1991) 'TQM and the Management of Labour', *Employee Relations*, 13 (1), 24–31.

Wilkinson, A., Redman, T. and Snape, E. (1993) *Quality and the Manager: An IM Report*, Corby: Institute of Management.

Wilkinson, A., Marchington, M., Goodman, J. and Ackers, P. (1992) 'Total Quality Management and Employee Involvement', *Human Resource Management Journal*, 2 (4), 1–20.

Willmott, H.C. (1992) 'Postmodernism and Excellence: The De-differentiation of Economy and Culture', *Journal of Organizational Change Management*, 5(17), 58–68.

Willmott, H.C. (1993) 'Strength is Ignorance; Slavery is Freedom: Managing Culture in Modern Organizations', *Journal of Management Studies*, 30, 4.

Willmott, H.C. (1994) 'Business Process Reengineering and Human Resource Management', *Personnel Review*, in press.

Wilson, D. (1992) *A Strategy of Change*, London: Routledge.

Witcher, B. (1993) *The Adoption of Total Quality Management in Scotland*, Durham: Centre for Quality and Organisational Change, Durham University Business School.

Xu, Q. (1993) 'Three Manifestations of TQM: A Paradigm Shift in Management', paper presented to the British Academy of Management Conference, Cranfield, September.

# 1

# FROM QUALITY CIRCLES TO TOTAL QUALITY MANAGEMENT*

*Stephen Hill*

## THE LIMITS OF QUALITY CIRCLES AND THE POTENTIAL OF TQM

In 1987, I set out on what I thought would be a self-contained and fairly brief study of the quality circle movement in the UK, an updating of work done earlier in the decade when circles were in their infancy. The investigation was completed three years later, during which it had transmuted into an analysis of total quality management (TQM). The issue had then become whether this new philosophy of managing might live up to the extravagant claims of the gurus of quality management and deliver the benefits to companies and employees that quality circles, which are part of the same family and which were similarly hyped at the outset, had failed to do. A brief discussion of the genesis and outcome of the circle investigation helps make sense of TQM.

The initial research agenda was to assess competing views within the academic community as to the nature and viability of quality circles. Advocates believed they would flourish, because they successfully realized the objectives of the managers who had set them up: enhanced operational efficiency and product quality; greater employee involvement as a consequence of participation; improved human relations and a new company culture comprising

---

* This is a substantially revised version of 'Why Quality Circles Failed but Total Quality Management Might Succeed', which appeared in *British Journal of Industrial Relations*, 29, December 1991, pp. 541–68. The original has full details of the research referred to in this chapter.

greater openness and a shared commitment to continuous improvement. Sceptics believed they would inevitably wither, although there were different reasons for this view.

From an organizational behaviour perspective, there was the problem of organizational dualism and its effects on middle management: quality circles were effectively outside the existing line of command and unaccountable to their managers, people at the top seemed indifferent to how managers dealt with circles, thus middle managers would be expected to have little interest in making circles work.

The other explanation, deriving from a different intellectual perspective, had to do with the imputed motives of senior managers in introducing quality circles in the first place. Circles were seen as components of a strategy to bypass trade unions and create an individualistic relationship with employees, in order to increase the legitimacy of management in employees' eyes. Ramsay (1977; 1985) has argued, of participative schemes in general, that companies extend participation on a cyclical basis. His 'cycles of control' thesis is that, historically, top management has responded to periods of crisis in industrial relations, when labour has challenged its legitimacy, by offering greater participation, only to revert to conventional ways of managing when the crisis is over. Moreover, the offer of more participation during crises is largely an ideological appeal, with little real substance in terms of changing the way of managing; on investigation, all participative schemes turn out to be small beer. The ideological aim of schemes such as quality circles is to repair managerial legitimacy. From this perspective, quality circles were a response to the industrial relations crisis of the late 1970s and the start of the 1980s, with a lag while managerial perceptions adjusted to the new realities emerging in the early 1980s, which should have faded once managers had become convinced that the traditional balance of power in employment had returned.

In the event, I found no support for the claims made by the advocates of quality circles (Hill, 1991a). Investigation of thirteen companies which had introduced circles in the early 1980s showed that only two still retained them by the end of 1989. Circles had led to minor operational improvements, but had done little to increase involvement, improve the human relations climate or change company cultures. It was rare for more than 10 per cent of the eligible employees to join, and non-members disparaged circle programmes, despite a widely held belief among employees that more participation in managerial decisions was highly desirable. The evidence supported the sceptics' claim that circle programmes inevitably fade away. The major feature was lack of management support. Middle managers were recalcitrant, mainly as a result of organizational dualism, although managerial culture was also unsympathetic to the participation of subordinates. Senior managers who had started the circle programmes subsequently failed to back the initiative and were indifferent to management recalcitrance.

There was some evidence to support the thesis of a cycle of control. First, participation was introduced partly to solve a perceived crisis in industrial relations earlier in the decade. Second, participation was restricted to a narrow range of issues and middle managers reduced its effectiveness even in this limited area. Third, circles decayed once the crisis had passed. However, other evidence qualified the predicted pattern. Senior management in several companies continued with circles through to the late 1980s, long after the changing environment of employee relations had reduced the need to repair managerial legitimacy and the economic returns from circles had been shown to be small. Circle members themselves reported that their participation had real substance and disagreed with non-members who saw it as a sham. Finally, more than half the companies had persevered with some form of participative quality improvement after the demise of quality circles. These included four firms that were managing on the basis of TQM.

Comparison of the British and Japanese experience of quality circles shows that the British borrowers of Japanese techniques of participative quality management in the 1980s failed to comprehend the broader context of quality management and that, in Japan, circles were only one part of the *total* system of quality improvement that we now call TQM. Lillrank and Kano (1989: 37) state that it is rare in practice for Japanese companies to have circles without TQM, while circles 'are by definition part of a company-wide effort of quality improvement and change' (ibid.: 40). Japanese quality theorists are well aware of the pitfalls of taking circles out of context, and Ishikawa (1985: 144), for example, is highly critical of the Western use of circles, which he thinks are bound to fail. He believes that a basic premise of starting quality circles must be that top management is also embarking on TQM.

Top management in the four TQM companies specified enhanced business performance as their goal, and cultural change as one of the means to achieve this. Cultural change subsumed the participation, involvement and intrinsic reward elements that circles had been aimed at. The crucial difference was that these desirable outcomes were now seen to depend on prior changes in the attitudes and behaviour of *managers*, which required an organization-wide cultural change. Moreover, TQM seemed to avoid the organizational design problem (dualism) which had contributed significantly to managerial resistance in the past.

## TQM THEORY

There is no single theoretical formalization of total quality, but the American quality gurus, Deming (1986) and Juran (1988), and the Japanese writer Ishikawa (1985) provide a set of core assumptions and specific principles of management which can be synthesized into a coherent framework. Total quality management is a business discipline and philosophy of management which institutionalizes planned and continuous business improvement. The real test of quality management is its ability to satisfy customers in the marketplace. TQM assumes that quality is the outcome of all activities that take place within an organization. Accordingly, all functions and all employees have to participate in the improvement process and, to ensure this, organizations need both quality systems and a quality culture.

For the purposes of this discussion, certain principles of quality management may be described briefly. First, top management is the main driver of TQM. Quality is a strategic issue for corporate management and is not just an operational issue for lower levels of the hierarchy. Quality includes innovation, which is the search for more effective ways of meeting customer requirements, as well as improving the efficiency of existing operations. Top management determines quality priorities, establishes the systems of quality management and the procedures to be followed, provides resources and leads by example. Oversight of the improvement process normally resides in a steering committee of senior managers reporting directly to the top of the organization.

Second, quality improvement occurs in two places. One is the existing 'vertical' structure, where improvement activity takes place within naturally occurring organizational units, such as departments, sections and work teams, rather than outside. However, since many issues cut across these units and the divisions between functions, new arrangements for the 'horizontal' coordination of improvement are also required. Cross-functional management is an essential feature of TQM. One principle of horizontal activity is the idea of the internal customer: organizational units discuss the quality of their performance with those who receive their output, in order to improve the service they provide to these 'customers'. The use of *ad hoc*, multifunctional or interdepartmental project teams is a second way of organizing across the vertical lines. An implication of this is that a matrix organizational design may provide a particularly appropriate structure within which such activity can take place.

Third, the crucial role in business improvement lies with management. Major innovation is clearly a managerial task, but the incremental improvement of existing operations is also primarily the responsibility of management. Most quality problems occur in systems controlled by managers and they have the power to resolve them, whereas rank and file employees are less to blame and usually lack the authority to put things right. Deming and Juran estimate that 10 per cent or less of quality issues in manufacturing operations can be tackled by workers and foremen on their own. Ishikawa (1985: 130–5) further suggests that, within the management group, middle managers have a distinct place in improvement: they stand at the cross-roads of the vertical and horizontal planes, and they are also responsible for the activities that take place among rank and file employees, notably quality control circles in the Japanese case.

Juran's notion of self-control is of particular interest here. He maintains that responsibility for quality should be assigned only to people who can control the quality of what they do. People have to be able to regulate what they do and have the authority to implement improvements. Even when they have the ability, shopfloor and office employees usually lack the authority, and should not be asked to accept responsibility for what is beyond their control. One implication of this is that responsibility should pass up the hierarchy to those with the authority or, alternatively, that authority should be decentralized downwards. The conditions necessary for greater self-control among shopfloor employees include job enrichment and more workgroup autonomy.

Fourth, there are rigorous and systematic techniques of issue identification and problem-solving which every employee should be trained to use. These include: measures of non-conformance and, where appropriate, statistical methods of process quality control; measures of the cost of quality; cause and effect analysis and decision-making procedures. These in turn rely on accurate and relevant information on every aspect of the business. Hard data are a requirement of what has aptly been labelled as 'management by fact' (Garvin, 1991).

Finally, the improvement process both creates and depends on cultural change. The appropriate culture has many elements. It includes: the internalization of quality and continuous improvement as a goal of all activities; the absolute priority of customer satisfaction; a systematic and rational approach to quality improvement issues; more open communications, so that those further down are listened to by those further up; the greater involvement of a wider range of people in the decision-making process; and the creation of high-trust social relationships. Deming and Juran believe that US companies have to change their managerial styles and personnel policies in order to incorporate rank and file employees into this quality culture, recognizing that traditional practices have led to a cultural divide between managers and other employees which makes their participation in improvement problematic.

The British Quality Association distinguishes a range of 'soft', 'hard' and 'mixed' forms of TQM (Wilkinson *et al.*, 1992). 'Soft' TQM emphasizes customer awareness and the duty of employees to take responsibility for quality. The principal strategy is the development of customer care programmes, in order to improve the quality of delivery and company culture. This is achieved by means of employee education and training, and the relaxation of supervision for quality control, so that employees can be empowered to deliver quality to internal and external customers. Employee motivation is crucial for successful customer care. 'Hard' TQM uses the traditional techniques of quality control and assurance, and corresponds to 'management by fact'. Mixed forms combine the two approaches. The BQA typology generalizes from the practices of UK companies that claim to be implementing TQM but, in doing this, dilutes the concept to include forms that do not embody the core assumptions of the quality gurus and would fail the practical test of the premier quality awards; for example, the Baldrige Award (Garvin, 1991). There is a familiar phenomenological issue here: if people believe something is real, then it *is* real to them. However, for the purpose of this analysis, 'real' TQM contains both 'hard' and 'soft' elements that give practical expression to the principles outlined above. (See also Wilkinson, 1994.)

The inadequacies of British quality circle programmes can now be seen more clearly. Top management did not take an active role in improvement, middle managers were excluded by the dual structure, the issue of cultural change was only partly addressed, and those whose responsibility was quality improvement were not given the requisite authority (quality circles proposed improvements, but it was usually up to managers to implement them). The ultimate absurdity was to train rank and file employees to use modern techniques of quality management while their managers remained largely in ignorance of these. Quality circles were in any case not on their own an appropriate means to realize the objectives that senior management had for them. The bulk of quality improvement issues and all the really important ones are beyond the competence of circles, because they transcend the workplace or exceed the authority of workers and foremen. Outside the framework of TQM, circles encounter the problem that companies are not structured to respond to bottom-up initiatives and managers do not understand the improvement process, with the result that, even in the limited area where circles have competence, managers may obstruct improvement. Employees are probably correct to disparage the circle method of enlisting their involvement in improvement, which clearly fails to meet their aspirations for more say when introduced into a quality management vacuum. A number of companies did change their communications and personnel practices in a 'quality' direction, introducing new methods of communicating with employees and their union representatives and, in five cases, bringing in single-status terms and conditions of employment. However, these changes plus quality circles were insufficient to enlist the full involvement of people at the bottom and raise their commitment in the way senior managers desired.

The TQM literature regards quality management as a core component of every job and the organizational arrangements for quality as integral to the operating systems of companies, thus dualism ceases to be an issue. However, the analysis of how companies might successfully implement the principles of quality so that continuous improvement is in fact established as the normal organizational state is not adequate. While solutions to the technical issues of designing appropriate systems and procedures are fully specified, there are obvious lacunae in the treatment of the social factors. Resistance to improvement is properly highlighted, but its nature and extent are not understood and the proposed solutions are too restricted. First, commitment is seen as a problem among rank and file employees, but there is little recognition that this is an issue throughout an organization, including the managerial grades, and that different groups typically do not share the objectives of top management. Second, the mechanisms required to persuade people to 'buy into' quality management are limited to leadership from the top, systematic education and training, learning the benefits by doing and recognition for achievements. The thrust of these prescriptions is that top managers should win hearts and minds without compulsion, and quality management theorists lack a proper understanding of how companies operate, the difficulties faced in introducing planned change and the academic literature on organizations. Cultural change is a major objective of quality management and this has been discussed extensively in the organizational design literature. Schein (1985: 223–43) has noted that structures, systems and procedures are important but secondary mechanisms of change. The primary tools used to embed a culture include leadership and education, and the more coercive levers of persuasion available to top management by virtue of their command of organizational power, namely the deployment of organizational rewards and punishments. Yet the consensus among advocates of TQM is that the financial incentive, for example, should never be used, as this 'does not form part of the TQM culture, and would defeat many of the objectives' (Oakland, 1989: 303).

The following discussion shows how certain companies have implemented TQM and largely overcome the pitfalls of circles, but in doing so have had to go beyond what the gurus of quality management believe to be desirable.

## TQM IN PRACTICE

Four companies with TQM were investigated. One was the European subsidiary of a US office automation company, which was in its fifth year of TQM in 1988 (when most of the fieldwork in this company took place). It had extended TQM to all employees two years earlier. The second was a British office automation company. This had a fairly active quality circle programme, which predated TQM by many years, and TQM was applied first to managers and after two years to everyone else. The programme was tracked from the second through to the fourth year in 1990. In late 1989 and early 1990, the British subsidiary of a US manufacturer of components for the automotive industry was investigated. This had started TQM in 1985 and extended it to the shopfloor in 1988. A British manufacturer of precision engineering components whose programme was a year old and confined to management, the company being unsure when it would extend the scheme, was also investigated. Case-study methods were used. These included interviews and discussions among all levels of management and with union representatives and other employees, and inspection of the companies' own documentation.

Three companies illustrate the seriousness and care with which top managers have approached TQM, in contrast to the 'quick fix' mentality that typically marked the introduction of quality circles. The US office equipment company spent nearly two years on preparatory work before introducing its scheme. Implementation started with top management and slowly cascaded down the organization until it reached office and shopfloor employees about two years later. The automotive company launched TQM among its managers with far less prior preparation, but then spent three years developing its procedures with extensive help from outside consultants, before extending them to all employees. The British office equipment company had substantial and long-term experience with various aspects of quality management, including circles and an earlier programme that trained every manager in marketing and customer care, but still took nearly two years to design and implement a scheme among its managers, before all employees were brought into the net. The commitment of top management was rarely questioned in any of the firms, since top managers provided the very substantial resources that were necessary for such a major and long, drawn-out change, created the appropriate systems and were quick to iron out any problems that arose as TQM developed.

The US office automation company differed from the others in two important respects. First, it had the most explicit view of total quality as requiring new ways of working and treating people and as covering all transactions and employees. Managers were required to work more in teams, to consult before making decisions, to encourage openness and trust and show respect for others, to assist subordinates and act as role models. They were obliged to place the satisfaction of external and internal customers ahead of other considerations. The company also prescribed the use of formal techniques to identify, assess and resolve quality improvement issues. In the fourth and fifth years, TQM was incorporated into individual performance appraisals and business objectives. Adherence to prescribed TQM procedures and behaviours (rather than improvement outcomes) became a part of annual appraisals, salary reviews, promotions and dismissals. Corporate management aligned divisional business objectives with TQM, putting customer satisfaction ahead of return on assets and market share. This was the only company to make TQM obligatory in all these ways. Second, when it began to implement TQM, it did so with a better and more fully worked out scheme than the automotive company, which was also in the fifth year at the time of the research. In effect, its programme was about two years further on. This may be significant for the following discussion, because it is generally accepted that TQM takes several years to become established as a normal way of working, and differences among the companies may reflect these differences of timing.

Middle managers in each company said that they had become more involved in quality management than previously. The integration of the improvement process into the existing organization and as part of normal working practices meant that managers could now direct their subordinates to work on specific issues and keep control of initiatives from below. Improvement activity was seen as more focused, coherent and relevant, less time-consuming and delivering quicker and more substantial benefits, in comparison with circles and other schemes. In the British office automation company where TQM was introduced alongside circles, these continued to operate as voluntary groups which remained detached from managerial control, but managers could now assign all employees, including circle members, to quality improvement groups and corrective action teams. Indeed, quality circles achieved a new lease of life and grew in numbers, although they were less numerous than other group activities. Managers found circles easier to live with under TQM, and dualism was less of an issue. The addition of managerially directed groups allowed them to meet their own immediate improvement objectives, the broader understanding they now had of quality improvement made them more appreciative of the value of voluntary commitment to quality, and they suggested that circle activities themselves were now more tightly focused on issues relevant to the quality objectives of the company. In the fourth year, however, following an internal survey which showed that many employees were not convinced of the company's commitment to quality as its first priority (see below), it was decided that managers should be required to develop group improvement activities as an integral part of their job; these were not optional activities. As a result, senior departmental managers were set targets for the involvement of their subordinates in group activities, which carried financial bonuses. The upshot was that group activity, including working with circles, was worth getting right.

Managers in the US office automation firm reported that they had begun to delegate more as they came to rely on the abilities of their subordinates to solve problems. A notable example of this was the relocation of a production facility from one building to another in one of the British plants. The departmental production manager delegated the entire operation to his first-line section managers and operatives, who worked with production engineering on the design of the new layout, arranged the move and supervised the installation of the equipment. He reasoned that they were more likely to get the transfer right than he was, given their practical experience with the machinery. His role was to be kept informed of progress and to sign the authorizations for the required expenditures. Describing the event, the manager stated that previously he would have taken charge, although he would have involved his section managers, but the idea of delegating and involving operatives would not have crossed his mind. The fact that it now seemed both sensible and natural to do so had brought home to him how much TQM had changed his style of managing.

There was a movement towards more involvement of various layers of management in decision-making in each company. The TQM structure of participative issue identification and problem-solving gave managers more input into decisions taken above them in the hierarchy and horizontally across departments and functions. Discussions with managers suggested that this had gone furthest in the manufacturing division of the US office automation subsidiary, where all levels of management reported that decisions were now routinely made after greater consultation, both vertically and horizontally, and on the basis of greater consensus.

The centre of activity also shifted over time. Each company noted a tendency for middle rather than senior managers to become the main actors, with senior managers responding to issues by delegating to subordinates and not participating actively in the teams. In the early days, multi-level groups of managers within naturally occurring units were common, but with time managerial involvement in improvement teams tended to be among managers of similar status on projects that ran horizontally across the organization. All the companies except the US office automation firm regarded this development as evidence that quality management was becoming ingrained and no longer needed to be driven from above, although senior managers continued to monitor the process in terms of the amount of improvement activity and reductions in the cost of quality and non-conformance. The US office automation company regarded the withdrawal of senior managers as an issue, however, and introduced measures to enforce their participation. A major review of the TQM programme in its fourth year, commissioned by US corporate management, had found that senior managers across the company failed to exercise the required leadership, refusing to become involved in teamwork and neglecting to use routinely the formal improvement and problem-solving processes (the failure to use formal techniques was widespread among all levels of management). Thereafter, senior managers were appraised more rigorously in their use of procedures, while all managers were required to convene at least one unit improvement team per annum.

Middle managers appreciated the increased decentralization and their greater influence over the decisions taken elsewhere in the organization that affected their activities. Many also believed that TQM could advance their careers, by bringing them to the attention of more senior managers if they performed well on a major improvement project, and that it gave them a better understanding of the wider organization. Decentralization and participation represent a major change in the style of managing for most companies, a shift from individual decision-taking and authoritative, top-down communication towards a more collective style with greater two-way communication and less emphasis on giving and receiving commands. It can also promote more teamwork and flexibility within the management group. The literature on employee participation strangely has ignored the desire among managerial employees for more influence and involvement, yet the extension of managerial participation under TQM is a significant gain for people who, like the employees they supervise, have a real interest in a more participative system of managing. The language of teamwork is of course the standard discourse among managers, but, in practice, this has been more exhortatory than real among the middle and lower levels of management where functional specialization and authoritative management have been the norm. TQM has the potential to align reality with rhetoric by means of participation.

Nevertheless, quality management is not universally welcomed and these organizations reported a lack of involvement among some employees at all levels. The British office automation company surveyed all its employees in the third and fourth years of TQM. They were asked to rate themselves, their immediate bosses and the company in terms of commitment to quality on a number of dimensions of quality management. Two-thirds of the respondents had a high personal commitment to quality, 60 per cent reported that their immediate managers were highly committed and 50 per cent regarded the company as giving quality an absolute priority. The first two proportions increased slightly between the two surveys, while the third declined. The US office automation company asked all employees to assess the behaviour of their immediate bosses in a number of areas in the third year of TQM, about eighteen months before this investigation. In the manufacturing division, between 60 and 70 per cent of subordinates assessed their bosses' behaviour as conforming to the company's specifications regarding the appropriate ways of working and treating people, and the consideration of customer requirements, although their assessments of how frequently the formal techniques of quality improvement were used were lower. These results are obviously of unknown value, given the limitations of company-sponsored surveys, but they are the only data available that provide some idea of the level of acceptance. They give flesh to the claim in every company that it takes a number of years to persuade everyone to 'buy into' quality management and explain the decisions to make adherence to quality procedures obligatory. On the other hand, the self-assessments and assessments of others also suggest that a majority does subscribe to a culture of quality.

The quality improvement outcomes were significant. Every firm had substantially reduced the level of defects in the final product and at intermediate stages in the manufacturing process, as well as having increased customer satisfaction as assessed by customer surveys, and reduced costs. New measures of operating efficiency, such as the cost of non-conformance and the more all-embracing cost of quality, were introduced as part of TQM and showed continuously increasing efficiency each year. The two office automation companies also measured levels of quality improvement activity, although in slightly different ways. The US firm logged over 600 projects in its manufacturing division in the fourth year of TQM, this division employing around 5,000 people, while in the major manufacturing plant of the British company there were 250 improvement groups covering 46 per cent of the 3,000 employees in the fourth year.

Line managers in the three companies which had extended TQM to the office and shop floors were satisfied with the measurable outcomes at these levels, such as reduced defects and costs. In every case, rank and file employees were assigned responsibility for inspecting their own output, routinely informed of any faults found subsequently and encouraged to solve problems with their co-workers. The most significant change in working practices associated with TQM was experienced in the automotive company. This had abolished supervision and introduced autonomous teamworking in a new, automated assembly facility. Operators were trained in multiple competences and the teams decided who would do what. Production engineers and business coordinators (as middle line managers were now titled) acted as facilitators and consultants to the labour force. In another company, a work group operating a CNC machining centre cell was given responsibility for production scheduling, tool management and minor changes to the cell's programmes. In the absence of consistent and independent information on attitudes and perceptions, and before-and-after measurements, the extent of rank and file involvement or cultural change cannot be established. But there are indications that TQM may be well received. People appear to identify with the quality improvement aspect of the new culture. This emerges from the attitude data collected by the British office automation company and the revival of quality circles after the extension of TQM to all employees (the proportion of employees in circles having increased from 10 to 17 per cent). In the US office automation company, interviews with operators, union representatives and section managers revealed that large numbers of the direct labour force were thought to have absorbed the ethos of quality improvement and enjoyed the opportunity to put quality training into practice, and that they seemed to regard the company as a better employer as a result. However, the union stewards in all three firms made the point that other important changes in personnel policy during the 1980s, notably single-status employment, would also have contributed significantly to changing views about the companies as good employers.

Finally, TQM unites routine management and managing for innovation in one set of organizational arrangements and practices. Most of the improvement activity that takes place near the bottom of companies deals with incremental innovation for efficiency – that is, finding better ways of doing existing things. This was the thrust of quality circles and remains so with new forms of employee involvement in improvement. Finding new things to do is also central to TQM, and this more radical form of innovation is usually located in the middle and higher reaches of companies. Indeed, top management is even more concerned to get TQM working effectively in this part of the organization, because the potential benefits of improvement here are much greater than further down (Hill, 1991b). While much quality improvement activity among the managerial strata in these companies was incremental in nature and oriented to the more efficient performance of existing tasks, TQM did provide a method of facilitating changes of a more radical and innovatory kind. New product development, new manufacturing methods and new supplier relations were all handled by multi-functional project teams arising out of TQM and using quality management techniques to work to a conclusion. In some cases these were one-off teams, while in others they were permanent features of new structures of cross-functional liaison and decision-making. An essential feature of both was that the people responsible for dealing with the outcomes as part of their routine managerial duties were also responsible for handling change, and this linkage was believed to produce better outcomes.

## DISCUSSION

The late 1980s was a period of significant transition in the search for improvement and cultural change in British companies, a time when TQM emerged from the relative obscurity of the pioneering firms that had taken it up in the mid-1980s, to become the new 'corporate religion' of the 1990s (*Financial Times* report, 3 February 1992). Three of the cases studied were among these pioneers: by 1990, one firm had been working along TQM lines for nearly six years, another for five and a third for four. However, one must be cautious in seeking to understand how TQM works in Britain. As shown above, it takes several years to introduce, develop and institutionalize full-blown TQM, even among firms that pursue the approach wholeheartedly, so it is reasonable to assume that most companies will be on the learning curve and still developing their procedures. In addition, many British companies have introduced aspects of modern quality management but apparently have not embarked on full TQM (Wilkinson *et al.*, 1993). For both reasons, full TQM is unlikely to be normal. Moreover, it looks as if many British companies which claim to have introduced TQM have done so on the cheap and in the hope of a quick fix, ignoring the principles of best practice and the substantial investments required, and proceeding in a half-hearted, unsystematic and partial way, with the result that they have got it wrong (Cruise O'Brien and Voss, 1992; Wilkinson *et al.*, 1992; 1993). Finally, the range of applications now described as 'TQM' is so wide, including, for example, what are essentially customer-care programmes as well as real TQM, that one must take care to compare like with like.

Most of the blame for the failure of quality circles to realize the business improvement and cultural change objectives of senior managers should be assigned to middle managers; the response of the middle levels of the organization must be related, in turn, to the failure of senior managers to establish appropriate organizational designs. TQM avoids the problem of parallel and dualistic structures, by integrating quality management into existing hierarchies. The point at which each reporting line converged in these companies was the top establishment manager. This was also where overall responsibility for quality management resided. Every company also modified its operating systems and procedures, to include quality management as part of the normal method of managing and as a component of every managerial job. Quality control professionals had a facilitating role, training and advising people in other functional areas, but no direct responsibility for quality improvement. Improvement was therefore part of a unified structure that prevented organizational dualism.

An appropriate design consists of more than just the right structures, systems and procedures, however, and these companies found they still had to contend with backsliding and a lack of commitment among certain middle and senior managers. In particular, a number of people failed to develop participative teamworking among subordinates and to pursue improvement using the tools of quality management systematically. Both the office automation companies had started with the assumption that TQM should be taken up voluntarily and that managers would willingly adopt the required attitudes and behaviour, provided the people at the top created the appropriate organizational arrangements and climate, but introduced significant changes in the fourth years of their programmes when they decided to use their normal methods of rewarding desired behaviours and punishing deviations in order to make TQM stick. These developments extended the assimilation of improvement into the everyday fabric of management. The automotive company remained less concerned than the others to monitor the process and was more interested in outcomes, but managers were clear that delivering improvements would be rewarded in career terms. In sum, managers came to understand over time, as the result of their experience of using quality management procedures and the actions of their bosses, that TQM directly affected their own interests: it helped them to manage more effectively, it increased their own participation and it carried both positive and negative sanctions. One may conclude with the simple proposition, that top management will increase the likelihood of a successful outcome to planned organizational change – in this case, quality management and its associated cultural shift – when it finds ways to align this with the self-interest of individual managers.

While there is firm evidence of the tangible business benefits of TQM, and clear indications that cultural change within management was under way, it is not possible to be so definite about cultural change among shopfloor and office employees. Anthropologists and ethnographers define culture as comprising standardized and patterned behaviours, as well as mental constructs such as values, beliefs, attitudes and assumptions (Singer, 1968), although organizational theorists have placed more emphasis on the latter than the former. Taking attitudes and perceptions, there is some evidence that people identify with elements of the TQM culture – in particular, they take pride in good work, are aware of quality issues and endorse their firm's activities to improve quality, but the validity of this evidence is unclear. However, research on Japanese firms operating in Britain has shown that British employees value the opportunities that Japanese systems provide for high-quality work and to rekindle the work ethic, as well as the more 'egalitarian' style of Japanese managers (White and Trevor, 1983). There is also considerable evidence that job redesign which widens the range of tasks and increases responsibility can create what people regard as better jobs. Thus, a positive evaluation of TQM would not be unexpected. Wilkinson *et al.* (1991) also report favourable employee responses in two companies which have recently implemented TQM. The behavioural evidence is much firmer, and by their actions many employees show that quality management has been internalized and is becoming a normal way of working. The effects of the other changes that preceded the formal adoption of TQM, such as the upwards harmonization of terms and conditions of employment and new production concepts, do not confuse the issue, because these developments are treated within TQM theory as components of quality management. Thus there is some support for a second proposition – that non-managerial employees are receptive at least to parts of TQM culture.

A criticism levelled against cultural change strategies is that they attempt to indoctrinate employees into managerial ideologies that serve corporate interests rather than those of employees. In Foucaultian terms, they are discourses of power that mould employees' subjectivities. The way TQM is projected in some companies may indeed verge on brainwashing, and 'corporate religion' assumes a sinister meaning. People, however, are not cultural dopes, they can judge such ideological appeals for what they are and test the exhortations of top management against reality. Middle managers, lower-level employees and their union representatives were not seduced by the rhetoric, and endorsed TQM only when they were convinced that corporate management meant what it said, and could see benefit to themselves. Even then, acceptance was conditional and it seems unlikely that 'strong' corporate cultures can succeed if they rely primarily on ideological manipulation.

The firms studied have maintained participation at the base of their organizations beyond the point in the cycle of control and legitimation where one might have expected it to be dropped; nor is it a sham. The author's own observations of work tasks and improvement teams in action, together with the perceptions of workers, stewards and supervisors, indicate that rank and file employees have become more involved in issues that were previously the prerogative of management. The examples of a quality improvement team taking charge of the plant relocation and of work group autonomy are dramatic illustrations, but the routine use of improvement teams and the enlargement of jobs confirms the picture. This is without being starry-eyed about the nature of participation at this level, nor to suggest that it necessarily empowers lower-level employees to any significant extent. In the main, participation has been confined to issues related to work tasks and work organization at the point of production. The area of autonomous decision-making varies from case to case, and it is most extensive where group working is also implemented. Where solutions to problems involve financial expenditures or have repercussions elsewhere in the organization, it is still common for employees to propose, while management makes the decision. Nevertheless, rank and file employees do have more say than before, so TQM meets at least part of their aspirations for participation.

The new approach was not experienced as coercive, but there is clearly the potential to increase stress and to facilitate control from above. Effort intensification can be one result of giving people more responsibilities, and this is especially likely to be felt as stressful when companies simultaneously move to lean production with reduced staffing levels. TQM also facilitates surveillance, because it generates information that is unprecedented in its scope and detail. Rank and file employees, however, did not report more intensity or control at the time of investigation, although it should also be noted that the state of the labour market and industrial relations in the 1980s meant that most British companies found they had all the control they wanted. The coercive potential of TQM applies also to managerial staff, of course — something that writers on the labour process often ignore. The only people to report stress here were a handful of first-line managers.

Finally, there are sound theoretical reasons for believing that top management now has a real interest in making participation work at all levels. One is simply the amount of money that they have chosen to invest in TQM. The others relate to different changes in

organizations over the last few years, that give enhanced participation a basis in the material conditions of production, rather than
just as an ideological prop of management. Quality circles were
introduced within traditional organizational structures that combined bureaucratic and Taylorist principles. Some of them showed
briefly that participation could deliver efficiency gains even in these
firms, by accessing the local knowledge of those doing a particular
job. The TQM firms, however, were trying to change on a broad
front and used quality management as a method of tying together
the components of change and as a model of the desired end state.
In common with many American and British organizations, they
had delayered and destaffed their lower and middle management in
order to reduce costs, while at the same time looking for a more
rapid and effective response to the contemporary product market
requirements of variety, change and quality. Delayering management promotes some decentralization of decision-making and an
enlargement of jobs that affect roles at and near the bottom of
companies. Rapid response puts a new premium on internal
flexibility and better horizontal coordination, which gives an additional impetus to wider roles at each hierarchical level as people
collaborate across the organization rather than push issues
upwards, shifting from mechanistic towards more organic ways
of working. TQM provides a workable method of handling such
changes and it must be viewed as an influential and effective
paradigm for flexible organizations, broadly conceived (Hill,
1991b).

It is therefore obvious that the strategy of changing organizations from below by means of quality circles was bound to fail. The
belief that change would convect upwards ignored the realities of
organizational power and inertia, and under-estimated the difficulty
of transforming companies in a 'quality' direction. The unwillingness of top managers to deal with the issue of organizational
design, by creating appropriate systems and structures and attach-
ing positive and negative sanctions – in other words, their refusal
to manage change – reduced what little chance circles may have
had. Even TQM, which is massively resourced, driven from the
top and works with the grain of management, is liable to falter
without the additional reinforcement of organizational controls.
The difference now is that the people who rule corporations
appear far more determined to succeed with this latest development than they ever were in the past.

# REFERENCES

Cruise O'Brien, R. and Voss, C. (1992) *In Search of Quality*, London: London Business School Working Paper.

Deming, W. (1986) *Out of the Crisis*, Cambridge: Cambridge University Press.

Garvin, D. (1991) 'How the Baldridge Award Really Works', *Harvard Business Review*, Nov–Dec, 80–93.

Hill, S. (1991a) 'Why Quality Circles Failed but Total Quality Management Might Succeed', *British Journal of Industrial Relations*, 29, 541–68.

Hill, S. (1991b) 'How Do You Manage a Flexible Firm? The Total Quality Model', *Work, Employment and Society*, 5, 397–415.

Ishikawa, K. (1985) *What Is Total Quality Control? The Japanese Way*, Englewood Cliffs, NJ: Prentice-Hall.

Juran, J. (1988) *Juran on Planning for Quality*, New York: Free Press.

Lillrank, P. and Kano, N. (1989) *Continuous Improvement: Quality Control Circles in Japanese Industry*, Ann Arbor, MI: Center for Japanese Studies, University of Michigan.

Oakland, J. (1989) *Total Quality Management*, Oxford: Heinemann Professional Publishing.

Ramsay, H. (1977) 'Cycles of Control: Worker Participation in Sociological and Historical Perspective', *Sociology*, 11, 481–506.

Ramsay, H. (1985) 'What is Participation For? A Critical Evaluation of "Labour Process" Analyses of Job Reform', in D. Knights, H. Willmott and D. Collinson (eds) *Job Redesign*, Aldershot: Gower.

Schein, E. (1985) *Organizational Culture and Leadership*, San Francisco, CA: Jossey-Bass.

Singer, M. (1968) 'The Concept of Culture', in D. Sills (ed.) *International Encyclopedia of the Social Sciences*, 3, New York: Macmillan and The Free Press.

White, M. and Trevor, M. (1983), *Under Japanese Management*, London: Heinemann Educational Books.

Wilkinson, A. (1994) 'Managing Human Resources For Quality', in B.G. Dale (ed.) *Managing Quality* (2nd edn), Hemel Hempstead: Prentice-Hall.

Wilkinson, A., Allen, P. and Snape, E. (1991) 'TQM and the Management of Labour', *Employee Relations*, 13, 24–31.

Wilkinson, A., Redman, T. and Snape, E. (1993) *Quality and the Manager: An IM Report*, Corby: British Institute of Management.

Wilkinson, A., Marchington, M., Goodman, J., Ackers, P. (1992) 'Total Quality Management and Employee Involvement', *Human Resource Management Journal*, 2 (4), 1–20.

# 2

# IDEOLOGY, QUALITY AND TQM

*Alan Tuckman*

## INTRODUCTION

Recent concern with total quality management – or TQM – has tended to see it as a part of a process of Japanization, subordinate to the more significant emergence of 'quality circles' (Hill, 1991, and in this volume) and just-in-time manufacture (JIT) or of TQM/JIT factory regimes (Deldridge *et al.*, 1991; Sewell and Wilkinson, 1992a). Submerged by the academic debate around the development of 'Japanization' is a more diverse development that expresses a growing and pervasive concern over 'quality'. Central to this development is the emergent ideology, practice and – importantly – discourse of TQM. The push for quality is being presented as both the means of industrial recovery – an aping of the perceived means of Japan's success – and of the attempt to construct a new managerial framework of industrial and social consensus. In this paper it is argued that the emergence of TQM is a central component within a broader attempt to create new forms of managerial and political control – not, principally, through coercion but by consent; what can be seen as part of a broader hegemonic project (see Gramsci, 1971; also Hall, 1988).

Commentators have tended to under-estimate the significance of TQM and the quality debate in the context of current social, political and industrial changes. Importantly, they ignore the move of formal systems of quality control and assurance out of manufacturing and into service industries and the public sector. In the process, consistent with *kaizen* – continuous improvement – quality assurance has been transformed into subtle, and subjective, modes of control over labour. The previous emphasis on statistical process control has shifted to 'culture change'; quality assurance has become TQM. Historically, 'quality control' was integral to craft and professional practice in the role, for example, of apprenticeship, training and peer control. However, within the framework of mass production in the 1930s, and the absence of such craft controls along with the increased scale of production, alternative means of quality control were established, based around systematic sampling, the statistical methods of quality assurance. Concern with quality in production – or service provision – is not therefore new; TQM has emerged not as a new concern with quality but as a critique of previous forms of quality assurance. What requires accounting for is the prominence given to 'quality' in the 1980s, reflected in the emergence of TQM.

The incorporation of this concern within that for a broader 'Japanization' process infers a recognition of one important reason for this increased prominence given to quality assurance in the shape of TQM. The late 1970s onwards saw under-performing Western industry outstripped by Japanese and other Asian producers, particularly in motor and electrical manufacture – the success of which was often seen as the very symbol of a healthy modern industrial economy. Growing internationalization of Japanese firms – with the establishment of their own plants in the West – contrasted with the closure of European and US plants.[1] The crisis was not restricted to manufacturing industry but was reflected in major changes in the relationship between the State and society. This change was characterized by an emergent 'New Right', which saw state intervention as the route to tyranny while 'the market' was the very expression of freedom (see Hayek, 1944), coupled with a view of bureaucracy as being synonymous with inefficiency and waste.[2] The decline of manufacturing in the West has been accompanied by major changes in the State and in public sector provision, with a shift away from planning and the Keynesian welfare state – and from more direct state provision, as in the former Soviet bloc – towards the market being seen as the key regulator of social as well as industrial and economic activity.

A central objective of this paper is to identify the emergence of TQM as a managerial ideology linked to these broader changes in the West. It seeks to examine both the long-term development of ideas about quality assurance and how this, in the 1980s, became linked to managerial notions of 'culture change' to establish TQM. Unlike the prolific literature that promotes TQM and argues that it empowers the workforce, or critics, such as Sewell and Wilkinson

(1992a; 1992b), who claim that – through its potential for direct surveillance – TQM achieves the opposite, here I argue that it is integral to the construction of consent to a broadly 'New Right' agenda within both politics and management. This is particularly important within the hegemonic shift represented by the New Right, with TQM promising significant savings by imposing a regime where workers – and managers – are supposed to get it 'right first time'. The goal of reducing 'waste' – congruent with New Right ideology – and particularly waste of paid labour time, is instilled through the ethos of the internal market, the customer/ supplier chain and the imperative for continuous improvement. This is not to deny that one of the objectives of this concern with quality is the improvement of products and services to the final consumer, but that, as a hegemonic project, the route to TQM is integral to obtaining workforce consent to new sets of – often far more intensified – working relations. Far from obscuring exchange relations within the labour process (see Burawoy, 1979), TQM presents the internalization of market relations as the only means of achieving quality. First, therefore, we will examine the very definition of quality and its links to the construction of the 'internal customer'.

## THE QUALITY CHAIN

### Defining quality

As a hegemonic project, TQM is founded on the notion – which is difficult to reject – that we should all strive to improve the quality of products and services. However, 'quality' is deployed within a particular technical discourse of quality assurance, which is rather different to common usage of the term. Central to TQM is this rejection of 'common sense' notions of quality: 'The first erroneous assumption is that quality means goodness, or luxury, or shininess, or weight' (Crosby, 1979: 14).

No less is 'quality' some transcendent, metaphysically or aesthetically defined – or more usually undefinable – notion. The very definition of 'quality' deployed within TQM discourse is down-to-earth, material and measurable. It grows out of, and conforms to, a relation between component manufacturer and assembler; quality means 'fitness for use or purpose', according to Deming (1982) or 'conformance to requirements', according to Crosby (1979), two of the gurus of TQM. Growing out of the emergent field of quality assurance within manufacturing industry, the central features of the problem of 'quality' in this context is uniformity in meeting the precise specifications of contracts and design plans (see e.g. Garvin, 1988). Quality is a by-product of the emergence of mass-production systems that introduced an increase in scale and volume of production, along with production being taken out of the hands of workers. If the control over the quality and standard of the product was taken out of the hands of the worker, then some means of monitoring the vastly increased levels of production was required, alongside the new production methods themselves. If we were to attempt to summarize this process, it must be that quality is being transformed into quantity.

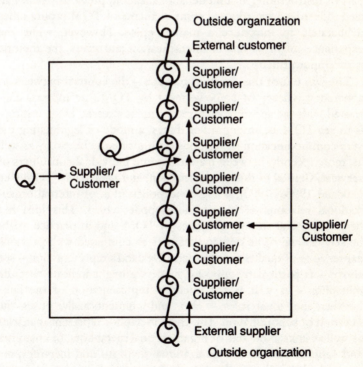

*Fig. 2.1.* The quality chain
*Source*: Oakland (1993)

## Customers and suppliers

In contrast to views that claim an initial reliance on the market, with organizational hierarchy meeting market failure (Williamson, 1975), it is argued here that the new quality is part of an attempt at post-crisis reconstruction that is based on the commodification of internal organizational relations and that previously non-market relations – at least in appearance – are being transformed into market transactions (see Offe, 1984). This draws into organizational relations the perceptions of a market transaction; relations internal to an organization are represented as those between a customer and a supplier. This often accompanies other changes that involve a more direct internal exchange system, like devolving budget-holding or other mechanisms by which the cost of an activity or service is measured, or of externalizing relationships through subcontracting and external suppliers. Most recently, as part of restructuring around denationalization, previously nationalized industries have adopted some elements of TQM programmes deliberately to introduce a market ethos. However, while the experience might be one of intensification and stress, the rhetoric is of empowerment.

The way out of this apparent paradox – the contrast between an apparent advocacy of empowerment by TQM's promoters, contrasted with the apparent disempowerment stressed by its critics – is to see TQM as, among other things, a mode of legitimating the very commodification of relations both inside the hierarchy as well as, more recently, between hierarchies and individual consumers of services. Central to this transformation, and arguably to TQM (see Oakland 1993, c.1990), is the conceptualization of internal organizational relations as a customer–supplier chain. This idea has become general among advocates of TQM, and in practice might be seen as one of its defining features as compared with previous expressions of quality management. Oakland's representation – see above – is particularly apposite, since we might indicate that the metaphor – as well as the intended representation of the links between individual roles – also, and unintentionally, poses the question of subordination. The chain metaphor represent manacles as well as links. New sets of organizational metaphors, of customer and supplier instead of organizational divisions and hierarchy, are established which are based on the internalization of market relations; a culture change programme is introduced which promotes the notion that it is only by seeing the next person down the chain in the labour process that quality can be assured. This, then, can be seen as the very penetration of New Right ideology into production – of an idealized market, but without concrete transaction. Thus, the notion of empowerment, which is also at the centre of TQM philosophy, borrows from New Right rhetoric in that empowerment is represented as the very product of the substitution of pseudo-market for bureaucratic relations.

Having identified the basic conceptualization of quality embedded in the emergence of TQM it is important to distinguish between particular approaches. The argument is not intended as one against quality, or quality assurance *per se*, but concerns the role of a particular approach – that of TQM – within a broader hegemonic project. TQM, which appeals to the universally acceptable striving for improved 'quality', has become part of a broader agenda that progressively commodifies social relations through the introduction of (ideologically and idealistically represented) market relations.

Some of the elements that draw TQM into the spectrum of New Right philosophy were already articulated within the approaches of some of the pioneer specialists in quality assurance prior to the 1950s. It was through them that the ideas spread to Japan. These pioneers have subsequently – in the 1980s and 1990s – become the gurus of TQM as the more submerged philosophy of market relations has gradually gained prominence. The basis of its conception of quality and social relations within the labour process is rooted in the development of mass production – the terrain where quality control and assurance were to acquire autonomy.

## FROM QUALITY CONTROL TO TQM

### Quality control and mass production

The establishment of modern quality assurance can be traced to the work of W.A. Shewhart on statistical process control in the 1930s at the Bell Telephone Laboratories, the research division of the Western Electric Company, where they were examining the best ways to sample for variation from the standardized equipment. Implemented around the earlier phases of the far more famous experiments – the Hawthorne studies – into the determination of 'restriction of output' and group behaviour, TQM has ultimately been seen as allied to their apparently humanistic management approach emphasizing employee motivation and involvement. In practice, however, the only relationship between the two sets of experiments – that giving rise to 'human relations' and that to 'quality control and assurance' – was the striving to resolve the problems arising from mass production. Management at the Western Electric Company – at the time at the forefront of electrical assembly work – were engaged in a process of 'continuous improvement' involving both human motivation with repetitive work and the control of the output of these workers.[3]

It was the application of statistical approaches to quality control to wartime mass production in the US, through the work of the Statistical Research Group, that saw the techniques become established. Even at the time, Deming was to make the distinction between methods of inspection out of faulty products and methods of avoidance; these were later represented as 'fire-fighting' and 'total' approaches to quality management, determining whether the new methods and techniques should be in the hands of a separate department or deployed generally. While there was this development of particular techniques, Deming was sensitive to the broader organizational setting for their adoption:

> Brilliant applications attracted much attention but the flare of statistical methods by themselves, in an atmosphere in which management did not know their responsibilities, burned, sputtered, fizzled, and died out. What the men did was to solve individual problems. Control charts proliferated, the more the better. Quality control departments sprouted. They plotted charts, looked at them, and filed them. They took quality control away from everybody else, which was of course entirely wrong, as quality control is everybody's job. *The put out fires, not perceiving the necessity to improve processes.*
>
> (Deming, 1982: 486; my emphasis)

Deming, then a government statistician and the intellectual heir to Shewhart, had offered his advice to a group of statisticians who were intent on applying their techniques to the demands of wartime production. The group included, incidentally, Milton Freidman, later the eminent economist and theorist of monetarism. Given the latter path of statistical applications into quality control, it is worth citing this advice:

Time and materials are at a premium [Deming argued], and there is no time to be lost. There is no royal short-cut to producing a highly trained statistician, but I do firmly believe that the most important principles of application can be expounded in a very short time to engineers and others. I have done it, and have seen it done. You could accomplish a greater deal by holding a school in the Shewhart methods some time in the near future. I would suggest a concentrated effort – a 'short' course followed by a 'long' course.

(Letter from Deming to W. Allen Wallis, April 1942, cited by Allen Wallis, 1980)

## Into Japan

Reputedly because of the inefficiency of the Japanese telephone system, the US occupation forces began to cultivate interest in quality control in their programme of reconstruction. In 1950 Deming accepted an invitation to give a series of lectures in Japan. The programme resembled his proposal for the Statistical Research Group in the US in 1943. Deming addressed a small group of top managers on the importance of statistical quality control (SQC) and, through them, this was meant to trickle downwards to the lower ranks of management and ultimately to the workforce through, and reinforcing, the established hierarchy. Importantly, and characteristic of the approach, this was complemented by an introduction into consumer research, thus drawing the links between production and consumption in the, as yet unarticulated, customer–supplier chain. This was followed by a series of conferences and lecture programmes carried out under the auspices of the Japanese Union of Scientists and Engineers (JUSE). Royalties from the publication of Deming's lectures, donated to JUSE, were used to fund prizes for quality improvement in Japan – the Deming Prizes – which have become the most famous quality awards to companies and individuals and are now copied in the West. Deming, who returned in subsequent years for further lectures, was followed by other statisticians – principally Joseph Juran and Armand Feigenbaum – who went further than Deming in developing the managerial and organizational dimensions of quality control.

As well as promoting the annual award of the Deming Prizes, JUSE produced a journal, *Statistical Quality Control*, first published in

1950. This built around an education programme designed for foremen, the journal being intended as a vehicle for discussion in workshop quality control study groups. In 1962 they published *Gemba-to QC* – 'Quality Control for the Foreman' – as one of a series of three pamphlets on quality control. The workshops for foremen were renamed 'QC circle activities' (Ishikawa, 1985; Deming, 1982).

Battling to reconstruct its industry and for a place in world markets while burdened by a reputation for shoddy and cheap goods, Japanese quality circle activity – contrary to the reports of many Western observers – was not concerned with working conditions. Rather, QCs had a purely pedagogic role in the education of foremen in the techniques of quality control. For the Japanese, the attraction of this method of training shopfloor workers in methods of detecting defects was that it saved the cost of inspection.

> If defective products are produced at different stages of the manufacturing process, even strict inspection cannot eliminate them. If instead of relying on inspection, we produce no defective products from the very beginning – in other words, if we control the factors in a particular process which cause defective products – we can spare a lot of money that is expended for inspections.
>
> (Ishikawa, 1985: 20)

The lessons were practical, applying the techniques learnt to address identifiable production problems. Problems were identified through brainstorming and the 'seven tools of quality control': Pareto charts, cause and effect diagrams, stratification, check sheets, histograms, scatter diagrams and Shewhart's control charts and graphs. While all employees were taught the techniques, usually by their foreman, the participation in the circles was voluntary. The origin and development of the circles, therefore, was not in the 'human relations' that had also emerged from the Hawthorne plant or in group participation, suggestion schemes or Scanlon plans, as some Western authors contended (Gorz, 1989: 63; Rose, 1988: 168). It was in the structured and controlled development of practical production skills. The circles sought workers' ideas – the 'gold in the mine' – in a way that was dictated and controlled by management. Juran's statement, which has been interpreted even by proponents of post-Fordism – particularly Murray (1990) – as indicative of the liberating, empowering side of quality management, actually referred to the savings that could be achieved by cutting waste through eliminating errors by management appropriating workers' informal work methods (see Burawoy, 1979).

## Doing it 'right first time' in the USA

While part of the historical transformation of quality assurance into TQM can be traced to Japan, it also developed in the West, and particularly in the USA, where it was to gain its most charismatic promoter. In July 1979 Philip Crosby left his Vice-Presidency of ITT, where he had had responsibilities for quality, to establish his own consultancy and offer training at his newly established 'Quality College' in Orlando, Florida. This move appeared to have been prompted by the success of his book, *Quality is Free*. The central message of the book, similar to that beginning to come out of Japan, was that quality should be built in and not, as was the general practice, inspected out. There was immense waste in the processes of inspection and in rectifying faults. The solution – which held the magic savings – was to 'do it right first time':

> Quality is not only free, it is an honest-to-everything profit maker. Every penny you don't spend on doing things wrong, over, or instead becomes half a penny right on the bottom line. In these days of 'who knows what is going to happen to our business tomorrow' there aren't many ways left to make a profit improvement. If you concentrate on making quality certain, you can probably increase your profit by an amount equal to 5 to 10 per cent of your sales. That is a lot of money for free.
>
> (Crosby, 1979: 1)

While the ultimate object of savings on cost is clearly spelled out by Crosby, managers are actually invited to engage in an act of conversion and faith; management enters into an evangelical crusade, becoming exposed to the true belief (ibid.: 8). In Crosby's words, quality management then goes through the stages of Uncertainty, Awakening, Enlightenment, Wisdom and Certainty (ibid.: 26–30). The appeal of this message was probably increased by workers' concerns over the quality of their work as well as – more significantly – by an increasingly vocal consumer movement (Moberg, 1978).

## Out of Japan

The evident success of the Japanese in riding out the international recession of the 1970s, to emerge as the industrial masters of the 1980s, served to bring together dimensions of quality assurance, or total quality control, in the Japanese context, with the more robust style of American management. It coalesced in 'total quality management'. Through the 1950s and 1960s, Japan had been considered a producer of cheap and shoddy copies of Western products, often presumed through the use of cheap labour. The issue in the 1980s was how Japan could have transformed itself into the world's leading industrial economy. In essence, the gurus' answer has focused upon concern for quality control, ignoring or discounting other explanations like the nature of state intervention and planning through, for example, the activities of the Ministry of International Trade and Industry (MITI). Again, this account resonates with the ideology of the new right. Not only do we have an eschewing of state intervention, but the interpretation of Japanese success promoted by the gurus of TQM did not prescribe greater expenditure but, rather, held out the promise of considerable savings by the avoidance of error and waste – of 'getting it right first time'.

This account of the causes of Japanese success and Western decline has become so embedded in TQM that one firm of consultants, in selling the idea, could use a photograph of a British motorcycle covered in cobwebs. This then carries the weight of a particular ideology. Motor cycles represented the first industry to collapse in the face of imported Japanese machines, despite a significant rearguard action by both Conservative and Labour governments in the early 1970s (see Boston Consulting Group, 1975; Smith, 1981; also NVT, 1974; Bruce-Gardyne, 1978). Central features of this intervention – including unsuccessful attempts at rationalizing the remnants of the industry, the establishment of the Meridan workers' cooperative and, more fundamentally, the long-term lack of investment that impeded product innovation – are totally ignored in the image presented. Total quality management is proffered as both the secret of Japanese success and the means to halt Western decline. The basic change is represented as a 'culture change' that covers both the devolving of quality inspection from specialist to operator, as well as the more fundamental subjective acceptance of the customer–supplier chain as the only means of achieving quality.

## THE COMPONENTS OF TQM

Drawing together the foregoing observations on the emergence of quality control and assurance, we can see TQM as the accumulation and transformation of four key components from existing practice that assumes a degree of a coherence by the latter part of the 1980s.

1 **Statistical process control** This developed out of the demands for regulation and monitoring of mass production, especially in wartime. It includes the seven basic tools that were the key to the emergence of quality circles as a pedagogic device in Japan and still forms the basis of at least some of the TQM training given in the West. One sign of the development of a quality programme is often the appearance of performance charts within the workplace. As TQM establishes itself, these 'hard' techniques are relegated in favour of 'culture change'.

2 **Procedures and audit** This has been the main activity of conventional quality assurance and is the context in which the tools were usually applied. It works on the assumption that if procedures are established to conform to the required outcome, then conformance in practice will lead to a product that meets the required specifications. If, through sampling, faults are found then this is seen as either a failure of conformance or a deficiency in the procedures. Increasingly, responsibility for this process is devolved to the shop floor, away from inspectors and quality departments, and monitoring has become standardized through BSI and ISO certification.

3 **Training** As can be seen from Deming's argument, training in statistical process control has been central to the development of TQM from its origins. In contrast to conventional views about the Japanese approach, it is very much a top or trickle-down method where the final stage is a foreman, team leader or facilitator teaching the methods to the shop floor to implement when appraising work standards. One feature of the introduction of such programmes is the appearance of performance charts displayed on the shop floor. TQM programmes tend to start with some trickle-down training. This is usually initiated by

consultants who train the management away from the plant and this is subsequently transformed into an in-house programme for the shop floor. With the establishment of TQM, quality assurance techniques tend to become submerged by the more evangelical dimension of 'culture change' and the recognition of internal customers and suppliers. The process is often represented as one of creating converts, of turning 'non-believers' into 'believers' (see e.g. Curtis and Boaden, 1988).

4 **Culture change**    Increasingly, with the formation of TQM out of quality control and assurance, the emphasis has moved to the idea of using the other three components to create culture change. There are a number of key elements and dimensions to this that themselves need disentangling. First, this might appear associated with a culturalist account of Japanese success, inferring that an appropriation of some aspects of Japanese work culture might have the required effect on Western performance. While from the US version, particularly in Crosby, there is an explicit rejection of this perspective, it clearly is part of a hidden agenda; the Japanese, it is felt, owe at least some of their success to 'meeting customer requirements'. Hence a second aspect of this notion of 'culture change' relates to the development of a work culture that internalizes the customer relationship as the only means of achieving the combined objectives of quality and business success. It is here that it must begin to challenge conventional representations of business organizations as bureaucracies.[4] TQM not only accompanies changes in the representation of organizational relations as internal markets, it also reinforces drives to cut down on levels of hierarchy through such things as increased use of teamwork. This, then, constitutes a third aspect of culture change: the apparent broadening of job responsibilities, with the devolution of quality assurance away from the quality inspector and expanding further the role of the productive worker. Within TQM this change is represented as an empowerment of the worker. Importantly, TQM did not appear fully formed, but evolved with management practice and state policy in the 1980s.

## THE DEVELOPMENT OF TQM IN THE WEST

In the last decade, quality management has been extended from an approach particularly designed for mass production industries to almost a panacea for all organizational ills across the spectrum of activity now encompassing health, welfare, education, etc. While drawing on specific methods and techniques it has, in management practice – and the policy of the State – moved into the mainstream of the New Right project in turning the appearance of all relationships into market transactions – it has helped to construct the 'cult(ure) of the customer' (Du Gay and Salaman, 1992). This can be represented as four phases of development, with considerable overlap between the phases:

| First phase: | Late 1970s to early 1980s | Some experimentation with quality circles. Mostly affected firms in direct competition with industrial sectors in which Japan had concentrated, e.g. electronics and motor industries. |
|---|---|---|
| Second phase: | The 1980s | Major companies, often affected by world recession, concerned with control of suppliers and subcontractors. |
| Third phase: | From mid-1980s | A growing concern with customer service, particularly in the service sector. |
| Fourth phase: | From late 1980s | Penetration of concerns with 'customer service' in areas which previously had not recognized the existence of customers. |

**Phase one: late 1970s to early 1980s**

In the late 1970s and early 1980s we can identify an initial concern from a number of Western companies facing direct competition from Japanese firms, particularly in the motor, electronics and computer industries. In a reversal of the process initiated by the Japanese government after the Meiji Restoration in the late nineteenth century, delegations of managers and experts converged on Japan to try to discover its secrets. As *Time* magazine was to observe: 'Like pilgrims to the temple of success, they [were] travelling to an ancient land . . . to learn how Japan does it' (30 March 1981, cited in Rees and Rigby, 1988: 173).

No longer did Japan's success appear to stem from their ability to produce cheap and shoddy goods; quite the reverse. They now – it appeared – based their success on quality. Schemes began to emerge in the West to focus workers' ideas on quality production. From his vantage on the line at GM's plant at Flint in the 1980s, Ben Hamper noted:

> a strange new entry into the GM vocabulary. The word was 'Quality'. The term itself was like some new intoxicating utterance that General Motors had pried outta the ass end of a golden goose. Quality, quality, quality. Suddenly, you couldn't raise your head without having your lobes pummeled with slogans and exhortations hailing this new buzzword. Up until this time, the maxim had always been Quantity. Quantity and Quota. Herd them trucks out the door. Quick, quick . . . QUICKER!
>
> (Hamper, 1992: 111)

The schemes to promote this appeared to play totally on the subjective: 'Some of these game plans were so utterly farcical, one would have been tempted to guffaw if it weren't for the fact that it was *your brain* that these follies were bein' foisted upon' (ibid.: 112; emphasis in the original). The key folly promoting quality was 'Howie Makem' a man dressed in a cat outfit who wandered around the plant to the, unintended, amusement of the workforce. This took the idea slightly further than GM's Shreveport plant, where quality was symbolized by a stuffed alligator, the 'Qualigator', kept in a glass case in the canteen and symbolized on the overalls (Parker and Slaughter 1988: 128).

The main discovery was the quality circle, and there developed a fad for their introduction, although this was also rather superficial. As Bradley and Hill (1983) were to note, these circles were seen as a 'high-trust' option and, as vindicated in a follow-up study, might not be integrated into existing organizational arrangements, thus gaining the suspicion of both middle management and unions. However, when interpreted as a voluntary 'bottom-up' mechanism for tapping the initiative of the workforce, they lacked the managerial controls and the basic methods of the Japanese variant (Hill, 1991, and in this volume). Most seemed to fail rapidly, either through tension within the wider company organization, with middle management, or through a decline in motivation and inertia as enthusiasm waned (see Dale and Haywood, 1984; Lawler and Mohrman, 1985). Quality circles have often remained part of TQM programmes, although frequently under some other title and always as the lowest rung within a hierarchical structure. No longer are they voluntary associations – they have become the means by which initial problems are identified and either dealt with directly or channelled up to an interdepartmental 'quality improvement team'.

Not all attempts at implementing some form of quality scheme were as superficial as many of the circle experiments. A number of firms, particularly in the areas that felt most vulnerable to Japanese competition, took a more systematic approach to their perceived production methods (see Hill, in this volume). For example Hewlett-Packard began to generalize the experience of a joint venture, Yokawa in Japan, which had received the Deming Prize in 1982. As their President and CEO observed:

> One should not believe that quality is the exclusive property of the Japanese. While HP's Japanese joint venture started out to improve quality a bit earlier than some other parts of HP, the rest of the company will surely obtain the same results and the same payoffs.
> The growing competition US firms face from Japan and all the 'new Japans' can have a healthy effect. It should drive today's business managers to make the kind of quality improvements that are possible.
>
> (Young, 1985: 9)

Likewise, the motive of competition was also beginning to affect the British motor industry, which was confronted with growing demand for Japanese cars. Clearly they seemed to meet customer requirements for reliability – in contrast to the reputation of the UK product. According to the study carried out by Marsden *et al.* (1985: 176–7):

> The use of automated techniques and the advent of Japanese competition served during the 1970s to highlight the relatively poor quality of the products of the UK industry, and while the adoption of automated techniques by the UK industry could in part remedy the problem, full solutions required improving the quality of labour input. At least two solutions were possible.

One relied on the intensive monitoring of the quality of labour input and product output through increased numbers of supervisors and inspectors. However, this was a much more expensive option than the second, which consisted of the attempt to involve employees in a concern for product quality through self-inspection of work and various consultative devices. In pursuit of this second option, UK manufacturers have explicitly sought to remove what they see as one comparative advantage of the Japanese industry.

### Phase two: during the 1980s

One difficulty encountered in the effort to improve quality was the control required over the quality of materials and components from suppliers and subcontractors. This was compounded by the realization of the cost-cutting potential of just-in-time inventory control. JIT prescribed the removal of buffer stocks of components that were instead meant to be delivered 'just in time' – often contrasted with the position where components were stockpiled 'just in case'.[5] We can identify a broadening of concern by major manufacturers, during the 1980s, over control of subcontractors and suppliers. The problem of control was increasingly taken up by the development of standards of procedure, and their monitoring carried out by external assessors sponsored by the State.

In 1982 the British Department of Trade and Industry (DTI) produced a paper entitled *Standards, Quality and International Competition*. This noted (p. 2) that:

> Success in world markets increasingly depends on a supplier's ability to satisfy customers on non-price factors, as well as price. Quality, which embraces the fitness of a product to meet throughout its life the customer's expectations (including good design, reliability, ease of maintenance, safety, energy consumption, environmental considerations – some of which may flow from regulatory requirements) is often the first consideration in purchasing decisions.

Here we can see a recognition of the role of quality in world markets, the internalization of the terminology of quality management in both definition and the customer chain, and also the role of regulation through procedures. The paper contended (p. 11) that:

70

Quality assurance, in the form of sound technical and administrative procedures for ensuring quality, offers more scope for reducing costs and enhancing competitiveness and profitability than many other management controls. It does this by reducing materials wastage, lost production time, re-work, extra handling and rejections. Improved quality, and reliability, by improving customer satisfaction, leads to increased sales competitiveness, reduced warranty claims and premium pricing.

Clearly part of the problem that is being identified in this DTI document relates to military procurement, in which there were both Ministry of Defence and NATO standards. The process of evaluating these standards is presently devolved to the British Standards Institute to implement, through government support, its standard for quality assurance, BS 5750. This is not, it must be noted, an evaluation of the quality of the product or service, but of the practices and procedures of manufacture and provision. Such systems had existed before, established by particular companies to control their suppliers or by procurement agencies within government but here nationally – and later internationally, through the equivalent ISO 9000 – an attempt had been made to produce a universally recognized standard of quality management.

The establishment of standards for use in the monitoring of procedures allowed a devolvement of responsibility away from customers, a pruning down of the number of potential suppliers, as well as a closer match between suppliers and customers in the reduction of stock with JIT. A quality consultancy industry mushroomed to facilitate the writing of procedures, although increasingly voices were heard arguing that there was more to total quality management, that this development required a more fundamental 'culture change' (Atkinson, 1990). One manifestation of this was under way when the DTI launched the National Quality Campaign in April 1983, subsequently incorporated into the Enterprise Initiative in 1989. During the period up to July 1987, about 50,000 companies contacted the DTI concerning information about certification and quality management more generally (Lascelles and Dale, 1989). A series of publications and videos was produced and financial assistance was offered to smaller firms to offset consultancy fees.

In short, in phase two, we can see both the strengthening of relationships between firms within manufacturing chains and the growing involvement of the State in shaping industrial strategy. In their evaluation of this, Lascelles and Dale (1989: 20) indicate the distinctive nature of the change in management approach being facilitated, in contrast to the more direct intervention of the Japanese state:

> Companies must accept intellectual ownership of the total quality management concept and devise their own quality improvement strategies. There has been a tendency to see the National Quality Campaign in terms of a Government economic strategy. But the DTI does not possess the kind of influence enjoyed by, for example, the Japanese Ministry of International Trade and Industry to enable it single-mindedly to co-ordinate the competitiveness of the national economy.

Nonetheless, as we shall see, another dimension of government's recommodification process – the denationalization of key industries and the introduction of internal markets – gave a further impetus to 'culture change' programmes.

## Phase three: from the mid-1980s

Paralleling the changes in manufacturing, there was a move to implement forms of quality management in the service industries which initially were concerned with technical issues. For example, in the financial sector, a number of banks became increasingly concerned with customer service. A growing emphasis was placed on the question of 'culture change', increasingly seen as a recognition of the demands of internal and external customers in the quality chain. Part of the message of the 'quality gurus' – particularly Deming – was that the purpose of a company was first and foremost to 'meet customer demand'. Since, in most situations, only a few employees actually had contact with the final customer, mechanisms were introduced, such as temporary job-swapping, to inculcate the idea of the link. However, the very metaphors that were being deployed within quality management's conceptualization of organizational relations were deliberately constructed to break down this distinction between internal relations and external customer. Indeed, this was the idea behind the customer–supplier chain.

The emphasis in the training programmes that accompanied the introduction of total quality increasingly moved from the tools of quality assurance – essentially statistical process control – to discussion of the internal customer. The customer whose requirements were to be met was the next person in the chain. The notion of 'quality' as a central corporate objective became a metaphor for the internalization of pseudo-market relations. The market as metaphor didn't just permeate into organizational relations, but was intended to embrace attitudes and behaviour within the organization; this was the nature of the culture change (see Kerfoot and Knights, in this volume). In a number of key instances this articulated a broader context of change in which denationalization was being experienced and competition, supposedly, opened up. Fitness for the market was increasingly internalized through the culture change of TQM. An interesting example of this was British Telecom. Recognizing its own position as a popular euphemism for the inefficiencies of state monopoly, BT had begun experimenting with statistical process control in monitoring and evaluating their quality indicators of call connection rates, etc. The introduction of TQM began in 1986 with PA Consultants employed to bring about a more fundamental, top-down transformation (see Dodsworth, 1988; Dixon, 1989). Increasingly, there was the view that they should become 'more like a business', that BT ought to 'transform their civil service mentality'. This became linked to a systematic training programme which explicitly located customers as the focus of activity.

## Phase four: from the late 1980s

Finally, there is the recent incorporation of quality discourse – with its TQM pedigree – into debate about the public sector services. What begins to appear is a universalization of the TQM prescription of meeting 'customer requirements' in such areas as health, education and welfare. 'Customers' are constructed where none had existed. This links TQM with two interrelated processes – commodification and managerialism – the context of which is the growth of financial accountability in the public services. Pollitt (1990) has indicated the level of tension that can follow the introduction of quality assurance into the public services where there is a significant professional involvement. As he indicates: 'professions provide their own quality assurance'. But the development of professional managers within the health service can lead to an increase in internal conflict between the positions of managers and those of healthcare professionals. In practice it means a separation of domain of the Directors of Quality Assurance, deploying patient surveys of customer requirements, and others (e.g. consultants) concerned with medical provision.[6]

This account of the development of TQM opens up a number of issues that need addressing concerning both power and control of the labour process, as well as the construction of a wider political hegemony. These two are integrally linked since the very discourse of the new hegemony, while articulated around citizenship and the consumer, is clearly rooted within these changes in production.

## POWER AND THE EMPOWERMENT OF LABOUR

### Subjectivity and hegemony within the workplace

The introduction of TQM is often represented as the very anti-thesis of classical Taylorism and Fordism. Instead of taking power and control away from the shop floor, it is represented as both a broadening of skill and an empowerment of the worker; they are taking control of their own production away from external inspection. Against this we might indicate the counter-tendency inherent in TQM, equating it quite centrally within a Taylorist tradition. The establishment and formalization of working procedures exemplify a Taylorist strategy: it takes what is in the heads of workers and presents it to management; it is clearly a separation of conception from execution (Braverman, 1974). Moreover, the preoccupation with constructing a measure of quality parallels the pseudo-scientific methodology initiated by work study. Instead of a reversal of the tendency for the 'degradation of work in the twentieth century', we might see the establishment of TQM as its culmination.[7]

The struggle around TQM, therefore, might be seen as a monolithic one concerning the control of workers' subjectivity. If we accept that Fordism subordinated the time and motion of the worker to management control, then the current changes associated with TQM are concerned with the subordination of employees' subjectivity. Gramsci – the theorist of hegemony – in his discussion of *Americanism and Fordism*, indicates this distinction

74

between the objective controls over workers' actions and their remaining freedom of thought:

> Once the process of adaption has been complete, what really happens is that the brain of the worker, far from being mummified, reaches a state of complete freedom. The only thing that is completely mechanised is the physical gesture; the memory of the trade, reduced to simple gestures repeated at an intense rhythm, 'nestles' in the muscular and nervous centres and leaves the brain free and unencumbered for other occupations. One can walk without having to think about all the movements needed in order to move, in perfect synchronisation, all the parts of the body, in specific ways that is necessary for walking. The same thing happens and will go on happening in industry with the basic gestures of the trade . . . the worker remains a man and even that during his work he thinks more, or at least has greater opportunity for thinking, once he has overcome the crisis of adaption without being eliminated: not only does the worker think, but the fact that he gets no immediate satisfaction from his work and realises that they are trying to reduce him to a trained gorilla, can lead him into a train of thought that is far from conformist.
>
> (Gramsci, 1971: 309–10)

Some of the available accounts, especially when linked to broader initiatives, 'management-by-stress' (Parker and Slaughter, 1990) or of JIT/TQM regimes (Deldridge *et al.*, 1991; Sewell and Wilkinson, 1992a, 1992b), seem to confirm Gramsci's analysis. Certainly, in the context of developed Fordist labour processes, there are classic signs of the intensification of labour and increased surveillance and little by way of a terrain of conflict. However what I have indicated is that the scale, and scope, of the introduction of TQM as a management strategy is not limited to mass production.

Indeed, the rhetoric of TQM actually appears to draw it closer to the labour process of the professional than of the mass-production worker; there appears to be a move towards autonomy and discretion. We might represent this development as an attempt at the internalization of surveillance – of the 'normalized gaze' (Foucault, 1977). In principle, the work discipline that is claimed to follow from an appeal to market relations is internalized as the only means to achieve quality, enabling power/knowledge to devolve not to the subject but to management. The organizational representation of this transformation, the work team, legitimates this external control through the demand for *quality*. This, it is worth stressing, is quite unlike the empowered professional where the appeal and control is characteristically through at least professional association with their own code of ethics. In TQM the ultimate appeal is through its own particular definition of quality. A new legitimacy is devolved on to management themselves, a rationale for their practice, that of the controllers and arbiters of quality. However, in this process, quality itself is transformed into a measurable quantity denying alternative approaches. The appeal to managers is also variegated. In manufacturing industry, quality gives them the rhetoric of empowerment and a human relations philosophy of involvement; for the public services manager the origins of TQM in the traditional areas of manufacture give a set of authoritative 'hard' techniques. But, as I have argued, the development of TQM is broader than the immediate demands of control within the workplace – be it a subjective chaining to managerial imperative – and is integral to the establishment of a New Right hegemony, of Thatcherism and its heirs.

## Quality and the State

A 1991 British Treasury White Paper, *Competing for Quality*, clearly argues (p. 2) for the culture change embedded in TQM practice in the workplace; that:

> Greater competition over the past decade has gone hand in hand with fundamental management reform of the public sector.
>
> This means moving away from the traditional pyramid structure of public sector management. The defects of the old approach have been widely recognised: excessively long lines of management with blurred responsibility and accountability; lack of incentives to initiative and innovation; a culture that was more concerned with procedures than performance. As a result, public services will increasingly move to a culture where relationships are contractual rather than bureaucratic.

In Britain the issue of quality has been broadened further into the basis of a political consensus. The idea of the quality revolution has become central to the repertoire of political debate and the construction of citizenship in a market society. In his forward to the

Conservative Party Manifesto for the 1992 election, John Major stated that:

> ... under the seal of the Citizens Charter ... (p)eople in schools, hospitals, public offices of all kinds are rising to the challenge. I knew they would. They just needed encouragement, incentive and a system that is outward-looking too.
>
> It is all part of a revolution in quality in Britain. British goods are once more winning the toughest markets abroad. There is new vigour in the businesses liberated from state ownership; better management and better industrial relations. These are the firm foundations of economic recovery.
>
> We are raising the quality of our education and training. We are raising the standard of our housing, as more people own and improve their own homes. We are concerned for the quality of our environment. And in government we are leading a drive for quality throughout our public services.

This is the current position within a longer trajectory of a war of manoeuvre, through the combative stance of Thatcherism through to the more urbane 'Majorism', in which the notion of citizenship has increasingly been reconstructed as of a consumer on the market.[8] The ideology of quality yoked to the notion of producer/citizen as consumer in a customer–supplier chain is increasingly dominant.

## QUALITY STREET: SOME CONCLUSIONS

This paper has not been addressed to a critique of 'quality' *per se*. It has attempted to show how the methods and techniques of quality management have been appropriated and developed within a particular agenda of the 1980s and 1990s which poses all relationships as variants on market transactions. The road to achieving quality is then presented as the acceptance of the customer–supplier chain; we must all see ourselves as meeting customer requirements. In posing as a new – and the only – way of achieving quality, it has obscured the roots of quality control within the labour process and has challenged, in the name of empowerment, the autonomy and control of labour. Like Taylorism it has attempted to initiate a 'mental revolution', addressing subjectivity through the notion of improving quality. At the same time it

77

challenges and undermines existing modes of quality control which have been established within the labour process.

A report on new management techniques for the Transport and General Workers' Union makes the point that:

> the idea of 'better quality' is a difficult one to resist. However, 'quality' used under 'Total Quality Management' is a much broader and more dangerous concept.
>
> Unions have been pressing for quality for years – more employees, safer working, more investment, better quality raw materials, opposition to built-in obsolescence, and so on. However, 'quality' in TQM does not really mean this, it really means **complete flexibility and absence of opposition to management's goals**.
>
> (Fisher, 1991; emphasis in the original)

Such challenges open up an alternative – and potentially more empowering – notion of quality that might support the opposition to current managerial and government strategies. One which recognizes the roots of quality control in the autonomous control of labour.

## NOTES

1 The practices of Japanese management, and particularly of Nissan in Sunderland, are promoted by Wickens (1987), although alternative views of this are presented by Garrahan and Stewart (1992), with reference to the Nissan plant, or to the Mazda plant in Flat Rock, Michigan, by Fucini and Fucini (1990). An interesting vantage on the decline of the US industry in the face of Japanese expansion can be found in the autobiographical account of life at GM offered by Hamper (1992).

2 I discuss the relationship between TQM, bureaucratization, and the 'dysfunctions' of bureaucracy more fully in Tuckman (forthcoming).

3 See Rose (1988) for an account of the Hawthorne studies and the Human Relations School. For an important account of 'continuous improvement' and the development of the Ford Assembly plant, see Williams *et al.* (1992).

4 When interviewing quality managers, in public, private and newly privatized settings, I have repeatedly been informed that the introduction of TQM represented the first time that they began to think 'as a business'.

5 Womack *et al.* (1990) indicate that all motor firms outsource a large proportion of components, with the exception of Fords during the

heyday of the Rouge plant, while Williams *et al.* (1992) indicate that at Fords, in this period, there existed an essentially JIT system of inventory.
6 The problem, as outlined by a number of such Directors of Quality within the NHS interviewed by the author, is that patients do not see themselves as customers of a service but as receiving free provision.
7 As one manager within the chemical industry interviewed by the author actually suggested: 'We've de-skilled the workforce so much that we now have to give them something to think about.'
8 The strength of this hegemonic position can be seen in publications of the Labour Party (1991; n.d.) which also appropriate some of the rhetoric of TQM.

## REFERENCES

Allen Wallis, W. (1980) 'The Statistical Research Group, 1942–1945', *Journal of the American Statistical Association,* 75 (370), June, 320–31.
Atkinson, P. (1990) *Creating Cultural Change: The Key to Successful Total Quality Management,* Bedford: IFS Ltd.
Boston Consulting Group (1975) *Strategy Alternatives for the British Motorcycle Industry,* London: HMSO.
Bradley, K. and Hill, S. (1983) 'After Japan: The Quality Circle Transplant and Productive Efficiency', *British Journal of Industrial Relations,* 21, 291–311.
Braverman, H. (1974) *Labor and Monopoly Capital: the Degradation of Work in the Twentieth Century,* New York: Monthly Review Press.
Bruce-Gardyne, J. (1978) *Meridan: Odyssey of a Lame Duck,* forward by Keith Joseph, London: Centre for Policy Studies.
Burawoy, M. (1979) *Manufacturing Consent: Changes in the Labor Process under Monopoly Capitalism,* Chicago, IL: University of Chicago Press.
Conservative Party (1992) *The Best Future for Britain: The Conservative Manifesto 1992,* forward by John Major, London: Conservative Central Office.
Crosby, P. (1979) *Quality is Free: The Art of Making Quality Certain,* New York: McGraw-Hill, New American Library edition.
Crosby, P. (1989) *Let's Talk Quality: 96 Questions You Always Wanted to Ask Phil Crosby,* New York: McGraw-Hill.
Curtis, B. and Boaden, S. (1988) 'Quality – Making it Happen' in J. Oakland (ed.) *Total Quality Management: Proceedings of the International Conference,* Bedford: IFS.
Dale, B. and Haywood, S. (1984) 'Quality Circle Failures in UK Manufacturing Companies – A Study', *Omega,* 12 (5), 475–84.
Deldridge, R., Turnbull, P. and Wilkinson, B. (1991) 'Pushing Back the Frontiers: Management Control and Work Intensification Under JIT Factory Regimes', paper presented to the 9th Annual Organisation and Control of the Labour Process Conference, 10–12 April.
Deming, W. (1982) *Out of the Crisis,* Cambridge: Cambridge University Press.
Dixon, H. (1989) 'BT lays its reputation on the line', *Financial Times,* 27 December.

Dodsworth, T. (1988) 'BT: stakes its future on its ability to deliver', *Financial Times*, 19 September.

Du Gay, P. and Salaman, G. (1992) 'The Cult(ure) of the Customer', *Journal of Management Studies*, 29 (5).

Fisher, J. (1991) *New Management Techniques,* TGWU Education Document, Supplement to TGWU Region 1 Regional Committee Quarterly Report (April).

Foucault, M. (1977) *Discipline and Punish: The Birth of the Prison*, Harmondsworth: Allen Lane.

Fucini, J. and Fucini, S. (1990) *Working for the Japanese: Inside Mazda's American Auto Plant,* New York: The Free Press.

Garrahan, P. and Stewart, P. (1992) *The Nissan Enigma: Flexibility at Work in a Local Economy,* London: Mansell.

Garvin, D. (1988) *Managing Quality: The Strategic and Competitive Edge,* New York: The Free Press.

Garvin, D. (1991) 'How the Baldridge Award Really Works', *Harvard Business Review,* November–December.

Gorz, A. (1989) *Critique of Economic Reason* (trans. G. Handyside and C. Turner), London: Verso.

Gramsci, A. (1971) in Q. Hoare and G. Nowell Smith (eds) *Selections from the Prison Notebooks,* London: Lawrence & Wishart.

Hall, S. (1988) *The Hard Road to Renewal: Thatcherism and the Crisis of the Left,* London: Verso.

Hamper, B. (1992) *Rivethead: Tales from the Assembly Line,* London: Fourth Estate.

Hayek, F.A. (1944) *The Road to Serfdom*, London: Routledge & Kegan Paul.

Hill, S. (1991) 'How Do You Manage a Flexible Firm? The Total Quality Model', *Work, Employment and Society*, 5 (3) (September), 397–415.

HM Treasury (1991) *Competing for Quality: Buying Better Public Services*, Cmnd 1730, HMSO.

Ishikawa, K. (1985) *What is Total Quality Control? The Japanese Way* (trans. D.J. Lu), Englewood Cliffs, NJ: Prentice-Hall. JUSE.

Labour Party (1991) *The Quality Commission: A Consultative Paper*, London: Labour Party Policy Directorate.

Labour Party (n.d.) *Quality Street: Labour's Quality Programme for Local Government*, London: The Labour Party.

Lascelles, D. and Dale, B. (1989) 'The UK Department of Trade and Industry National Quality Campaign: 1983 to January 1989', *International Journal of Operations and Production Management*, 9 (6).

Lawler III, E.E. and Mohrman, S.A. (1985) 'Quality Circles after the Fad', *Harvard Business Review,* 63, 65–71.

Mann, N. (1989) *The Keys to Excellence: The Deming Philosophy,* forward by W. Edwards Deming, London: Mercury Books.

Marsden, D., Morris, T., Willman, I. and Wood, S. (1985) *The Car Industry: Labour Relations and Industrial Adjustment*, London: Tavistock.

Moberg, D. (1978) 'No More Junk: Lordstown Workers and the Demand for Quality', *Insurgent Sociologist*, VIII (2 and 3), Fall, 63–9.

Murray, R. (1990) 'Fordism and Post-Fordism', in S. Hall and M. Jaques (eds), *New Times: The Changing Face of Politics in the 1990's*, London: Lawrence & Wishart, in association with *Marxism Today*.

(NVT) Norton Villiers Triumph Ltd. (1974) *Meridan: Historical Summary 1972–1974*, Meriden, Norton Villiers Triumph Ltd.

Oakland, J., (n.d. *c*1990). *Total Quality Management: a Practical Approach*, London: Department of Trade and Industry.

Oakland, J. (1993) *Total Quality Management* (2nd edn), Oxford: Butterworth-Heinemann.

Offe, C. (1984) in J. Keane (ed.) *Contradictions of the Welfare State*, London: Hutchinson.

Parker, M. and Slaughter, J. (1988) *Choosing Sides: Unions and the Team Concept*, Boston, MA: South End Press.

Parker, M. and Slaughter, J. (1990) 'Management-by-Stress: The Team Concept in the US Auto Industry', *Science as Culture*, 8, London: Free Association Books.

Pollitt, C. (1990) 'Doing Business in the Temple: Managers and Quality Assurance in the Public Services', *Public Administration*, 68.

Rees, J. and Rigby, P. (1988) 'Total Quality Control – the Hewlett-Packard Way', in J. Oakland (ed.) *Total Quality Management: Proceedings of the International Conference*, Bedford: IFS.

Rose, M. (1988) *Industrial Behaviour: Research and Control* (2nd edn), Harmondsworth: Penguin Business.

Sewell, G. and Wilkinson, B. (1992a) 'Someone to Watch Over Me: Surveillance, Discipline, and the Just-in-Time Labour Process', *Sociology*, 26 (2) (May) 271–91.

Sewell, G. and Wilkinson, B. (1992b) 'Empowerment or Emasculation? Shopfloor Surveillance in a Total Quality Organization', in P. Blyton and P. Turnbull (eds), *Reassessing Human Resource Management*, London: Sage.

Smith, B. (1981) *The History of the British Motorcycle Industry 1945–1975*, Birmingham: Centre for Urban and Regional Studies, University of Birmingham, Occasional Papers.

Trade, Department of (1982) *Standards, Quality and International Competition*, Cmnd. 8621, London: HMSO.

Tuckman, A. (forthcoming) 'The Yellow Brick Road: Total Quality Management and the Restructuring of Organizational Cultures', *Organization Studies*, Summer.

Wickens, P. (1987) *The Road to Nissan: Flexibility Quality Teamwork*, Basingstoke: Macmillan.

Wilkinson, A., Allen, P. and Snape, E. (1990) 'TQM and the Management of Labour', *Employee Relations*, 13 (1), 24–31.

Williams, K., Haslam, C. and Williams, J. (1992) 'Ford versus Fordism': The Beginning of Mass Production', *Work, Employment and Society*, 6 (4), 517–55.

Williamson, O.E. (1975) *Markets and Hierarchies: Analysis and Antitrust Implications*, New York: The Free Press.

Womack, J.P., Jones, D.T., and Roos, D. (1990) *The Machine That Changed the World*, New York: Rawson Associates.

Young, J. (1985) 'The Quality Focus at Hewlett-Packard', *Journal of Business Strategy*, 5 (5), 6–9.

# 3

# QUALITY THROUGH MARKETS
## The New Public Service Management
### *Kieron Walsh*

The public service is argued to be undergoing a management revolution (Major, 1989) intended to ensure that services are provided 'efficiently and effectively' and are responsive to the needs and demands of users. The Citizen's Charter constitutes an agenda for the 'long march' through government services, introducing market processes in order to break down traditional approaches to management and organization. Public services, from housing to education, and from police to refuse collection, are being subject to fundamental reorganization on market principles. The aim is to introduce the sort of total quality management approaches that have been developed in the private sector. The language of the new public management is one of standards, quality, empowerment and customers, in contrast to the traditional language of professional bureaucracy that had developed in the post-war years. As William Waldegrave argues:

> This [the Citizen's Charter] is part of the wider transformation of the way public services are moving away from the old command structure to more open responsive management by clear published contracts, which empower managers with the authority to run their organisations in the way that best suits the needs of those who actually use the services.
> 
> (Quoted by Tritter, 1993: 1)

In this paper I shall examine the way that quality management is being developed in the public service. In the first section I consider the problem of understanding the meaning of quality in the public service. The second section outlines the specific approaches that have been introduced to improve the quality of public services.

The third section discusses the impact of the changes that are being introduced on management, workers and service users.

The argument of the paper is that there are strong tensions in the patterns of quality management that are emerging. The rhetoric is often at odds with the reality of management change. As Tuckman (1992: 5) argues: 'while the experience might be intensification and stress the rhetoric is of empowerment.' Students of public sector management, such as Pollitt (1993), have argued that what is happening is that traditional Taylorist principles are being applied to public services. At the same time there are claims of genuine changes in the involvement of staff in service delivery, despite increasingly difficult financial circumstances. As Hawkey (1993: 14) maintains: 'far from total quality being difficult to maintain in turbulent times, it provides an anchor and a route for managing through significant problems in ways which enhance staff understanding and maintain their commitment'.

The tension between control and commitment derives from two contrasting streams of thinking about the nature of public service management in the last decade. The one derives from the belief that public services were inherently inefficient and wasteful, and that what was needed was greater efficiency and value for money (Chapman, 1979); the other derives from the belief that public services are anonymous, distant, and unresponsive to the needs of the public, and need to be closer to the 'customer'. The contrasts that are apparent in approaches to the management of public service derive from attempts to address these two issues of efficiency and responsiveness at the same time, and often with the same mechanisms.

The contrasting approaches to the reform of public service management reflect different views about the nature of government. On the one hand there is the idea that public services are provided for citizens as individuals who have rights as consumers, who are the purchasers of services which they pay for through taxes – an idea which was most obviously expressed in the 'poll tax'. On the other hand, there is the concept of citizenship as the expression of community membership, involving duties as much as rights, and expressed through mutual obligation. The introduction of market processes to public service management is the natural expression of the individually based concept of citizenship. The emphasis on community is expressed through approaches to the reorganization of government services that are based more on participative democracy and mutual obligation – for example, through processes of decentralization and user control of service delivery.

## THE MEANING OF QUALITY

The meaning of quality is more difficult to determine in the case of services than manufacturing products in the private sector, because of their non-material character (Gronroos, 1984; Normann, 1984). It is difficult to specify services in terms of conformance in the way that is common for manufactured goods. Services have been distinguished from material, manufactured goods along a number of dimensions (Bowen and Schneider, 1988). They are intangible, while material goods are tangible; they cannot easily be stored or owned, and do not persist through time, while, in the case of manufactured goods, exchange typically involves transfer of ownership, and inventories can be maintained to meet fluctuations of demand. In the case of services it is often the user that is maintained as an inventory, through the use of waiting lists. Services are difficult to standardize, and quality cannot easily be guaranteed. Perhaps the most important characteristic of services, though, is that they involve a close relationship between the producer and the user in the process of production. Peters and Waterman (1982) argued that what makes companies excellent is that they 'really are close to their customers'; in the case of services, the involvement of the user is difficult to avoid. The delivery of services involves what Normann calls the 'moment of truth', in which the producer and user come together in the creation of the service, which is more like a dramatic production than a manufacturing process. Service production and service delivery are not processes that can easily be separated in time and space. Closeness to the customer is not avoidable for the teacher, doctor or social worker, though that closeness does not necessarily mean that the producer is sensitive to the needs of the user.

The personal nature of many services means that the identity of the partners to the relationship matters for the quality of service. There is little need for the producer and user of manufactured goods to have personal knowledge of each other. The psychology of services is different from that of the consumption of manufactured goods. As Foa and Foa (1974) argue, services involve particularistic exchanges, in which the identity of the partners contributes directly to the nature of the product and the quality of the service experience. In the case of services, knowledge of quality is likely to be difficult to obtain for those who are not parties to the exchange. It is not easy to evaluate, for example, the performance of a surgeon or a social worker. As manufactured products become more complex, it can be argued that they increasingly involve a strong service component, but the nature of that component is less likely than for many services to require a personal relationship of user and producer. While I am likely to care about who is my doctor, or who teaches my children, I am not likely to be concerned about who, precisely, made the car that I drive or the clothes that I wear.

The character of services makes it more difficult to organize their production through automated, mass production systems, and to apply the principles of work measurement and control, than is the case for manufactured goods. Clearly there are examples of technologically based approaches to service management and delivery – for example, in banking or fast-food services – but the more personal the service, the more difficult it is to develop such methods. Developments in information technology have certainly had an effect upon the management of the public service, but have had only a very limited impact on the way that core services such as education or social care are delivered. Traditional approaches to production management, introduced to protect the technological core against fluctuations in demand (Thompson, 1967), are more difficult for services which are produced at the edge of the organization rather than in the core. As we shall see, much of the development of public services in the post-war years involved attempts to introduce mechanistic systems, but there was always a high level of discretion by 'street-level bureaucrats' (Lipsky, 1980). If the work of such service producers is to be controlled, the method is likely to be one of influencing values as much as control through technology; as Hochschild (1983) puts it, the 'heart' must be managed.

Public services must be distinguished from those produced in the private sector. The public character of the various services produced by government means that they are discussed in terms of contrasting and conflicting political values. Health, education, police and other public services are basic goods, and, whether they are actually produced in the public or the private sector, will be the subject of political regulation, because of the need for distributive justice. The issue of what are to be accepted as basic goods will, itself, be a matter of political dispute (Rawls, 1972), but there will be such goods in any but the most attenuated social system. Political values will be involved, both in the determination of what services the public sector should produce, and in determining the principles on which they should be distributed. The methods of public service production will also be a matter of political debate – for example, the degree to which they should involve participation by users (Burnheim, 1988).

Debate over the quality of public services involves normative as well as positive questions (Walsh, 1991a). It is perfectly possible for the same service to be seen as being of high quality from one political perspective, and low quality from another. The definition of public service quality is politically contestable. In education there is a continuing debate about whether comprehensive schooling provides quality education. There are, similarly, debates about the quality implications of service delivery mechanisms from a political perspective – for example, whether centralized or decentralized approaches are most appropriate, or whether contracting out is politically acceptable. The measurement of quality is also a matter of contention – for example, in the attempt to use quality-adjusted life years (QALYs) as a measure of the value of different health interventions. The debate over the nature of public service quality is a debate about the values of the public sector.

If we are to understand the way that quality management has been introduced in the public service, then we must consider a number of dimensions. There is, first, the development of approaches to defining the quality of public services, through the emphasis on standardization and contract-based approaches to service delivery. The second dimension concerns the methods of working and organizational changes that have been introduced in order to implement quality initiatives – for example, decentralization of service or devolved budgets. The third dimension is concerned with the measurement and control of quality. Each of these dimensions of quality can be contested, with different political perspectives resulting in different evaluations. The debate over the proper approach to production and delivery of public services in the last decade, both in Britain and other countries, has reflected a revival of the debate over the relative effectiveness of planning and markets as methods of decision-making. The quality debate is, therefore, part of a wider conflict of different political systems.

## THE QUALITY REVOLUTION

At the base of the developing approach to quality management in the public sector is the attempt to develop clear standards for services. The first principle of the Citizen's Charter is 'setting, monitoring and publication of explicit standards for the services that individual users can reasonably expect' (*Citizen's Charter First Report: 1992*).

The government's argument is that the public service will only be effective if it is required to meet explicit, preferably quantified, standards. Central government is laying down standards that must be met by public services at the local level – for example, the national curriculum in education, and the 'Litter Code'. The Patient's Charter specifies waiting times in hospitals; planners must deal with development applications within a given period. In other cases, standards are specified in contracts for services, which are increasingly used throughout the public sector, as compulsory competitive tendering and market testing are extended. The statement of precise standards, which are made known to the public, is seen as basic to the new public service management. Standards are also embodied in the service contracts with the public developed by local authorities such as those of Islington, Lewisham and York, for such services as refuse collection, swimming pools and housing repairs. The development of explicit standards for the public service can be seen as an attempt to reduce the power of the producer. Right-wing governments, such as that of Margaret Thatcher, have been concerned to reduce the power and dominance of producers in the public sector. Services such as education and social care are seen as having been unaccountable because the professionals have dominated the process of determining what services should be produced and how, if at all, they should be evaluated. This battle between government and producer interests was most obvious in the confrontations between government and teachers in the mid-1980s, leading up to the abolition of key bodies of professional influence such as the Schools Council. More generally, the development of clear standards can be seen as part of a confrontation with the power of public service trade unions over the control of public services and the determination of how they should be delivered. Centrally defined standards are seen as being necessary to ensure that service quality is not undermined by local authorities being dominated by trade unions. The statement of clear standards is also seen as enhancing the ability of users to control public services by making it possible for them to be clear about what services they are supposed to receive. Complaints procedures, for example in health and social services, have been central to the development of the new public management. The development of standards is part of the attempt to ensure increased transparency in the operation of public services, which is seen as making possible user influence and redress for failure. The statement of standards provides the basis for the organization and evaluation of public services.

There are a number of types of organizational change that have been introduced in the attempt at a quality revolution in the public service. First, there is the separation of purchaser and provider roles, most obviously in the National Health Service and social care, but more generally throughout the public service. Purchasers are responsible for defining service policy, specifying the service to be delivered and monitoring the quality of the service actually delivered. Providers are responsible for the delivery of service within the parameters laid down, and for meeting performance targets. Those who provide the service may be part of the same organization as the purchasers, part of another public service organization, or operating in the private sector. The most explicit expression of the purchaser/provider split is contracting out, or operation according to internal quasi-contracts. The public sector is becoming a 'nexus of contracts', in contrast to the traditional pattern of professional bureaucracy and integrated hierarchies. The ultimate expression of the division between purchaser and provider and the development of contracts is the 'enabling' state, which no longer provides services but rather commissions them from other providers (Ridley, 1988).

The creation of the purchaser/provider split makes possible the operation of internal markets within public service organizations, a development that has been most apparent in the National Health Service. Purchaser and provider relate to each other through quasi-contracts (LeGrand, 1991), and internal charges operate as the means of ensuring the match of supply and demand of services. The internal market is an attempt to mimic the operation of the market within the public service itself. The provider must set charges that will ensure that financial targets are met. Purchasers are free to search for the provider who will deliver the most cost-effective service. The result is that there is pressure on service costs, and incentives to increase productivity and efficiency. The requirement that producers operate on a trading basis is seen as reducing the abilities of providers, particularly professionals, to dominate the service. Purchasers are intended to operate as surrogates for end-users, and are forced to be explicit about the decisions that they make over what services are to be provided, particularly over rationing issues.

The second approach to changing the traditional public service management system is the breaking down of the large organizations that have been particularly characteristic of the British public service. If the market is seen as the most efficient mode of integration, then it is not necessary to persist in management through large integrated hierarchies. The arguments of Hayek, about the inevitable failure of planned systems to cope with the information demands that their operation requires, are widely accepted by public service reformers. The anonymous, unplanned, adjustment mechanisms of the market are seen as more efficient, and the creation of a large number of smaller public service bodies is seen as making it possible for the market to be mimicked in the way that they relate to each other. Mutual adjustment procedures replace planning as the mode of coordination, and the excessive information demands of public service bureaucracies are avoided.

Individual service-providing units, such as schools, colleges and hospitals, have been allowed to opt for independent status. About one thousand schools have opted for grant-maintained status, and the majority of health provision is now carried out by trusts. In the Civil Service, executive agencies – the so-called 'Next Steps' agencies – have been established, which are intended to be independent of ministers and government departments in the delivery of service. The majority of civil servants now work in executive agencies. Local authorities, such as those of Berkshire, Bromley and Westminster, have been establishing parts of their organizational systems as independent agencies through various forms of externalization – for example, management buy-outs, buy-ins and quasi-franchising. Many local authorities increasingly see themselves as 'enabling' bodies engaged in the purchase and commissioning of services, rather than their production. Various forms of relationship with producers are being established – for example, facilities management agreements and contracting out. The local authority then acts as a strategic body, specifying the services that are to be delivered, and monitoring the process of provision, rather than itself providing services directly. Residential care has been privatized in a number of cases, and other authorities have transferred housing provision to independent housing associations. Central government has contracted out a wide range of services, as have health authorities.

The public service is going through a process of disaggregating the large-scale bureaucracies that were built up in the post-war years. Devolved budgeting is a major element of the process of disaggregation and involves the establishment of cost and profit centres that are given direct control of the finance they need, with strong powers of virement – that is, the ability to move money from one budget head to another. In 1983 the government introduced the Financial Management Initiative into the Civil Service, in order to:

> promote in each department an organisation and system in which managers at all levels have:
> a. a clear view of their objectives and means to assess and, wherever possible, measure outputs or performance in relation to these objectives;
> b. well-defined responsibilities for making the best use of their resources including a critical scrutiny of output and value for money; and
> c. the information (particularly about costs), the training and the access to expert advice that they need to exercise their responsibilities effectively.
>
> (Massey, 1993: 47–8)

In the National Health Service there have been various attempts at clinical budgeting and other forms of devolved financial control, most notably the Resource Management Initiative (Packwood *et al.*, 1991), though they have had relatively limited success. Budgetary control in education has been devolved to schools though the introduction of local management of schools. Local education authorities must hand over the greater proportion of finance to schools to spend as they choose. Individual local authorities have engaged extensively in the devolution of budgetary control to cost centres, which may act with considerable autonomy.

Contracting out and market-testing go along with the development of internal markets and the breaking down of large hierarchies. Local authorities have been required to submit a range of manual services, such as refuse collection and building maintenance, to competitive tender, and the competitive regime is now being extended to professional services, such as legal advice and housing management. Tendering for domestic laundry and catering services was introduced in the National Health Service in 1983. Trust hospitals are now contracting for services such as financial management. In the Civil Service there is an extensive programme of market-testing, affecting both traditional support services, such as building cleaning, and 'areas closer to the heart of Government' (*Citizen's Charter First Report*: 59). Many thousands of public service contracts have been let and the value of the work involved runs into billions of pounds. Even such quintessentially public services as prisons and policing are being subjected to market disciplines.

The measurement of quality, and the linking of the achievement of quality to individual reward and the distribution of finance, is the third stream of the 'new public management'. Performance measures have advanced rapidly in the National Health Service and central government. In the National Health Service the number of performance indicators rose from seventy in the early 1980s to 450 in 1988 (Flynn, 1992: 109), and in the public expenditure White Paper from 500 in 1986 to 1,800 in 1987 (Carter *et al.*, 1992: 20). In education, testing and the publication of examination results are being used as the basis for national league tables.

Performance indicators have been developed on a statutory basis for local government in order to 'inform the public about the standards of performance of their council, and to facilitate comparisons with other councils, and from one year to another' (Audit Commission, 1992: 1). The Audit Commission has been given the responsibility of policing the local government performance measurement system. Performance pay has advanced rapidly in government services, covering both manual and non-manual workers. Loosely controlled bonus systems introduced in the late 1960s and early 1970s have been increasingly tightened to create a much closer link between pay and performance for manual workers.

Inspection, audit and regulation have become increasingly

important in the public service. The Audit Commission has extensive powers to investigate and report on the performance of local and health authorities. Existing inspectorates, such as those for police and fire services, have become more influential and new inspectorial bodies have been created, for example for the magistrates' courts and for social services. Inspection reports for prisons and schools, for example, are now published. Quality assurance is being developed, partly in response to contractual requirements. Public service organizations are pursuing certification of quality assurance systems under British Standard 5750, notably in local government; by 1992, seventy authorities had been awarded a total of 106 quality management certificates (Freeman-Bell and Grover, forthcoming: 8). Contracts for public services commonly require that contractors shall have developed quality assurance systems that are certificated by third parties.

The purpose of these changes is to separate the management and delivery of services from politics, and to establish the citizen as a customer. The political role is defined as involving the specifications of service and the establishment of standards, rather than any concern with direct service delivery. The development of political strategy for services is seen as a separate exercise from the process of service delivery, and politicians are seen as strategists. In the case of the National Health Service, for example, there is a Policy Board and a Management Board to reflect the separation of politics and management.

> The central management of the NHS must reflect this division of responsibilities. The Government proposes that responsibility for strategy will be for an NHS Policy Board chaired by the Secretary of State of Health. Responsibility for all operational matters will be for an NHS Management Executive chaired by a Chief Executive.
>
> (DHSS, 1989: 12)

The establishment of executive agencies in central government reflects a similar desire for the separation of the political and the managerial, as do the requirements of the Local Government and Housing Act 1989 in local government. Accountability is, then, divided into political and managerial, and the traditional notion that politicians are responsible for everything that happens in the organizations that they head is no longer accepted.

The new public management conceives of the citizen as a

customer for services, and citizens should be able to choose freely what they want on a basis that is as market-like as possible. Elderly people are to have enhanced choice over the residential establishments that they enter. Parents, through choice over the schools that their children attend, will influence the finance that is available to schools, since this is determined by pupil numbers. Patients may choose the doctors with whom they register. Choice is seen as essential to the empowerment of citizens as consumers, and the effective operation of markets for public services. 'Empowerment' is seen as being reflected in the establishment of clear individual citizens' rights. In part, this definition of service users as customers can be seen as part of a more general emphasis that has characterized management thinking since the 1980s, and which involves a reconceptualization of work organization as a set of producer/customer relations (Du Gay and Salaman, 1992). Citizens are seen as having acquired rights to services through the payment of taxes, and are defined as individuals rather than as members of communities. Individual rights of citizenship are then property rights. The state's primary role is to protect the rights of individual citizens rather than to provide services. Where services fail to meet the standards defined for them, then citizens should have the ability to complain and to obtain redress. The logic of citizenship, as expressed in the Citizen's Charter, is illustrated in Figure 3.1 (Prior *et al.*, 1993).

The values that dominate the system are those of traditional market liberalism, and the relationship between individual and state is understood in a contractarian form.

The move to a consumerist perspective on the nature of public

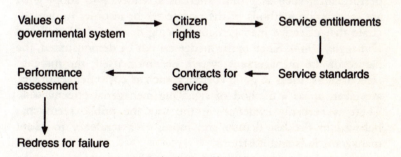

*Figure 3.1* The Citizen's Charter

93

service is reflected in organizational change and in the search for better information systems. Change in public organizations typically involves decentralization, in order to get 'closer to the customer', and the establishment of one-stop shops. The desire for better information about public activities and wishes is reflected in the increasing use of surveys, user panels and user control of services. The centre of gravity of public service organizations is moving more towards the point at which they interact with the public, with direct service providers within public organizations being defined as the customers of support services.

## WORK ORGANIZATION

The redefinition of government along managerialist and consumer lines is transforming the nature of organizational work in the public service. Indeed, it can be argued that the level of change in work organization in the public sector is greater than that which has happened in the private sector. As Pollert (1988: 308) has argued: 'There is, indeed, considerable research suggesting how the public service sector and the nationalised industries might pioneer employment restructuring.' This judgement is reinforced by the fact that it was only after 1988 that the major reforms of the organization of government finally emerged, and they are having a major effect on the nature of public sector work.

Some of the reason for change in the management of the public services is the need to demonstrate that they are effective. The public service will always find it difficult to demonstrate its effectiveness, because there is no immediate measure of overall performance, such as profit. There is a tendency to adopt what are seen as the methods of the private sector in order to demonstrate that effective management is being developed (Powell and Dimaggio, 1983). Since performance cannot be demonstrated, the nature of the management system becomes, itself, the mark of effectiveness. Ideas in good currency, such as customer sensitivity, are taken up as a method of signalling managerial effectiveness. There is certainly evidence, in the way the public sector has behaved in the last decade and more, of a tendency to adopt managerial fads and nostrums.

A central component of the new public management is the reassertion of the 'right of managers to manage'. The emphasis has been upon the role of top managers as the service strategists, and cost centre managers as responsible for the direct delivery of service, with control over their own finances. The role of middle management has come under pressure, as public service organizations attempt to restructure in a way that enables them to put more finance into direct service delivery. In a number of local authorities, for example, there have been programmes of delayering, with contracts between internal purchasers and providers and performance targets substituting for control based upon hierarchical authority. The role of management is also being asserted against the role of the professional, who has dominated the public service in the post-war years. In the Civil Service there has been an emphasis on management in executive functions being independent of the 'policy professionals'. In the National Health Service, general management was introduced, following the Griffiths Report in 1983, partly to reduce the influence of doctors. In local government, competitive tendering and contracting out has led to an emphasis on the effectiveness of service management. In education, local management of schools and grant-maintained status has enhanced the managerial role of headteachers, and the mixed economy of social care is leading to a more managerialist emphasis in the operation of social services.

The impact of the pursuit of quality in the public service, through the use of market-based mechanisms, has been a significant reduction in the number of staff employed. Competition is seen as ensuring the delivery of better-quality services at lower cost, which, given the labour-intensive nature of public service, inevitably means lower staffing. Tighter management, for example of absenteeism, which has declined considerably since 1989, has reduced the number of staff required. Flexibility in working methods has also reduced labour demands. There were major reductions in the size of the Civil Service in the first half of the 1980s. In local government there was a reduction of more than 114,000 manual worker jobs between 1988 and 1991 (LGIU, 1993). Many trust hospitals have made significant reductions in staff and there is evidence that the pupil:teacher ratio in schools has increased following devolved control. As well as changes in the number of jobs, the pattern of work organization has changed. There has been a tendency for the ratio of non-manual to manual jobs to increase. The reason for this is that internal market systems, contracts, and performance management are complex and involve

95

their own bureaucracy. Contracts must be monitored, performance recorded, invoices sent and bills paid, all of which demands staff. As the Audit Commission found, in its study of Family Health Service Authorities:

> Each member of the FHSA's staff engaged on administration supports on average about five GPs – a high cost reflecting a considerable administrative 'paper chase'. There is a corresponding administrative burden within practices. Paying practices by the number of activities undertaken (vaccinations, cervical smears, etc.) generates a large amount of paper.
>
> (Audit Commission, 1993c: 16).

Similar findings have been made in the case of the local management of schools and the effects of competitive tendering in local government and the National Health Services (Audit Commission, 1993a; National Audit Office, 1987; Walsh, 1991b; Walsh and Davis, 1993). It is difficult to argue, on the evidence available so far, that the reform of the public service is leading to a reduction in bureaucratic overhead costs. The transaction costs (Williamson, 1985) of the new systems of management – for example, the costs of writing and managing contracts, or of measuring performance – are high. Investment in information systems, in particular, has been costly, as a result of the development of the new public management.

There is substantial evidence that the reform of the public service has led to improved efficiency. Studies of contracting out and competitive tendering in particular have found that unit service costs have been reduced, while quality of service has been maintained. Headteachers, managers in trust hospitals, and heads of government agencies all tend to argue for the value of changes that have been made in leading to a closer focus on performance. What is more debated is the source of changes in costs.

Three reasons are put forward for changes in efficiency and quality of service. First it is argued that there have been technical improvements in the organization of work, for example through investment in capital, and consequent productivity gains. The second proposed source of efficiency gain is that work has been speeded up, and the workforce required to work harder. The third source of change in service costs is argued to be a reduction in the pay and conditions of the workforce. Studies of refuse collection have found that contracting out has led to savings largely as a result of technical improvement rather than wage cuts (Cubbin *et al.*, 1987). In other services, though, there is less evidence for technical improvement, and more for the speed-up of work (Walsh and Davis, 1993). Despite their positive attitude to the changes made, headteachers and managers in the health service are able to point to little evidence that they have had a substantive impact on the nature of services. It is also clear that competition and contracting out have led to worsening of pay and conditions, particularly in highly labour-intensive services such as cleaning. The savings that have resulted from contracting out have resulted from a combination of technical change and worsening the position of the worker. What seems to be happening is that a clear concept of the nature of public service management is emerging, though there is little evidence of its effect on quality of service.

While the introduction of competitive mechanisms have been worsening the position of many workers, there has been an emphasis on the importance of front-line workers, as the crucial point of contact with the public as customers. As the Audit Commission (1993b: 7) puts it:

> Good people are essential for any organisation, particularly in service businesses where they account for a large element of the cost, are a major part of the service, and have a decisive influence on the way the organisation is perceived by its customers.

Front-line workers are then defined as internal customers within the organization. There has been an increase in commitment to training in many public service organizations, commonly using structured approaches organized around National Vocational Qualifications and the Management Charter Initiative. Training systems are being certificated under the Investors in People initiative. Despite strong pressure on public service finance, the commitment to training has been maintained in many government organizations, particularly those which see themselves as in the forefront of the development of new management approaches.

There has been a particularly strong element of 'customer care' training in the development of public service management in the last decade. More generally, public service organizations have been committed to the development of their own internal programmes of training. The purpose has been to generate a clear organizational culture, to which the training programme is intended to build

97

commitment. Corporate identity programmes, internal communications systems, such as briefing groups and staff magazines, and the use of logos and slogans have also been important in the building of staff commitment within the organizations.

The development of initiatives to get closer to the customer, such as decentralization and one-stop shops, are frequently resisted by workers because they are seen as imposing new demands and worsening conditions. Decentralization, for example, may be seen as involving transfer from convenient locations to much less accessible ones, and disrupting career structures. One-stop shops, where staff may have to deal with a wide variety of queries, are seen as a threat to professional identities. The emphasis on customer care has developed at the same time as public workers have become more concerned for their safety, following assaults and even murders, notably in housing, social services, health and social security. There are also emotional difficulties in producing what Hochschild calls 'short bursts of niceness many times a day'. Research shows that staff dealing with difficult emotional problems emphasize the importance of distance, and of not 'taking people's problems home with you' (Walsh and Spencer, 1990: 29). The nature of the interaction between purchaser and user is likely to be highly emotionally charged in the public service, and requires the management of emotion. Equally important is the feeling of staff in decentralized offices that they are frequently not able to help people adequately because they are not given the information or resources. While their role as front-line delivery staff may be emphasized, they feel that in practice they are operating within a strict rule system established by a distant senior management (Walsh and Spencer, 1990).

There are dual messages for workers in the pursuit of quality in the public services. On the one hand it is argued that only by empowering the staff who are involved in direct service provision will it be possible to develop effective services. At the same time, many of the initiatives have the result of worsening the position of front-line workers. As the Trades Union Congress report on quality in the public services (1991: 21) argues:

> So-called 'employee involvement' for service quality looms large in most quality programmes, especially those which seek to fundamentally change an organisation's culture and working practices. The assumption behind the management push for

improved service quality is that employees are willing converts to the new ethos and gladly welcome any moves towards increasing self-management and closer team working.

In general this may be true, but union officers have expressed some anxiety about the way in which 'worker empowerment' schemes have been foisted onto often disquieted, over stretched and underpaid workers. The agenda is set by management and the strategy for enhancing worker participation is designed and executed with minimum consultation. This is not to say that the workforce is always hostile or apathetic, but that greater responsibility for the job is often presented without altenatives and more importantly is not perceived as a negotiating right. Indeed employee empowerment is often concerned with obligations and duties rather than rights and collective representation. The language is of worker empowerment, with the stress on individualism, consensus building and openness. It is not a procedure to facilitate a formal relationship between representative groups where a collective agreement is negotiated. The main objective is usually to tie the employee's performance and behaviour more closely to overall goals of the organisation.

In the extreme, those who criticize a customer service programme can then be defined as 'renegades, subversives and opposers of what is being attempted' (Seifert, 1992: 400).

The pattern of organization that is emerging in the public service is one of radical fragmentation. The traditional organizational approach of large-scale, centralized, self-sufficient bureaucracies is giving way to a multiplicity of institutions, organized in networks rather than hierarchies. The differentiation and specialization that previously happened within organizations is now moving to an inter-organizational level. Wholly new types of organization, such as Training and Enterprise Councils and Urban Development Corporations, operating solely in a strategic and purchasing role, are emerging. Some have seen this development as a move from a Fordist to a post-Fordist pattern of administration (Sanderson, 1992; Stoker, 1989), with flexibility, both of organization and workforce, as a central feature of the change. There is a growing division between the central core staff of public organizations and less attached peripheral staff. Part-time and fixed-term contracts have been much more commonly used over the last decade than previously – not only for manual staff, but for professional workers such as teachers. Organizations must work together if they are to be able to deliver services effectively, for example in the case of community care, in which voluntary and private providers are playing an increasingly important role. Staff are no longer seen as members of large public services, but as attached to smaller local service delivery units – a development which is reflected in the decline of national bargaining for public sector workers. A number of local authorities have opted out of the national bargaining system. In schools, hospitals and government executive agencies diversified patterns of pay and conditions are slowly emerging. Within large public service organizations such as local authorities, unified central bargaining systems are being broken down.

The extent of change should not be over-emphasized. The public sector still employs a large proportion of those who deliver public services. Competitive tendering in local government, for example, has only resulted in about 20 per cent of work in those local government services involved being contracted out. Public service organizations remain large employers and operate in a bureaucratic fashion. As Cochrane (1993: 87) argues: 'One consequence of the new arrangements may, in any case, be an increase in formal hierarchy, determined by detailed contracts in some areas, leaving still less scope for practical initiative at the level of delivery.'

The contract-based system may, as Stinchcombe (1990) argues, strongly resemble a hierarchically based organization system of control. The long-term movement, though, is clearly towards more disaggregated systems of service delivery, controlled through explicit statements of standards and performance-based management systems with decentralized patterns of bargaining. The emerging system exhibits a tension between trust and mistrust, and commitment and control. The language of empowering staff to respond more directly to citizens as customers goes along with a low-trust syndrome (Fox, 1974), embodied in increased direct management control, for example in the management of direct labour and direct service organizations (Walker, 1993). The management stance in the public service is now much firmer than it was ten years ago, and services that received little attention are now strongly controlled. The development of trust and control may be seen as alternative sides of the same coin. As Armstrong (1989: 316) argues:

The sheer expense of securing trust in the immediate agency relationship therefore involves employees (and existing senior managers) with a strong economic incentive to find cheaper alternatives. It is in this sense that the expenditure on monitoring and bonding which figures so prominently in positive agency theory may make sense. . . . At the same time, the economic privileges and social status associated with high trust positions within the agency relationship provide individuals and social groups within management hierarchies with powerful incentives to bid for, or to hang on to such positions.

Senior managers in the public services have experienced considerable increases in pay, and additional benefits, such as private health insurance, in recent years, which serve to tie them more firmly to the organization. Many lower-level staff, by contrast, have experienced an erosion of their position. The definition of the public service as 'among the first rank of good employers' no longer informs the employment relationship of the government workforce.

What is emerging is a gradation of attachment to the organization and centrality to its operations, in contrast to the previous hierarchy of position. There are core staff who are central to the organization's activities, particularly highly paid central strategists, and those who control contracts and procurement. Direct service deliverers are less central, depending upon the character of the local market for services. Where there is a plentiful supply of labour, then staff can be less directly attached to the organization, operating on service contracts. Contract staff in relatively unskilled manual jobs, for example building cleaning, have a very loose attachment to the organization. The system of public service management has been going through a process of radical decoupling.

## CONCLUSION

The definition of quality in the public service through the estalishment of standards and performance management can be seen as the basis for the emergence of the 'evaluative state' (Henkel, 1991). The first step in this development is the separation of politics and management. The second is the establishment of processes of audit and inspection to provide a check on the freedom of management. The statement of clear standards and performance measures makes it possible to exercise control at a distance. Intermediate layers of management and, indeed, government may then be dispensed with. This development is most apparent in the education system. Local education authorities are gradually being abolished, to be replaced by a system of standards embodied in the national curriculum, and central control from the Department for Education, through testing and tightly defined processes of inspection. Such, at least, is theory. Practice, as the problems of the Secretary of State for Education have shown, may be more difficult.

'Contract' and 'customer' have emerged as the metaphors of the new public service management. In many cases, particularly in local and central government, there are real, enforceable, legal contracts with external, often private sector, service providers. In others, such as health, there are quasi-contracts. The relationship between staff and the organization, whether they are directly employed or not, is also seen in a contractual way, with clear expectations of performance. The delivery of service is seen as involving a chain of customers, both within and outside the organization. The approaches adopted to quality cut to the heart of the debate over the nature of the public realm. This debate is happening not only in Britain, but on an international basis. The role of the state in ensuring that public services are delivered does not necessarily require direct employment of the staff who deliver those services. As Osborne and Gaebler have argued, the role of the state may be 'to steer, not row'. The debate over the quality of public services is also a debate about the nature of government in market economies.

# REFERENCES

Armstrong, P. (1989) 'Management, Labour Process and Agency', *Work, Employment and Society*, 3 (3), 307–22.

Audit Commission (1992) *Local Authority Performance Indicators*, London: HMSO.

Audit Commission (1993a) *Adding Up the Sums: Schools' Management of Their Finances*, London: HMSO.

Audit Commission (1993b) *Putting Quality on the Map: Measuring and Appraising Quality in the Public Service*, London: HMSO.

Audit Commission (1993c) *Practices Make Perfect: The Role of the Family Health Services Authority*, London: HMSO.

Bowen, D.E. and Schneider, B (1988) 'Services Marketing and Management: Implications for Organisational Behaviour', *Research in Organisational Behaviour*, 10, JAI Press, 43–80.

Burnheim, J. (1988) *Is Democracy Possible? The Alternative to Democratic Politics*, Cambridge: Polity Press.

Carter, N., Klein, R. and Day, P. (1992) *How Organisations Measure Performance: The use of Performance Indicators in Government*, London: Routledge.

Chapman, L. (1979) *Your Disobedient Servant*, Harmondsworth: Penguin.

*Citizen's Charter* (1991) Cmnd 1599, London: HMSO.

*Citizen's Charter First Report: 1992*, Cmnd 2101, London: HMSO.

Cochrane, A. (1993) *Whatever Happened to Local Government?* Buckingham: Open University Press.

Cubbin, J., Domberger, S. and Meadowcroft, S. (1987) 'Competitive Tendering and Refuse Collection: Identifying the Source of Efficiency Gains', *Fiscal Studies*, 8 (3), 49–58.

Department of Health and Social Security (1989) *Caring for Patients*, London: HMSO.

Di Maggio, P. and Powell, W.W. (1983) 'The Iron Cage Revisited: Institutional Isomorphism and Collective Rationality in Organizational Fields', *American Sociological Review*, 48, 147–60.

Du Gay, P. and Salaman, G. (1992) 'The Cult[ure] of the Customer', *Journal of Management Studies*, 29 (5), 615–33.

Flynn, R. (1992) *Structures of Control in Health Management*, London: Routledge.

Foa, P. and Foa, U. (1974) *Societal Structures of the Mind*, New York: C.C. Thomas.

Fox, A. (1974) *Beyond Contract*, London: Faber & Faber.

Freeman-Bell, G. and Grover, R. (forthcoming) 'The Use of Quality Management in Local Authorities', *Local Government Studies*.

Gronroos, C. (1984) 'A Service Quality Model and its Marketing Implications', *European Journal of Marketing*, 18 (4).

Griffiths, E.R. (1983) *NHS Management Inquiry*, London Department of Health and Social Security.

Hawkey, P. (1993) 'Foot Down on the Quality Drive', *Local Government Chronicle*, 30 April, 14.

Henkel, M. (1991) *Government, Evaluation and Change*, London: Jessica Kingsley.

Hochschild, A.R. (1983) *The Managed Heart*, Los Angeles, CA: University of California Press.

LeGrand, J. (1991) 'Quasi-Markets and Social Policy', *The Economic Journal*, 101, 1256–67.

Lipsky, M. (1980) *Street-Level Bureaucracy*, New York: Russell Sage Foundation.

Local Government Information Unit (1993) *Realising Your Assets – Involving the Workforce in CCT*, London: Local Government Information Unit.

Major, J. (1989) *Public Service Management: The Revolution in Progress*, London: The Audit Commission.

Massey, A. (1993) *Managing the Public Sector: A Comparative Analysis of the United Kingdom and the United States*, Aldershot: Edward Elgar.

National Audit Office (1987) *Competitive Tendering for Support Services in the National Health Services*, London: HMSO.

Normann, R. (1984) *Service Management: Strategy and Leadership in Service Businesses*, Chichester: Wiley.

Osborne, D. and Gaebler, T. (1992) *Reinventing Government: How the Entrepreneurial Spirit is Transforming the Public Sector*, Reading, MA: Addison-Wesley.

Packwood, T., Keen, J. and Buxton, M. (1991) *Hospitals in Transition: The Resource Management Experiment*, Milton Keynes: Open University Press.

Peters, T. & Waterman, R. (1982) *In Search of Excellence*, New York: Harper & Row.

Pollert, A. (1988) 'The Flexible Firm: Fixation or Fact?' *Work, Employment and Society*, 2 (3), 281–316.

Pollitt, C. (1993) *Managerialism and the Public Services: Cuts or Cultural Change in the 1990s?* (2nd edn), Oxford: Blackwell.

Prior, D., Stewart, J.D., Walsh, K. (1993) *Is the Citizen's Charter a Charter for Citizens?*, Luton: Local Government Management Board.

Rawls, J. (1972) *A Theory of Justice*, Oxford: Oxford University Press.

Ridley, N. (1988) *The Local Right: Enabling not Providing*, London: Centre for Policy Studies.

Sanderson, I. (1992) 'Introduction: The Context of Quality in Local Government', in I. Sanderson (ed.) *Management of Quality in Local Government*, Harlow: Longman.

Seifert, R. (1992) *Industrial Relations in the NHS*, London: Chapman & Hall.

Stinchcombe, A. (1990) 'Organising Information Outside the Firm: Contracts as Hierarchical Documents', in A. Stinchcombe (ed.) *Information and Organisations*, London: University of California Press.

Stoker, G. (1989) 'Creating a Local Government for a Post-Fordist Society: The Thatcherite Project?', in J. Stewart and G. Stoker (eds) *The Future of Local Government*, London: Macmillan.

Thompson, J.D. (1967) *Organizations in Action*, New York: McGraw-Hill.

Trades Union Congress (1991) *The Quality Challenge*, London: Trades Union Congress.

Tritter, J. (1993) 'The Citizen's Charter: From Users' Perspectives', paper at The Public Sphere Conference, Manchester.

Walker, B. (1993) *Competition for Building Maintenance*, London: HMSO.

Walsh, K. (1991a) 'Quality and Public Services', *Public Administration*, 69 (4), 503–14.

Walsh, K. (1991b) *Competition for Local Authority Services: Initial Experience*, London: HMSO.

Walsh, K. & Davis, H. (1993) *Competition and Service: The Impact of the Local Government Act 1988*, London: HMSO.

Walsh, K. & Spencer, K. (1990) *The Quality of Service in Housing Management*, Birmingham: INLOGOV, University of Birmingham.

Williamson, O.E. (1985) *The Economic Institution of Capitalism*, New York: Free Press.

# 4

# QUALITY MANAGEMENT AND THE MANAGEMENT OF QUALITY*

*Janette Webb*

For more than a decade in Britain we have had a government which has sought to replace the ideology and structures of bureaucracy and regulation with those of enterprise and deregulation. According to the rhetoric of enterprise, one of the remedies for a weak economy and the lack of competitiveness of British businesses in global markets is the creation of a new type of customer responsiveness. Indeed most managements, regardless of the sector or type of organization they operate in, now use the language of the 'sovereign customer' and the 'customer care' package has become *de rigeur*. Whatever the public cynicism about the reality behind the rhetoric, most of us are implicated: when we are not the consumer targets of customer care, we are, as employees, meant to play enterprising supplier to the people who used to be peers or workmates, but who are now our 'customers' in the firm's internal supply chain. The language of enterprise is undeniably persuasive: it has 'established an affinity between the politico-ethical objectives of neo-liberal government in the UK, the economic objectives of contemporary business and the self-actualizing, self-regulating capacities of human subjects' (Du Gay and Salaman, 1992: 631).

---

* David Cleary was the research fellow for the project described here and has contributed to the paper through fieldwork, discussions and joint writing: many thanks.
The project was funded by ESRC/DTI as part of the 'New Technologies and the Firm' initiative.
Thanks are also due to the many managers, engineers and sales people who talked patiently to us about their work.

Total quality management (TQM) provides a central element of the prescriptions associated with free market ideology. TQM is inherently concerned with the 'sovereign customer' and uses the concept to promote a new 'vocabulary of motive' (Wright-Mills, 1940), legitimating the restructuring of the firm and translating enterprise ideology into material practices. This chapter focuses on the interpretation and use of TQM by managers and assesses its implications for managerial work.

## WHAT IS TQM?

Hill's discussion of TQM theory (this volume) provides an appropriate definition of the parameters of a TQM programme. I would add, for my purposes, that in the language of TQM, customers are not solely external to the firm, but are also internal. Workers and managers receive work from an 'internal supplier', add their contribution and then pass it on to their 'internal customer'. Through the use of quality improvement teams, the objective is to agree, and then meet, the requirements of each internal customer, creating a chain of quality ending with the external customer. In theory, no internal 'customer' should be given faulty or incomplete work, as a result of the poor quality work of their internal 'suppliers'. Workplace relations are thus translated into quasi-market transactions, but without the element of choice of supplier which is meant to operate for customers in the external market-place (Delbridge *et al.*, 1992). The code of conduct, emphasizing the virtues of initiative, self-reliance and commitment, in turn encourages members of the workforce to reconstruct themselves as personal TQM projects; a focus for continuous improvement, and in turn marketable commodities: 'even the most marketable employees need to take a proactive approach to their careers, because marketability rapidly fades unless it is conscientiously maintained' (Yvonne Sarch, *Observer* magazine, 21 March 1993).

Taken at face value, TQM is a philosophy which seems to promise an optimizing, rather than a satisficing, strategy for products and services, as well as a reversal of the separation between the planning and execution of work, which has been held accountable for progressive deskilling in many occupations. Yet TQM is at the centre of two extreme claims. On the one hand, its management-oriented proponents promise salvation for inflexible, traditional industries selling poor quality goods, made by an alienated workforce: 'most TQM experts get evangelical about their message' (Bank, 1992: 47). On the other hand, a number of academic analysts have charged its advocates with massive deceit, arguing that TQM allows management to disguise the fact of intensification of work, increased surveillance and management control over labour with the cosmetic language of teamwork and personal empowerment (Delbridge *et al.*, 1992; Sewell and Wilkinson, 1992). In fact there are two distinct strands to academic criticism of the vogue for TQM. One is the pragmatic, but broadly optimistic, view represented by Hill (1991 and this volume), Wilkinson *et al.* (1991; 1992) and Wilkinson (1993) where TQM is seen as having some potential to improve industrial democracy, albeit within management-determined limits, and to contribute to better-quality goods and services. In each case, however, the writers would argue that the treatment of social factors by the proponents of TQM is inadequate. The result for a number of firms is an overly narrow view of quality, a 'quick-fix' model of TQM and corresponding failure to align personnel or human resource management policies with TQM strategy (Wilkinson *et al.* 1991; 1992). Hill (1991 and this volume), however, reports companies where TQM was implemented with long-term top-level commitment, resulting in reduced costs and improved customer satisfaction. He also suggests that there is evidence that, by and large, both workforce and managers welcome TQM as long as some degree of self-interest is visibly tied in. On the other hand, the work of Delbridge *et al.* (1992) and Sewell and Wilkinson (1992), which concentrate on the shopfloor implications, is broadly pessimistic and sets out to show how a systematic application of JIT/TQM principles facilitates greater management control, individual surveillance and intensification of work, without meaningful 'empowerment' at the bottom of the hierarchy. Instead it is the managers who are the chief beneficiaries of TQM, with the potential to control the behaviour of the workforce through centralized management information systems and self-disciplining peer groups of workers.

## THE ROLE OF MANAGERS IN TQM

There is then a dispute about the character and implications of TQM. It could be argued that the final verdict depends on the role and intentions of senior managers, given that, like other process innovations, TQM could be used for contradictory political ends. Unlike other innovations, however, TQM is itself meant to focus on changing the nature of managerial work, as well as reducing the numbers of middle management and supervisory jobs. Managers 'have the major responsibility for quality improvement and managerially controlled systems are the prime sources of quality failures' (Hill, 1991: 401). The popular management texts on the cultural aspects of TQM concentrate on change at managerial levels, with top management expected to set the standards and to be an example through their conduct: they are no longer allowed to say one thing and do another (e.g. Kanter, 1990). Peters (1988) concludes his lengthy prescriptions with a call for absolute integrity and honesty: 'successful organizations must shift from an age dominated by contracts and litigiousness to an age of handshakes and trust' (p. 518). Hypocrisy and double standards, he argues, are a guarantee of failure. The implied managerial identity is that of a messiah, with talk of the 'crusade for quality': 'the pursuit of the goal of perfection in TQ has a monkish ring to it. The . . . conversion to TQ . . . is both personal and public. . . . There is also an element of personal witness' (Bank, 1992: 47). No doubt vows of poverty and chastity will follow shortly! The pursuit of TQM is meant to bring its own rewards and its advocates decry the use of financial incentives to enforce compliance (Oakland, 1989). There is implicitly an attempt to rediscover charismatic leadership, and to retreat from the dominant rational bureaucratic mode (Weber, 1948).

There are radical implications for middle managers. Instead of being guardian of a function, the middle manager becomes someone who facilitates and supports the workforce, in whatever ways they demand: 'the middle manager must practise fast-paced "horizontal management", not traditional delaying "vertical management"' (Peters, 1988: 369). According to Hill (1991: 403–4):

> organizational devices that cut across internal boundaries, a wider diffusion of information and improved communication, the decentralization of decision-making within management as a result of wider participation and a principled commitment to the sovereignty of the customer, are forces for debureaucratizing behaviour.

Of course, this ignores the threat to middle managers of the implied revisions of their role, and reductions in their numbers

(Preece and Wood, 1993). They may perceive themselves as losing traditional sources of power, as losing control over their specialist expertise (Wilkinson, 1993) and as having to work harder for no greater returns. Thus Wilkinson *et al.* (1992) found that TQM, rather than uniting managers, became a source of conflict between competing interest groups. Senior managers have to overcome existing ways of doing things in order to make TQM effective, even if this means sacking managers who resist and using the traditional sticks and carrots to enforce compliance. Indeed, Hill (this volume) reports that once managers began to see that adopting TQM could serve their own career interests, it began to be taken seriously.

## TQM IN OPERATION: CREATING THE 'CUSTOMER RESPONSIVE' FIRM

The case studies discussed below are part of a project which examined the management of a section of a supply chain in the computer systems industry (Webb and Cleary, 1994). The fieldwork focused on three firms and consisted of interviews with middle and senior managers, sales representatives and systems engineers, with some observation of meetings and workplace practices. The first firm, Midas, was a medium-sized disk-drive manufacturer. The second, Telewave Electronics (TE), was an international computer systems manufacturer. The third, Albion Spirits (AS), was a drinks manufacturer undergoing major restructuring, including the buying-in of distributed computer systems.

Each firm was pursuing some aspects of TQM but with different objectives, derived from the context in which they were operating and the aims of senior management. None of them appeared to regard TQM as a 'quick fix', though Midas operated with the most instrumental, short-term approach. Midas's customers, all larger and better resourced, were moving to 'strategic partnerships' with vendors. Midas was effectively forced to adopt the language of TQM in order to stay in business. They perceived themselves as being in a race to gain authorized vendor status, which meant controlling cost and product quality against highly efficient competition. TQM was at a very early stage, with discussions beginning during fieldwork. As in Hill's study, it was the US-owned company, TE, which had the most systematically elaborated version of TQM. It had been experimenting with many of the ideas for about a decade and saw the techniques as a way of responding to heightened competition from the Far East. The corporate objective was to make sales and production structures more responsive to customers, by increasing the rate of product innovation and new product releases, and controlling the cost of production. In AS, TQM was a tool for creating a debureaucratized organization, under central corporate control, out of a collection of semi-independent brand companies. TQM was at a relatively early stage, and the main motivation was the search for increased profits, following a recent takeover by another firm, Corporate Booze (CB).

It was only in TE that all levels of the workforce were involved in TQM. In both Midas and AS, managers and engineers were the first targets for change. In all three firms, TQM was seen as having the potential to transform the management of development, manufacturing, supplier relationships and sales, with radical implications for the jobs of managers and engineers. Functions and relationships between functions were restructured, in line with senior management's perceptions of the market and desired supply chain relationships. In each case the ambition was to create a 'customer-responsive' organization, where functions, and cross-functional teams, from R. & D. through to marketing, materials procurement, manufacturing and sales, facilitate not only continuous improvement in existing processes but technical innovation.

## Telewave Electronics

TE is a US-owned multinational corporation employing 87,000 people, with 4,000 in Britain distributed between two manufacturing sites, four R. & D. sites and twenty-two sales offices. It is the epitome of the expertise-based company, with labour costs heavily weighted towards graduate engineers. Its engagement with TQM appears to have been highly profitable: unlike many other suppliers, TE is continuing in profit.

The corporation is well known for its human resources style of management, which is underpinned by a unitarist corporate ideology known as 'the TE way.' Managers are regarded as playing a critical role in creating 'a work environment in which the contributions of all people can be recognized' (TE corporate literature). Managers and supervisors are highly trained and their accessibility is facilitated by integrated production and office areas; there are no closed offices and there is only one canteen. The ideology is reinforced by single-status terms and conditions of employment and above-average pay rates. The majority of the workforce has security of employment, but job flexibility is the norm. TE is a non-union employer, and the employment contract emphasizes the individualistic relationship between company and employee. Security of employment and an internal labour market sustain the belief that opportunities for improved pay and status are dependent not on collective action but solely on the individual's ability and motivation: the ideology is strictly meritocratic. Continuous improvements in performance are expected and there is considerable peer-group pressure on individuals to fall into line.

By implication, individuals carry the blame for their own relative failure and since there are in reality a very small number of promoted posts, most people will be relative failures. It is typically those in middle management who experience the contradictions between the espoused ideals and the reality of restricted career mobility most strongly, particularly when recession means little or no job mobility. In general, however, pay and benefits are relatively high, many people have intrinsically interesting jobs and there is a high degree of acceptance of the ideology: 'The opportunities are there, it's up to the individual to take them' is an often-heard comment.

## TQM in TE

Despite the seeming informality with which TQM techniques filtered down, there was a clear corporate agenda: TQM was seen first as a means of overcoming the firm's historical reputation for prioritizing R. & D. over and above what would sell. The language of the internal customer was used to overcome barriers between sales, marketing, manufacturing and R. & D. functions, and between divisions, which emerged over a forty-year period, despite the corporate ideology. Vendor management policies were introduced. TQM techniques were taught across the workforce as a strategy for continuous improvement of processes and as a way of decreasing production costs. Production arrangements increasingly relied on the use of a combination of just-in-time and TQM techniques (Dawson and Webb, 1989). The sales function moved to a form of consultative selling, which promises to solve the customer's business problems through computer applications.

Corporate motives could thus be summed up as cost-cutting plus more effective direction of innovation. Greater corporate control over product development, marketing and manufacturing was effected first by means of extensive international seminars, second by the 'carrots and sticks' of performance measures, and third by restructuring to create a clear-cut division between the location of R. & D. and that of manufacture, gradually concentrating R. & D. expertise, while siting manufacturing plants close to targeted markets.

At divisional level there was an attempt to institutionalize customer responsiveness through the redirection of product development. After ten years, development was no longer the sole preserve of the lab engineers. Instead there was a commitment to a triad of R. & D., marketing and manufacturing, who were each other's internal 'customers': product designs had to be saleable, easy to manufacture and competitive. Pressure was put on divisions to shorten development timetables. The main vehicle signifying the change was the business team, comprising middle managers and engineers from each function. In part this was meant to provide a channel for insights from less senior staff into the development cycle, preventing the domination of strategy by senior management. The 'internal market' thus created was, not surprisingly, a place with some tensions. Middle managers felt that senior managers were not as responsive to the teams as they should be, but that there was greater accountability and more routine exchange between functions and a more efficient development process. Work was less 'like a party' than it used to be, and the feeling of being under pressure was greater. Far from developing their charisma, for middle managers TQM meant revealing to subordinates their 'feet of clay', when they were unable to solve problems on the spot. Informally the status hierarchy of R. & D., marketing and manufacturing remained. The lab engineers regarded themselves as the locus of technical creativity, and although they viewed themselves as increasingly market-driven, they did not regard themselves as marketing-driven, which was described by the lab manager as resulting in a 'laundry list approach' to design. From an R. & D. perspective, TQM had not resolved their major managerial problem, which was how to foresee the next technical breakthrough. Reliant on the informal technological community for inspiration, and under threat from the centralization of R. & D. in centres of excellence, the anxieties about technical innovation were particularly acute and no doubt made channels to the customer via marketing seem cumbersome and inadequate. Even in an organic system like that used by TE, the search for a structure suited to continuous innovation was far from over.

## *'Partnership with customers'*

The convergence on computing industry standards has resulted in loss of technical differentiation between manufacturers who have sought to find alternative 'unique selling points'. In TE's case, these were characterized as 'knowledge and people' (account manager) and the new strategy was presented to customers as a 'strategic partnership'. The moral code of TQM was brought into play to provide a sales vocabulary of trust, a warm, caring dependency, heart-to-heart support and 'healing of the raw nerves of the [customer's] business' (TE support engineer). For sales staff the role meant persuading the customer that they were buying, not technology, but 'added value' in the form of solutions to business problems:

> 'We're not selling computers, we're selling money . . . we are really saying we can provide solutions that will put X amount on your bottom line. . . . The fact that we use this technology to do it is to some extent irrelevant to a finance director, as long as he believes what you're saying is true.'
>
> (Account manager)

The reputation and social worth of the supplier was foremost: 'It is establishing TE as a reputable computer supplier to that organization that is my primary objective. . . . So I very rarely get involved in discussions about what computers can and cannot do' (account manager). 'TE are trying to generate a culture of honesty, commitment and all those good nice words. But they actually mean something in TE' (account manager).

The sales function was thus one of those which saw its overall status improve as a result of TQM. The reformed role constituted a form of professionalization: getting 'to the heart of the [customer's] business' (account manager) required the licence and mandate of the professions, with their metaphorical clean hands and a demonstrable possession of valued technical knowledge. Such knowledge was carefully cultivated – first, through the creation of centres of business expertise which provided the commercial knowledge for the sales team to demonstrate their competence to potential customers. In addition, sales work had become more segmented, with a distinct division of labour between the moral 'front' and the 'back stage' technical support used to specify the system requirements.

Sales reps had to walk a tightrope between over-promising in order to win the sale and setting customer expectations at a manageable level. Hence negotiating customer requirements was itself carefully managed. Routines and procedures were constructed as a means of protecting sales reps from failure and a distinction was made between a successful sale and professionally correct handling of a sale. If the work was 'done properly', it allowed responsibility for relative failure to be placed on the user's business contingencies, despite the user's natural desire to blame the supplier. The first important step to proper handling was getting in at the right level – senior management – bypassing the in-house data-processing function: '[When] the selling process [is] from the internal technical people to the users, they oversell the system often to get it justified and then we are struggling to deliver everything to that expectation' (account manager).

Setting customer expectations was ideally achieved by pre-sales consultancy by the supplier, which the user paid for. Everyone was well aware that a company spending perhaps tens of thousands of pounds on such consultancy was already halfway committed. If things did go wrong, there were routines for cooling out the customer. The division of labour between the sales reps, who upheld the moral front, and the technical back-room team who were the repository of 'the knowledge' was highly valuable in this process. The technical experts could conduct a combined technical and organizational analysis, without threatening the reputation of the sales front person.

Overall, the changes introduced under the umbrella of TQM were a continuation of past traditions, rather than a radical break. The moral rhetoric of TQM, and its ethos of 'partnership' with internal and external customers, fitted easily with the pre-existing corporate ideology. As far as managers were concerned, the changes in their work were asssimilated into a corporate context adapted to flexible job content, endless negotiating around responsibilities and divisions of labour, and indeed to the acceptance of change itself. TQM made the managerial role more visible because of the emphasis on solving quality problems as they arise, rather than setting them aside for later, but the management process in TE was already actively researched, debated and experimented with and managers were encouraged to be analytical and reflective about the social relations of management. The result was a highly polished processional 'front' which facilitates continuous change, whatever the career dissatisfactions of middle managers. However, as our next case-study company showed, one firm's meat is another firm's poison. An attempt to institutionalize customer responsiveness can have disastrous consequences when it is mismanaged.

## Midas plc

In Midas, TQM was part of the rescue operation for a restructured firm verging on bankruptcy, after a period of massive profitability. Midas plc was a medium-sized British company, of ten years standing. In 1990 it employed approximately 800 people, distributed between Britain, the USA and Singapore, developing and manufacturing disk drives for the work station market. The company had initially enjoyed tremendous success, having started with a technological lead in an open, expanding market. By the latter part of the 1980s, however, large profits had turned to large losses. Other suppliers had eroded Midas's technological lead and were able to sell the product more cheaply. In March 1989 the auditors' report closed down operations, but the company was refinanced with $20m. in new money, supported chiefly by one of the clearing banks and 3i plc.

The new senior management team set out to replace what was perceived as the 'closed and arrogant' style (vice-president of engineering) with an open, collaborative approach to the definition of business strategy. A number of experienced managers were appointed to prominent roles in design, production and quality engineering. Formal structures were created to control development timetables and to create a perceived missing communication link between the design team, manufacturing and customers. In the purchasing function, the development of integrated relationships with suppliers was espoused as a key to quality and cost control. The reality of 'partnership', however, was rather different for Midas. With declining market power and struggling with cash flow, it was treated less favourably by vendors, who prioritized orders from prompt payers. Yet increasing interdependence tied

115

Midas in to suppliers' timetables which were outside its control. Such suppliers were well aware of their threat potential: 'The problem is next week will do for them and yesterday will do for us' (design engineer).

### Product development and the internal market-place: what went wrong

Business strategy prioritized retrieving the OEM customer base through intensive liaison and competitive benchmarking. A customer support organization was created with responsibility for customer feedback on products and for negotiating technical standards. The other formal structure for customer feedback was the marketing group, which sought to gather intelligence on customer requirements and competitor products. In practice 'the partnership bandwagon' (marketing manager) meant that customers had to be actively courted, as they set higher standards of quality. While some customers were seen as constructive, others were perceived as expecting perfection first time. Visits to these firms were fraught: customer engineers used the opportunity to introduce new requirements into a tentative design specification, pushing up costs for the supplier and testing out the supplier's willingness to promise to meet them. This was particularly prevalent as a negotiating tactic with Midas, because of its weak market position. The result was a set of internal 'customer–supplier' relations which were equally fraught: marketing wanted firm specifications and precise dates for prototypes, in order to be seen as credible by its external customers, while it was in development's interests to retain as high a degree of freedom as possible.

Attempts at competitive benchmarking proved disastrous: the marketing manager continually alluded to 'being in the race', dragging the development group along with claims and rumours about the competition. In the attempt to shorten development timetables and find a quicker route to market, the product specification was repeatedly changed by senior managers. New technology was dropped or compromised:

> 'The longer [the design project] slips, the more chance it has of changing. . . . And the more it slips . . . the more other suppliers who announce products cause all sorts of changes and you never actually get to a point when you say that is what we will go and design. . . . Before you know where you are you

116

have slipped six months. And you can't really afford to do that
... otherwise you don't get in to the key accounts ... then
you don't have enough business to sustain you.'

(Chief mechanical engineer)

Instead of the prescribed equal dialogue between the 'internal customers', marketing, development and manufacturing, the development team was at the bottom of the status hierarchy. Marketing had emerged at the top as a result of the rhetoric of customer responsiveness. It was able to use its direct contact with customers as a legitimating device – who can argue against what the market wants, after all? – and have the final say in timetabling and performance specifications. For development, marketing symbolized the difficult and elusive external customer, with its ever-changing and ever-increasing demands. The difficulty of staying within tight schedules was further worsened by the ability of manufacturing to make repeated demands on development for help with routine production engineering.

The result of the customer-responsive ideology, its accompanying race to market mentality and the emergent informal status hierarchy, was anxiety, increasing labour turnover and poor performance. Development timetables became shorter and shorter, with development engineers routinely working overtime and still failing to meet deadlines. Although going through the motions of a formal development process, in practice there was a sense of inertia, sometimes described as a death wish, in engineering. The management response to disaffection was not, however, to seek improvement through collaborative project management, but to adopt an increasingly directive stance, deepening the motivational crisis yet further: 'It's all geared up for what the company can get from the individual. There's no sort of "what can the company do for you" sort of thing. It's just all work, work, work and no play; pressure, pressure, pressure' (design engineer).

For many of the engineers, the actions of the new development manager opened up a gulf between the TQM rhetoric of participation and the reality of a mechanistic style of control. He had eradicated the old structure, where senior engineers had had relative autonomy in project mangement, in favour of a matrix structure, intended to incorporate some of his own appointments in key roles. These changes were viewed with suspicion by the engineers, who interpreted them as a way of excluding them from both project planning and from the higher-paid management roles. In the face of continuing distrust, and with the short-term objective of meeting deadlines, a system of direct control was imposed and the espoused progressive management never transpired. Instead informal, historically based authoritarian norms continued to dominate practice: 'It was always "who's to blame for this or that", never "OK that's wrong, let's fix it"' (senior engineer).

### *The consequences for product innovation – continuous non-improvement*

'There is never enough time to do the job properly, but there is time enough to do it again and again and again' (design engineer).

Distrust between senior management and the senior design engineers undermined the development process. The engineers increasingly used their knowledge as a defensive weapon, controlling access to knowledge and implicitly refusing to delegate aspects of design or to train junior engineers. Their defensiveness was particularly damaging to any attempt to build continuous improvements into the design cycle. Existing knowledge was not routinely incorporated into new projects and new expertise remained unused. Design mistakes went uncorrected from one generation of products to the next:

> 'Someone comes up with an initial design. You get it on to the board, you find all the problems. The initial designer leaves the project and goes on to something else, and then it's us, the junior engineers, left to tackle the problem and try and fix it. . . . They'll probably make the same mistakes over and over again and I'll have to keep fixing the same mistakes over and over again.'
>
> (Design engineer)

By August 1991 the company was in receivership. For Midas's management, the attempt to apply TQM principles resulted not in continuous improvement, but in an inability to control timetables, costs and products. They espoused the virtues of total quality techniques, but acted according to a short-term, instrumental rationality. Ironically, the very measures taken to exert control undermined the achievement of their own objectives, producing a motivational crisis among the engineers, the collapse of management legitimacy and loss of control over the development process (Webb, 1992). In this case the gulf between the moral code of conduct prescribed by TQM and the reality of work experience undermined whatever commitment had existed among the technical experts to the goals of senior management. The experience of Midas represents a potentially common crisis for many small and medium-sized engineering firms, locked into a highly competitive and unstable supply chian, dominated by bigger firms. Under the guise of TQM, such 'strategic partnerships' represent anxious bargaining, intensification of work and increased monitoring and control for the workforce.

## Albion Spirits

The intention of the buyer in a TQM system is to improve the quality of its bought-in technology, including making use of the vendor's expertise, implicitly or explicitly, as part of the contract. Buyers try to use such 'partnerships' to impose higher standards in relation to quality and price on suppliers in exchange for a relatively stable source of revenues. Indeed, 'strategic partnerships', as conceived by the senior management of Albion Spirits, implied keeping vendors on their toes and playing them off against each other, in order to ensure that they delivered on their promises.

AS is a large firm in the food, drink and tobacco sector. It has a turnover of approximately $3.5bn. and employs 14,000 people in Britain. The context for TQM was a contentious takeover by a company whose directors saw the opportunity for windfall profits simply by the device of reorganizing a number of autonomous brand companies, with their duplicate clerical, data-processing and engineering functions, into a 'slimmer' corporate structure. The immediate consequences were job losses and serious damage to AS's reputation for being a nice, friendly place to work. Before the takeover, AS was a hierarchical company with a paternalistic attitude towards its employees. It had not been the place for young, ambitious types: 'Very rigid structure, the only way you got X or Y's job was when he died!' Five years later, it was well on the way to fitting the entrepreneurial image. TQM was central to the reorganization and was principally regarded as a means of promoting 'entrepreneurial' activity among managers and engineers. An integral part of the 'customer-responsive' project was the replacement of fragmented, incompatible computing systems with integrated management information systems, organized around distributed computing.

### Information services: managing the internal market-place

The new 'internal market-place' was tense, turbulent and shrinking! A period of intense structural upheaval began as soon as the takeover was completed. The new systems, designed to bring the unruly provinces of AS under tight federal control by creating centralizing lines of managerial authority, were implemented by senior managers who were either moved from CB or recruited externally: 'People left in their droves, totally changed; the whole focus was different.' The old brand companies were reordered into three cross-cutting business units: production, exports and bottling.

A new information services (IS) organization played a central part in creating the TQM 'business team' mentality and was instrumental in overcoming prevailing traditions of regional autonomy. For senior management, TQM meant the collapsing of barriers between production and business functions: IT strategy, business strategy and production processes had to form an integrated whole, with IS providing the delivery system that links business units and circulates information between them. Senior managers make up the brain, transmitting instructions and formulating strategy. The explicit agenda for IS was to provide the required 'business service' through the creation of the MIS. Senior IS management organized the department by allocating account managers to each of the three business units, and IS became the organizational link with IT suppliers.

The IS manager faced some early difficulties in drawing jurisdictional boundaries with other established centres of computing expertise and in policing IT acquisitions, but it would probably be fair to regard these as the teething problems which are inevitable after a wide-ranging business reorganization. In the long term, it seems likely that IS will bring the other centres of expertise to heel, for two reasons. First, traditions of regional autonomy are on the wane. Second, new IT acquisitions are likely to precipitate the kind of organizational changes which will make the life of IS managers a great deal easier. The three largest projects all attempt to break down once and for all the organizational legacy inherited from the takeover. They are cross-functional systems designed to pull AS into a federal management structure where even the idea of regional autonomy would be unthinkable. By the mid-1990s, the strategy supposes, all business units will be linked together via systems which will produce the sophisticated information base to enable the company to respond immediately to changes in market conditions. The initiative is from CB senior management and is concerned above all with the creation of an integrated operational division, where previously there had been a number of separate units. The planning and tendering is coordinated by IS but organized on a project team basis, orchestrated, in a way unthinkable in the past, by outside consultants. Finally, each of the three projects is several orders of magnitude greater than previous IT acquisitions. The projects are the creation of a product data base; the construction of an integrated network allowing AS to manage its supply chain by linking it into joint venture partners and distributors; and the creation of a single bottling system, allowing common working practices to be introduced across bottling plants.

Nevertheless, there are two problems. The first is the significant number of employees who will become surplus to requirements. This is already apparent in the most advanced of the three projects, the common system being introduced in the bottling division:

'We are moving from a company where the departments are very much operated by their own internally integrated system. Instead of you having a lot of clerical transferring of information on paper, it will be given to the system . . . there will be manning savings. . . . Your skill level changes and you need people who can look for something that is not right and then investigate . . . [you] can't retrain everyone but we try to upgrade their level from being a doer to an interpreter, and . . . that you see a problem and investigate it.'

(Project manager)

Job losses are not only at the level of clerical workers. Many programmers and analysts who used to work in the brand company DP shops now find themselves with redundant skills. Clerical workers are likely to find that they are laid off on a relatively large scale, but those who have redundant IT skills will probably be retrained, to make up a reservoir of expertise targeted on the specific technologies defined by senior management as strategically important. The reason for doing so leads into the second of

AS's problems: managing its external relationships in such a way as to buy in expertise as and when needed, without becoming entirely dependent on third parties in areas vital to company operations.

IT suppliers were managed by project teams which negotiate requirements and supervise implementation. These teams were made up of representatives from middle management in the plants affected, one or two IS representatives, and a number of consultants coordinating business planning. The project teams worked within parameters set by the CB board member responsible for, and the head of, IS. As a result, the pre-takeover situation, where AS obtained most of its IT equipment from a single supplier, has been replaced by a wider portfolio of suppliers competing against each other in 'strategic terror':

> 'Suppliers [are] coming in and talking about strategic partnerships. Well, that's fine and dandy, but what they are actually doing is selling a mechanism to negate the fact that they don't have any differentiation between themselves in terms of price, performance, operating systems and portability. So the only way they can do that is get closer into bed with you. Now, if there is something tangible on the end of that that you get as a result, fine. But I think that all of the things that they could give you as a result of the strategic partnerships can be obtained as a result of strategic terror.'
>
> (Head of IS)

## CONCLUSION

TQM did not represent guaranteed salvation for ailing businesses and alienated workforces; nor, however, was it seen primarily as a means of super-efficient exploitation of labour. In line with Hill's findings, it was viewed as having a significant role in the restructuring of middle and senior management and technical functions. It was also seen as holding out the promise of improved product quality, cost and innovativeness. In fact TQM had different manifestations, dependent on the purposes of its proponents. Its content and interpretation (and hence its effects) depended on: (1) the structure of the organization using it and the performance appraisal and reward systems in place; (2) the ability and will of senior managers to translate the philosophy of TQM into specific forms relevant to the business; (3) the political-economic operating environment of the business as construed by managers; and (4) the dynamics of trust and distrust between the workforce and senior management over the introduction of TQM.

TQM techniques did not negate the fact that supply-chain relationships are power relationships, and are about the ability of either user or supplier to gain advantage at the other's expense. To the extent that this segment of a supply chain was typical of the computer systems industry in a recessionary context, TQM was bad news for the smaller suppliers. Supposed strategic partnerships actually meant prices pushed down and expectations raised. Hence Midas was forced to pay lip-service to TQM, but failed to solve its internal management problems. Not surprisingly, TE's market power meant that it was far more successful in its pursuit of active supply-chain management. TE corporate management was able to adapt TQM to their own ends, gaining increased control over innovation, without damage to the collaborative ethos, or serious threat to internal labour markets. In AS, TQM was used far more instrumentally to create the new internal market-place, overturning the former hierarchy and cutting layers of management and specialists out of the structure.

In each case, TQM had radical implications for managerial and technical roles, not least the loss of significant numbers of jobs in the lower and middle layers of the white-collar hierarchy. The required knowledge base changed, undermining established exper-tise and ways of doing things. Functionally specialized definitions of jobs were replaced with generalist or hybrid technical/business roles. Managers and specialists were meant to become business rather than function-oriented. The informal status hierarchy, and intra-managerial power relations changed accordingly. The struc-ture used to effect such transitions was the ubiquitous business team, which was meant to enforce collaboration and identification with corporate goals. The reward for the loss of autonomy was the promise of access to higher management for some, as technical and managerial career grades were combined. The resultant inter-nal customer–supplier relationships were not necessarily more harmonious than the old competing interest groups; indeed, in the Midas case, the rhetoric of customer-responsiveness became part of the armoury in the struggle for control over resources and business directions. Hence the formal dimension of TQM cannot be taken at face value: one approach to the management of the supply chain may be proclaimed by senior management, and even institutionalized, but this does not mean that senior management's objectives will be shared or implemented by the actors involved at different organizational levels.

For managers and technical experts, the quality ideal appeared to be subjectively powerful because of the connection between the rhetoric of enterprise, the ethical concept of the self-regulating, responsible individual and the technology of TQM. The latter provided the means for the regulation of conduct, in the form of business teams, continuous improvement projects, consultative selling, and so on. The rhetoric of knowledge-based enterprise appeared to open the door to new forms of 'organizational professionalism' (Abbott, 1988), but the managers and experts occupying such roles are unlikely to have the autonomy of the traditional professional, and their knowledge is meant to be dedicated unstintingly to the pursuit of profit. Managers and engineers were in fact subject to greater centralized control and increased monitoring by corporate management.

Whilst the appeal to individual autonomy is seductive, it is also deceptive because it replaces the fact of class-, race- and gender-divided workplaces with an ideology of egalitarian relations, where the determinant of success is individual merit, motivation and commitment to the corporate ideal. Workplace relations become market transactions and collective action in pursuit of a cause has even less legitimacy than before. Although the 'virtuous' code of conduct for the treatment of the internal customer is about ideals of service and meeting the needs of others, the other face of market relations – as exploitation based on power – is unlikely to be displaced. Nor does TQM provide the means for questioning corporate objectives, or, at the end of the day, for redistributing real power over business direction down the hierarchy. If anything, it seems to raise the profit motive to new heights and, as Wilkinson *et al.* (1991) found, the apparent market logic works to convince employees at all levels of the legitimacy of senior management directions.

Conversely it is possible to think of TQM as a code of conduct similar to that of an equal opportunities code. Just as the rhetoric of equal opportunity has been used, despite its limitations, to the benefit of some groups of women, for example, so the rhetoric of TQM could conceivably be used in campaigns for more democratic management practices, improved safety systems, socially useful services and products. If it forces managers to think critically about their role, overcomes some forms of British management authoritarianism, challenges vested interests in the hierarchy, and opens up to question the relative power, perspectives and values of different segments of the firm, then it must serve a useful purpose. It is difficult, however, to feel optimistic about the chances of the participative scenario becoming reality, at least not while the main preoccupation for many people is finding or holding on to a job. At worst, particularly in a recession, the ideology of TQM reduces honesty, integrity, authenticity 'and all those good, nice words' to marketable commodities which have a price just like any other goods; it reduces workplace relations to the 'imperatives of the market' and becomes an excuse for managerialist, and immoral, expediency.

# REFERENCES

Abbott, A. (1988) *The System of Professions*, Chicago, IL: University of Chicago Press.

Bagguley, P. (1991) 'Post-Fordism and the Enterprise Culture: Flexibility, Autonomy and Changes in Economic Organisation', in R. Keat and N. Abercrombie (eds) *Enterprise Culture*, London: Routledge.

Bank, J. (1992) *The Essence of Total Quality Management*, Hemel Hempstead: Prentice-Hall.

Dawson, P. and Webb, J. (1989) 'New Production Arrangements: The Totally Flexible Cage?' *Work, Employment and Society*, 3, 221–38.

Delbridge, R., Turnbull, P. and Wilkinson, B. (1992) 'Pushing Back the Frontiers: Management Control and Work Intensification under JIT/TQM Factory Regimes', *New Technology, Work and Employment*, 7, 97–106.

Du Gay, P. and Salaman, G. (1992) 'The Cult[ure] of the Customer', *Journal of Management Studies*, 29, 615–33.

Hill, S. (1991) 'How Do you Manage a Flexible Firm? The Total Quality Model', *Work, Employment and Society*, 5, 397–415.

Kanter, R.M. (1990) *When Giants Learn to Dance*, London: Unwin Hyman.

Oakland, J.S. (1989) *Total Quality Management*, Oxford: Butterworth Heinemann.

Peters, T. (1988) *Thriving On Chaos: Handbook for a Management Revolution*, Basingstoke: Macmillan.

Preece, D. and Wood, M. (1993) 'Why Managers Might be a Stumbling Block to the Effective Use of Quality Measurements', unpublished paper, Business School, Portsmouth University.

Sewell, G. and Wilkinson, B. (1992) 'Someone to Watch Over Me: Surveillance, Discipline and the Just-in-Time Labour Process', *Sociology*, 26, 271–90.

Webb, J. (1992) 'The mismanagement of innovation', *Sociology*, 26, 471–92.

Webb, J. and Cleary, D. (1994) *Organisational Change and the Management of Expertise*, London: Routledge.

Weber, M. (1948) 'On Bureaucracy', in H.H. Gerth and C. Wright-Mills (eds) *Max Weber: Essays in Sociology*, London: Routledge.

Wilkinson, A. (1993) 'Managing Human Resources for Quality', in B.G. Dale (ed.) *Managing Quality*, (2nd edn), Hemel Hempstead: Prentice-Hall.

Wilkinson, A., Allen, P. and Snape, E. (1991) 'TQM and the Management of Labour', *Employee Relations*, 13, 24–31.

Wilkinson, A., Marchington, M., Goodman, J. and Ackers, P. (1992) 'Total Quality Management and Employee Involvement', *Human Resource Management Journal*, 2 (4), 1–2.

Wright-Mills, C. (1940) 'Situated Actions and Vocabularies of Motive', *American Sociological Review*, 5, 439–52.

# 5

# GOVERNING THE NEW PROVINCE OF QUALITY

## Autonomy, accounting and the dissemination of accountability*

### Dr Rolland Munro

## INTRODUCTION

Quality, it seems, becomes the territory of middle managers. Each company in Hill's study of TQM (this volume) notes a 'tendency for middle rather than senior managers to become the main actors'. Why should this be so? If TQM is to be recognized as distinctly different from previous quality agendas, as involving new philosophies of managing, how is it that the governance of quality comes to be the province of middle managers?

Hill appears to accept Ishikawa's reasoning to explain a shift of the governance of quality from top managers to middle managers. Noting that it is top managers who are typically extolled by consultants to be the main drivers of TQM, Hill follows Ishikawa's suggestion that a shift to middle managers is to be welcomed, precisely because TQM promotes decentralization and delegation.

Since Hill, particularly in his studies of quality circles, has been a

---

* The research for this chapter was conducted with Dara Kernan. The discussion draws considerably on our joint paper, 'Governing the New Province of Quality: from representations of economic reality to representing the customer', presented at the British Accounting Association conference, University of Strathclyde, 1993 and the eleventh International Standing Conference on Organisational Symbolism, Barcelona, 1993. In addition to helpful comments made by participants, I am particularly grateful to David Knights, Peter Miller and Mike Power for their comments on the earlier paper. The present chapter has benefited also from comments by Hugh Willmott and Simon Lilley.

leading sceptic over talk of decentralization, it is worth quoting him at length:

> Middle managers appreciated the increased decentralization and their greater influence over the decisions taken elsewhere in the organization that affected their activities. Many also believed that TQM could advance their careers, by bringing them to the attention of more senior managers if they performed well on a major improvement project, and that it gave them a better understanding of the wider organization. Decentralization and participation represent a *major* change in the style of managing for most companies, a shift from individual decision-taking and authoritative, top-down communication towards a more collective style with greater two-way communication and less emphasis on giving and receiving commands. It can also promote more teamwork and flexibility within the management group. The literature on employee participation strangely has ignored the desire among managerial employees for more influence and involvement, yet the extension of managerial participation under TQM is a significant gain for people who, like the employees they supervise, have a real interest in a more participative system of managing. The language of teamwork is of course the standard discourse among managers, but, in practice, this has been more exhortatory than real among the middle and lower levels of management where functional specialization and authoritative management have been the norm. TQM has the potential to align reality with rhetoric by means of participation.
>
> (Hill, this volume; emphasis added)

In the study which follows, we have little dispute with Hill's findings over the main domain of activity in TQM. In our study, it was also middle managers who were busy governing the new province.

Where we depart from Hill is over his analysis that autonomy has increased. First, that managers *claim* to 'have' more autonomy can hardly be considered sufficient to evidence the case. Second, attributing shifts in autonomy to TQM is surely inaccurate, historically. Budgeting, certainly since the 1950s (Argyris, 1952), has been argued to be the principal facilitator of delegation. While it may be difficult to see how accounting systems can be deeply enrolled in a new surveillance over quality, especially when they have been held to be part of the problem of control (Munro, 1987; Vollman, 1990), it is unfortunate that a discussion of budgeting plays no part in Hill's analysis.

Drawing on our own study, we suggest the omission is fatal. Any impression of greater autonomy, we argue, should be tempered by a detailed analysis of changes to accountability. For example, Munro and Hatherly (1993) have suggested that much of the 'new commercial agenda' is directed at intensifying a *lateral* accountability. As they point out, an interest in lateral account-ability may represent less a switch from hierarchical accountability, than an attempt to *extend* hierarchical accountability. For this reason, the scope of our study stretches beyond a direct focus on quality to include changes in the way managers draw on accounting numbers.[1]

It is important to be clear here about the focus of our argument. We are not dismissing Hill's point that TQM alters management style. We agree that a decisive shift in management style has accompanied the rubric of quality. Nevertheless, Hill's claim for a *major* change in management style could be expected to amount to more than observations of an 'increase' in decentralization and 'more' participation.

In our view, Hill is too quick to decide that shifts in autonomy are all mutually beneficial. He represents participation exclusively as a 'greater influence' on decisions and a greater 'involvement' within traditional management systems. He appears not to con-template the possibility that a redistribution of autonomy could represent power effects, symptomatic of changes in the politics of managing. In particular, his discussion lacks any analysis of a reshaping of interests which the advent of quality provides to actors in redrawing their territorial responsibility. In this respect our analysis concerns itself with examining the dark side of delegation: an intensification of accountability.

Accordingly, what we depict in our study are some ways in which quality may be constitutive of a new order. The chapter illustrates how the advent of quality can affect relations between senior and middle managers. After a general discussion on quality, we explore some specific changes in a UK subsidiary of a very large manu-facturer. The concern is to examine quality as a territory, a space of representation which is not only shaped by interests, but which, in turn, is shaping of interests.

# THE ADVENT OF QUALITY

A key matter to be grasped in the quality debate is that quality is *problematizing*. Within the wider debate, the nature of quality is being thrown open to question. The new techniques which form themselves under the rubric of 'quality' are multiple, hetero- geneous and uncertain. They include quality circles, statistical process control, auditable procedures, training in appraisal of standards, teamwork problem-solving, time-management, and much else (see Tuckermann in this volume for a fuller discussion on the differences among these 'tools').

Quality therefore plays an endless host to the new and the practical, and does so in ways which redefine that which is to be taken to be new or practical. It is important therefore for those who are interested in the 'issue' of quality, rather than its immedi- ate application, to note this aspect of the debate. Quality is a movable feast, which has the capacity to redefine itself towards 'quality being free', at the Philip Crosby 'conformance' end of the spectrum, or towards a call for 'thriving on chaos', in the Tom Peters emphasis on 'excellence'. Quality's elusiveness to definition appears to be part of its resource.

This elusiveness to definition goes beyond a refusal to settle the 'essence' of quality, at least in terms of the traditional meta- narratives of equating it with the 'good', the 'true', or the 'just'. Rather, the adoption of rubrics, such as 'fitness for purpose', appears to decentre discussion in ways which *disseminate* decision- taking away from the top of an organization. Only locally, at a place and a time of production (see also Giddens, 1984), can fitness for purpose be determined – at least this is the new myth of the real! Instead of decisions being made in the abstract spaces of head office, the accounting numbers and the CEO's head, decisions are now to be *grounded* in the existential realities of time/space. Only in this way can the US, Canada, Europe, Britain be saved.

In this context, empowerment should not be confused with a granting of autonomy to the individual, giving them discretion over a reconstruction of their work practices. Rather, empowerment is the creation of space within the organization that *extends* the scope for identity work: the identity of employees is no longer to be that which is constrained by a 'given' functionary role, something that must always make self *other* and, hence, create a need for a 'technical' role to be supplemented by a 'social' self. Nor is identity

130

to be limited to a 'persona' that is fixed in ways that helps create and cement differences between public and private spaces. Identity is now that which is to be forged more completely within the work space; quality is a space of representation which is being constructed to make the notion of work more complete and, further, in expanding the forms of work, which has the potential to colonize identity work.

The particular focus in the paper therefore is on the 'enactment' strategies (Weick, 1977; Smircich and Stubbart, 1985) which translate quality agendas into identity work and harness identity work as power effects. There is a double movement involved in translation: 'Translating interests means at once offering new *interpretations* of interests and *channelling* people in different directions' (Latour, 1987: 117). Channelling agents, including people, in different directions affects identity work by offering employees new interpretations of interests. The matter of identity therefore is not one of taking sides; for quality or against it. Initially this may be part of the bludgeon. But being 'for' quality is not itself part of the issue. Who can be against quality? (*And* still work for this company?) The question of quality becomes: *how* to be for quality? How do people reshape their interests in the context of quality? After a brief discussion of the setting, we will analyse some accounts to suggest *how* quality becomes 'enrolled' into accounts of their work by managers and employees.[2]

## THE SETTING

To see politics in the making requires entering the 'laboratory' (Latour, 1987). For the quality debate this is a manufacturing processing plant. We sought access to the UK subsidiary of a very large global manufacturer. The company, hereafter Component, manufactures replaceable components for cars. Concurrent to the study, the top managers were considering changing the accounting systems to activity-based costing.[3]

In brief, managers in Component perceived the subsidiary as having been subject to significant changes on a number of fronts. First, although not unrelated to the following matters, the internal strategy had altered. The previous emphasis on economies of scale had generated a taken-for-granted consensus on internal strategy as a 'drive on production'. This 'drive' had, however, all but collapsed. A heightened pressure on quality, more emphasis on delivery and greater scrutiny of unsold stock had made impotent the traditional emphasis on numbers as a form of control. As a consequence, this 'ulcer syndrome', the pressure on production to 'bust a gut', had shifted from production runs which concentrated on making the biggest single number to an emphasis on 'quality numbers', producing components for market demand.[4]

In terms of quality, the company considered itself to be at an advanced state. The quality management system was built round the philosophy of 'never-ending improvement'. The company had been granted its ISO 9000 and had a 'reasonable' Nissan audit rating. Although the quality manager claimed to 'preach the message of everyone being responsible for quality', formally, the quality department was responsible for setting standards and coordination of aspects of the quality management system, including statistical process control, a procedures audit programme, project teams, improvement teams and scrap analysis.

The company had also received what may be regarded as external 'kicks' (Laughlin, 1991). First, ownership had changed. Previously the US parent company was a family business with low family involvement. The picture we were given was one of little control over top management, with the former owners being contrasted as 'weak' compared to the purchasers, who were characterized as 'very hard' on financial targets. The new owners were seen as being 'strong on budget controls' and as having an 'engineering drive'.

Second, world markets were perceived as changing their nature and shape, for a number of reasons. Sales were made direct to automobile manufacturers and also to the wholesale market for replacement. However, due to product improvement, the latter market had shrunk to a third of its former importance. Added to this, a Japanese competitor had entered the market, taking up sales particularly in the Pacific Rim. A future threat lay in the opening of a European plant by this competitor. Since this would obviate Component's present advantage in import regulations for selling in Europe, it was felt that this made Component's future output a 'straight commodity product'.

## CHANGING IMPRESSIONS OF MANAGERS' WORK

In their accounts, managers in Component vigorously denied having a routine: 'There's no such thing as a typical day' was a standard response to our question about routines. Although this might seem to fit the extant picture of a manager with a two- to three-minute attention span, we sensed there was more to this than the phenomenon of interruptions. Managers commented about interruptions, but not that they were continual in the way Mintzberg (1973) indicates.

In contrast, as will now be discussed, managers in Component gave great emphasis to the changing nature of management.[5] It is possible therefore to link this impression of change to their resistance to 'having a typical day' and to further definitions of management, particularly the notion that management involves strategy work and setting 'goals' for subordinates. Managing was not to be confused with supervising. As one plant manager remarked: 'There's a vast difference between managing and supervising.'

In line with this, considerable emphasis in Component was given to delegation. For example: 'I try not to be in the plant as a supervisor-type job at all. The supervisors must become managers. You've got to stop running around telling people what to do, you've got to give them your knowledge and let them run it' (plant manager). Or again, in response to a question over priorities: 'I tend to delegate more. In the early days I tried to do too much myself – you must involve other people. We have project teams working now on problems' (quality manager). What is important to catch here is that this emphasis on delegation is being portrayed as *different* from before.

In this reiteration of 'the need to delegate', something new appears to be being exacted in Component over responsibility. We interpret this recitation over delegation as both an occasion and a cover for increasing distance. By a process of delegation, responsibility is being limited within the line. First, responsibility is being portrayed no longer as *line* responsibility, but as specific to a *point* in the line. Second, there is some asymmetry here about the nature of delegation. Responsibility pertains particularly to the matter of getting it right for one's senior. Blame cannot travel upwards – only credit can. Delegation in Component, therefore, means more than a transfer of authority for taking responsibility. Taking *ownership* implies a full transfer of responsibility for what goes wrong.

This trend we interpret to be one of increasing a manager's exposure. A general currency for the phrase 'between a rock and a hard place' is, we suspect, no accident, for that is the place in which managers live by their own doing. It is the space which they are busy creating for each other.[6] A current emphasis on 'macho' management, such as 'putting iron in your john', can only be expected to work alongside and interpenetrate the notion of distance as being essential to identity work. Creating distance, along the format of 'me Tarzan, you Jane', becomes definitional to being a 'good manager'.

This transformation from delegation into 'distance' is perhaps most clear in the comments of senior managers. They particularly resist the feeling that they were responsible for work not completed by their subordinates:

'I give them [the people who work for me] more and I leave them to suffer the ulcer syndrome, the production. I don't chase the production as much as I used to do. Four years ago, for example, you know I'd be chasing every line, and chasing it down through the ranks. Now I say it's no longer my business to that degree.'

(production director)

No longer *my* business! Here is a distancing equivalent to that of a traditional machismo, one which stands the responsibility of senior managers well back from the fray. This is a Teflon approach to accountability, but one that we suggest is becoming typical, not aberrant, as the words might have sounded less than ten years ago.

Whether or not the technical nature of managerial work has changed since Mintzberg's (1973) landmark study is a moot point. This, however, was not the focus of our study. What interested us in Component is this semiosis of delegation into distance. This changes the identity work. To 'do manager' is to be in a 'hard place'.[7] The manager presents 'himself' as ungiving and unforgiving. The artefact of 'distance' carries the facilitating rhetoric of empowerment, while turning it back to a constraint: 'If you are my subordinate, I'm not here to make your job easy, you are there to make my job easier.' In such ways, delegation and distance, do managers enact the great message that *their* time is money.

## ACCOUNTING, VISIBILITY AND DISTANCE

As has been discussed, managers pictured themselves as giving up the more technical work (see also Munro, 1991) – delegating more, but perhaps more importantly, becoming resistant to pressure to take responsibility for work not completed by their subordinates. This double-movement of 'delegation' and 'distancing' implies a break *within* the line, a limitation being placed on accountability coming back up the line. A resistance by senior managers to being held accountable for a subordinate's failings can be understood therefore, in part, as a *creation* of distance.

The conventional wisdom, however, is that accounting *overcomes* the distance created by delegation. The literature (e.g. Mouritsen, 1991; Robson, 1992) presents accounting as the technology which most successfully brings together the two features of distance and delegation. This suggests that closer attention should be paid to the use which is made of accounting numbers.[8]

Although textbooks on accounting invariably extol budgets as facilitating 'autonomy', autonomy is granted at the price of a readiness to account for deviations from budgets. Accounting numbers therefore go beyond the narrowly technical sphere of representing an 'economic' reality. Rather they can be considered as constructing a 'space of representation' in which *accounts* (Garfinkel, 1967) are given.[9] Typically this space of representation in manufacturing industry has revolved around variances from, say, a budget. Further, each level of managers can call on the person a level below to account for their specific variances. This is the 'surveillance' thesis in the accounting literature; progressing down the hierarchy, each set of variances will be more finely examined.

Certainly, in line with the surveillance thesis, little credence was given to the idea that accounting numbers are transparent to any 'economic' reality. Attempts to understand production through accounting numbers came in for especial contempt by managers at virtually all levels. Even senior managers in Component expressed antipathy to the budget, expressing it as a 'prop' for others:

> 'It's an administrative thing, people who run a business such as myself and the operations people, the tool is not to help us, it's that tool that's there to give to people who don't understand the business the perception that they know what's happening.'
> (production director)

Budgets were discussed as if they existed only for those who were unable to understand the 'real workings' of the company.

Given the traditional emphasis on budgeting, we were surprised, nevertheless, at the extent of the general hostility to budgets which we found. Difficulties with accounting systems resonated down the company, and here criticisms centred on standard costing: 'Standard cost is a pain to me, because I don't really believe in it anymore' (plant manager 2). Budgeting came under particularly heavy fire for more general reasons. Here is a not untypical comment about budgeting: 'It's a complete waste of time. . . It's bureaucratic, it's inflexible' (production director). In technical terms, the budget was 'flexible'. This inflexibility therefore should not be misunderstood as a technical oversight. Rather the budget was seen as inflexible due to a surveillance over variances, forcing action to be taken which production people saw as harmful to the company: 'It shouldn't be just to satisfy a variance, because that pushes you the wrong way' (plant manager 2).

Managers in Component expressed at length the pressure to avoid variances, reflecting a continuing, if ineffectual, reliance by Component's head office on accounting systems for surveillance. This matter might seem to raise a question here about how accounting techniques could be suitably amended and, indeed, as mentioned, there was interest at head office in the possibility of introducing activity-based costing.[10]

What interests us, however, is the strength of this disowning of the budget within Component. The question-mark is over how it is possible for middle managers not to believe in accounting numbers, if it is accounting numbers on which they are being held to account. The further question which arises is why senior managers were prepared to go along with 'rubbishing' the budget system. Once they had recognized the importance of relying on production numbers for control, were they not almost completely dependent on accounting numbers for their knowledge of the company? These questions can only be approached with some care.

A partial answer is achieved by reconceptualizing the type of identity work that is brought into being by abandoning the closeness and contact that is retained through calling for and examining accounts. Regardless of whether explanations are conducted at a geographical distance or within conditions of co-presence, explanations tend to be manufactured in ways that are hard for more senior managers to break (Roberts and Scapens, 1990). This has some particular effects on identity. For example, where middle managers find their concocted explanations are accepted, this can induce a loop that confirms the middle manager's impression over who is really running the company. Or again, even where a middle manager is being straight, which senior manager is to know, or can afford to care?

We suggest that in reformulating their identity work, senior managers were ditching only one part of the budget – standard costing. Since standard costing, by quantifying production in terms of costs and outputs, ostensibly 'drills' lines of sight into production, this implies that what senior managers were abandoning was surveillance. However, in abandoning surveillance, managers also appear to have been abandoning account numbers as the facility to 'overcome' distance. How then do senior managers compensate for any dilution in power effects from delegation? This is the crucial question that the foregoing analysis raises.

By dropping surveillance and no longer seeking explanation, senior managers can *benefit* from the increase in distance. In retaining only that part of the budget system which sets a single number, senior managers can effect a turn away from the calculation of a variance and, instead, treat the budget itself as mandatory. Meeting the number, at all costs to the individual who bids for resources under it, then becomes part of the identity work which middle managers accomplish. Miss the budget and you fail to deliver; you are not the sort of person who should be bidding for resources in the first place.

In this way, 'managing by distance' can be distinguished from 'managing *at* a distance'. Evolving a greater 'exposure' for middle managers not only requires a technology which can 'individuate' accountability (Roberts, 1991), but also to distancing. Budgets can help to introduce distance. By increasing the gradient for an account to pass muster, managing by distance puts pressure on middle managers to work to meet their budget and thus pre-empt any call to account. Essentially, managing by distance can make it harder for middle managers to offer explanations which convince, thus reversing any flow of power set up by a combination of delegation and information asymmetries.

Relying on budgets to create distance appears to propel top managers out of the mode of surveillance and into a new 'language game' (Munro, 1993), that of pseudo-markets. The effects are equally profound on middle managers, as will be further discussed in the next section. No longer need the budget be conceived of as a target calling for accounts, when missed or overshot. It becomes a number which *must* be met.

# THE NEW FOLD OF QUALITY

The ability to drill lines of sight into the production floor depends not only on technologies of representation, maps. Surveillance also requires a mapping out of the production floor. For someone to be able to read the map requires the territory first to be marked out. Together, the marking out of the production floor and the making of a map creates a 'space' between them which facilitates a surveillance of production. Drawing on Heidegger's essay on technology, together with post-structural writing, Cooper (1993) refers to this 'space' as a 'fold'.

Until recently the territory of production has been marked out in terms of machines and their costs. Only too literally were the written down values of the capital accounts reflected in the grinding machines being placed on one floor of a building and the drilling machines kept on another. Such geographical arrangements engendered a myopia around recovering 'capital' costs by driving down marginal cost through long production runs. In Component, this philosophy of economies of scale was embedded in conceptions of marginal cost and resulted in the belief that only the last 20 per cent of a production run was produced cheaply enough for the company to make money.

Although top managers in Component still clung to this belief as a fact of production, the consensus around standard costs driving 'economies of scale' had collapsed: 'You should deal with reality and not a standard . . . I don't believe it makes money. I don't believe it does anything except cause us a lot of bother' (plant manager 2).

It is this rejection of standard costing as a *discourse*,[11] and the construction of new discourses around alternatives like JIT, which makes transparent how accounting traditionally enters into the construction and reconstruction of the production floor (Munro, 1987). For example, while standard costing has encouraged a myopia over *machine* time, target costing (Hiromoto, 1988) may focus particularly on reducing set-up or throughput times.

Where the discourse shifts from costs to quality, the territory of production is remarked in terms of paths along which each unit can be named and tracked. As Sewell and Wilkinson (1992), among others, have indicated, *surveillance* paths can be constructed in the modern factory around concepts of quality not costs. Importantly the territory cuts across traditional functions, imposing lateral

138

production paths which intensify a lateral accountability (Munro and Hatherly, 1993). As a senior manager in Component expresses the 'new agenda':

> 'We've become much more formal in actually doing that [dealing with change], we've actually now understood that we bring together the multi-functional teams to tackle almost any situation. Whereas in the past it would just fall from one department to another, throw it over the wall into another department, the person had to understand miraculously and precisely where he was in that pattern or puzzle, now we're formalizing that much more where we get them together as a team so we can see the whole situation, understand the process, the diagrams, etc. and people begin to understand and say "This is now working and it's a better way." So from that point of view the reinforcing of change doesn't need me to drive it; they then say "This is the way to do it."'
>
> (production director)

At first sight this passage might seem to exemplify Hill's emphasis, discussed earlier, on greater participation in decision-taking and the capacity for more involvement. A question then arises as to how genuine this 'hands-off' approach really is. Is lateral accountability sufficient for control? And if it is, will traditional, pyramid hierarchies disappear?

Munro and Hatherly (1993) suggest not. They explicate how lateral accountability is likely to become subverted and be transformed into a tool to support and intensify hierarchical accountability. Note, therefore, the switch from 'we' to 'me' within the previous quote from the production director. The greater autonomy being granted is loaded. Yes, staff are to be incited by feelings of belonging, the inclusiveness of 'we' is all-embracing, but the responsibility is to be all 'theirs'. In being extended laterally, responsibility is also being distanced hierarchically: accountability equals 'we' minus 'me'.

## QUALITY AND REPRESENTING THE CUSTOMER

Middle managers contraposed their emphasis on quality with one on standard costing: 'It just makes you make things – it doesn't make you make quality items, there's no quality in standard costing at all' (plant manager 2). The issue plant managers were raising was that *either* they could manage the variances, *or* they could act in the best interests of the company. Quality, not quantity, is in the best interests of the company.

This issue is a pressing one for middle managers. Top managers were pictured to us as having gone 'back' to accounting numbers: 'When the recession came they went back to looking at variances, I don't blame the company but that's the frustration (they have shareholders to look after)' (plant manager).

Taken together, the implication of these two statements is that top managers do not look after the best interests of the company. This possibility requires further explication. First, as discussed earlier, top managers do not have the knowledge to look after the company. They are dependent on accounting systems, not first-hand knowledge. And accounting systems, as has also been discussed, with their base in standard costing, were no longer seen as relevant by anyone in production. In contrast, plant managers pictured themselves as uncircumventable. Plant managers disparaged the ability of others to see or to find out. They exhibited confidence about their own ability to 'know what's going on': '[My] isolated views may not reflect the total – they can only be my views if I'm isolated from that information. . . . I don't expect to have information from a corporate level, although I do know most things that are going on' (plant manager). As will become clear, this feeling of being central to information flows reflects less their position as being in the middle of the hierarchy and more an effect of their enrolment of quality. In Latour's (1987) image of networking, plant managers constructed themselves as a 'conduit' through which all information must pass.

Second, top managers are displaced by middle managers, who configure them as representing the interest of shareholders. However, while middle managers portrayed themselves as knowing the best interests of the company, they did not directly instigate claims to act for the company in the place of top managers. Instead, and most prominently, middle managers represented themselves as having the expertise over quality. In Latour's (1987) terms, they are establishing themselves as an 'obligatory passage'.

Middle managers are able to accomplish this translation by their contacts with Nissan, the accredited source for expertise on quality in Component. Here is a response to a suggestion for change: 'Charlie, you obviously don't know the way Nissan works' (plant manager). Knowledge of Nissan stands as knowledge of quality and acts to validate in Component plant managers' claims for having expertise over quality.[12]

An expertise over quality facilitates a further translation, one of turning the demands of the customer into a production schedule. This 'comes about mainly because we have a customer out there who wants a product. Then their demand is translated back into a schedule, so that's the thing that tends to drive us' (production director). While this translation sets up the responsibility of the plant managers, it is of particular interest to hear the basis of the network echoed in the accounts of their senior manager.

The important point is to see the process of enrolment through which middle managers achieve their title to speak for the customer. For example, given middle managers' link as spokespersons (Callon, 1986) of the customer, access to the source of expertise on quality was carefully guarded. Senior managers did not get invitations to visit Nissan – neither did the quality manager! Plant managers had established contacts and kept a close grip on these. Through their expertise in quality, middle managers represent the customer. Within the new 'ethos' of quality, middle managers stand ready to act as the spokespersons of the customer. In this way, accounting numbers become re-examined, but this time on the assumption that plant managers are serving the customer: 'I don't believe it's [standard costing] relevant to the present day if you are serving the customer' (plant manager 2). Standard costs become rubbished in the name of the customer.[13]

In summary, the specific processes which set up the title to speak on behalf of the customer are as follows: access to Nissan, expertise in quality, the translation of the demand from customers into schedules, and speaking on behalf of the customer; all these become tightly enrolled with each other in ways which represent the customer – see Figure 5.1. These are the 'intermediaries' which the plant managers mobilize and through which they ensure they retain their new title to represent the customer.

## CONTROLLING THE FOLD

In considering quality as instigating lateral accountability, the question that interested us was what moves might senior managers make to protect those power effects traditionally generated by actors accomplishing hierarchy? When lateral accountability is abroad, how do top managers ensure that middle managers

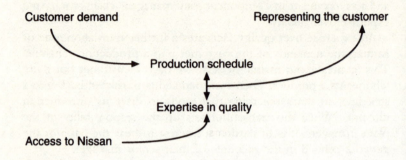

*Figure 5.1* The 'voice' of the customer

continue to work to accomplish hierarchy? Of especial interest, given the 'rubbishing' of standard cost systems, is whether accounting might play any role here.

As Cooper (1993) remarks, the map fails when the signposts on the ground have been removed and the roads have been torn up and obliterated. A tearing-up of the signposts of standard costing has been achieved through re-marking of the factory floor. This may happen, as discussed earlier, when the location of machines no longer accords with the cost centres of 'drilling' and 'grinding', but is arranged to facilitate 'manufacturing cells'.

A re-marking of the factory floor in terms of *quality* destroys the 'fold' of accounting numbers, within which the actions of middle managers have been previously observed. A new fold is created by plant managers marking out the factory floor and through schedules of production of their making. This new space of representation constitutes and is constituted by the new discourse of quality. Importantly, constructing the fold in this way places middle managers within a calculable space which makes them visible only to themselves.

It should be clear now why middle managers so strenuously opposed accounting numbers in our discussions with them. Were a 'new' cost accounting system instigated within Component, the principal danger to managers would be less one of more 'accurate' costings limiting and constraining action than that by reinstalling standard costs, plant managers are returned to the fold of accounting.

Once more under the gaze of accounting numbers, they could again become captive to the agendas of top managers. Without standard costs to underpin budgets, plant managers are free to manage their own agendas. Well, not quite free. There are limits. Whereas the *management accounting* numbers have been shaken off, the financial numbers still have to meet expectations. For the new governors of the province to be left alone, the surplus generated by the province must match up to the surpluses generated elsewhere. With a collapse of standard costing, budgets get rolled back, but not abandoned.

Budgets, if rolled back firmly enough, offer top managers the facility to switch from a mode of surveillance, a 'managing by the numbers' (Ezzamel *et al.*, 1990) into what has been described in this paper as 'managing by distance', a governing by *the* number. In a 'results'–oriented philosophy, numbers remain important, but with the greater potential to 'delayer', 'outsource' or hire in a replacement, an interest in the wealth of detail, previously held to lie 'beneath' accounting numbers, can vanish.

## A NEW TERRAIN FOR IDENTITY WORK

The advent of quality as an issue provides ample opportunity for the study of identity in a special sense. There is a new terrain for discussion, where questions of belonging and identity are themselves at stake. Quality becomes a space of representation, a territory in which identities have to be created and affiliations have to be settled. This statement requires clarification.

Quality is first and foremost a call for solutions. In this context, a ubiquitous problematizing to prove quality in terms of 'output' can be seen as both a displacement of collective surveillance and a time-compression on people's conceptions of the 'social'. Quality arrives in ways which encourage measurement of output in a much more intensive and individualized manner. This is one reason why 'attitude surveys' can only measure the most superficial changes in 'corporate culture', the swapping of one set of rehearsed beliefs for another. Rather than conduct surveillance over 'social' aspects, the incitement of quality is to use 'output' measures, ranging from those attributed to an individual to those attributed to the market, to question the sufficiency of colleagues' comportment towards the 'technical'.

Although much rhetoric over quality is expressed in terms of changing 'values', the advent of quality should not be interpreted as necessitating the induction of new values through training programmes and the like. Certainly, massive sums appear to be being spent on training, but a concern over values is frankly divisive. For example, such a concern can radiate a collective surveillance by members of organizations over 'social' aspects of belonging – such as what type of persons you feel your workmates are – in ways that may be harmful to production. An emphasis on quality, in so far as it is, for all the talk of culture, an implacably technocratic solution, is intended to change all this. The object of training, we suggest, is to inculcate a readiness to work within measures of output, not to 'educate'.

We suggest that the effect of the rhetoric of quality may be to embed employees more firmly in the specifics of time and space in which they each find themselves. If this is so, then *difference* can no longer be regarded as a matter of 'personality', colouring in the formalese of a job description. Instead, the logics of cellular position and measured performance prefigure identity work. Thus, at the same time as each employee is given space to announce an 'individuality', the telos of identity work is also being stabilized. Difference becomes harnessed in ways that instruct employees over the particular ways in which they are to be permitted to reconstruct their work practices and, in so doing, structure the very conditions of possibility which enable employees to be treated as *them*. Far from quality engendering a greater freedom to 'choose' identity, the effect of its rhetoric is to render the would-be Prometheus more bound in the ties of a moral discourse that makes a waiting customer more immediate and more pressing than alternative ties such as guild association or departmental loyalty.

The decisive switch is in the politics of managing. At the heart of quality as a strategic agenda, we suggest, is a dissemination of accountability. This amounts to less than a lauded decentralization of decision-taking and constitutes more an invention of lateral accountabilities in order to deflect responsibility away from the line and, simultaneously through the imposition of measures of output, individuate responsibility to a point in the line. Far from quality constituting accountabilities which are 'shared' in ways which might reflect the genuine participative decision-taking Hill anticipates, an individuation of accountability becomes intensified under quality regimes.

This dissemination of accountability, we suggest, explains much of the appearance of a 'drift' in quality, from 'hard' to 'soft' aspects of TQM (Wilkinson *et al.*, 1990), without recourse to drawing distinctions between manufacturing and service areas. We found no particular evidence[14] to substantiate the idea that quality works in manufacturing *because* of a set of 'hard' techniques (Tuckman, this volume). More cogently, an ability to individuate and intensify accountability is suggestive of why quality is a political weapon in the more established sense of politics. An individuation and intensification of accountability precisely fits with much of the thinking of the new right and could be expected to be forced upon an unwilling public sector exactly to undermine and destroy an ethos of collective responsibilities.

## CONCLUSIONS

Our concern over quality centres on politics in the making. As a strategic agenda, quality 'arrives' wefted together with a number of change agendas, such as autonomy, delegation, empowerment, and lateral accountability, not to mention more explicit competitive concerns, such as 'cost-down' and 'continuous improvement'. It is in this context that quality offers scope for a reshaping of territory, particularly related to responsibilities, resources and reporting.

There are many questions here which our focus on the creation of territory, of new spaces, can hardly begin to answer. If quality is a 'space', a new territory of interests, what is the nature of this space? Who controls this space? How is that control effected and how is autonomy brought into being? Is quality, as Sewell and Wilkinson (1992) represent it, a territory colonized by an electronic eye? Or is it more a 'visual' space which extends the collective surveillance of one's colleagues by one's colleagues, a 'neighbourhood watch' turned in on itself? Or, in contrast, is quality a 'disciplined' space (Foucault, 1979)? In what sense does a discourse on quality create a new truth regime? Are there governmentality effects?

Specifically, this chapter has examined the relation of quality as a *discursive* space to that of accounting. This turns out, as has been discussed, not to entail that a discourse on quality precisely replaces the accounting discourse. Rather, the advent of a 'new' discourse is a condition of possibility for a *mutation* in the accounting discourse, a shift from 'managing at a distance' towards 'managing *by* distance'. Drawing on findings with respect to Component, a leading UK manufacturer, this chapter links mutations in accounting discourse to the advent of a quality discourse.

Our findings are twofold. First, we illustrate how middle managers are enrolling 'quality' as an expertise to protect themselves and their status. Underpinning the rhetoric of quality is a remarking and remapping of the factory, which together instantiates the construction of a new 'fold' (Cooper, 1993). In so much as the effects of this fold are to create new lines of surveillance, this carries a number of implications for lateral accountability (Munro and Hatherly, 1993). For example, if control over the lines of surveillance is likely to remain in the hands of middle managers, as the holders of the expertise of quality, then the result is likely to create a new province ruled by middle managers and to radiate a governmentality effect over employees, through talk of 'empowerment' and the like. As discussed, this control is likely to remain in the hands of middle managers, since professionalizing over quality enables managers to represent themselves as the 'obligatory passage' over quality. Being the obligatory passage constitutes their legitimacy to act as spokespersons for the customer, and representing the customer, in turn, affirms the governing rights of middle managers.

Second, rather than be threatened by a quality discourse, top managers may seek to take advantage from a collapse of faith in the surveillance properties of accounting. As we have illustrated, they can do this by rolling back budgets to restrict responsibility to a point in the line. In this way delegation, without surveillance, accomplishes a 'managing by distance'.[15] Managing by distance, as we have described it, should not be confused with simply managing *at* a distance. To be sure, accounting is fully implicated with either, but managing by distance does not stop with an 'analytic detachment' (Miller and O'Leary, 1993: 188), whereby some explanations pass muster and others fall by the wayside as 'excuses'. Managing by distance takes the artefact of accounting numbers to its logical conclusion.

Previously it has been thought that accounting numbers should be used to instantiate a mode of surveillance, a scrutiny of reasons why the budget numbers have not been met. But this approach, as illustrated by Roberts and Scapens (1990), falters against the ingenuity of managers to 'manufacture excuses'. In contrast, a dissemination of accountability away from the line, through 'output' measures which individuate and intensify responsibilities, facilitates a switch to an *insistence* on a number being met, at all costs to the individuals concerned. In this way, a propensity by managers to give 'accounts' which excuse, legitimate or justify their failures is silenced.[16]

The decoupling here is, we believe, significant. Middle managers no longer have to rely on accounting techniques to meet the budget. The decoupling of budgeting from cost accounting means middle managers can draw up their own lines of surveillance. In Component, as in other companies, the discourse which is providing a new 'fold' and new lines of surveillance is one of quality, not costs. At first sight therefore, the discourse effect in Component is as Hill suggests, in that delegation appears to be centred on the necessarily ill-defined notion of quality.[17]

This said, the financial numbers will still have to be 'right', if top managers are going to sustain their rhetoric about 'managing by distance' and if middle managers are going to be allowed the governance of the new province of quality. The fold of quality – quality as a space of representation – sits within another fold, that of an 'internal' market of bids for resources, the pseudo-market of financial numbers.

While long-term implications of quality as a 'fold' are uncertain, Hill's suggestion that quality generates greater participation in decision-taking should be resisted. This idea stems perhaps from a wishful thinking that quality as a discourse is replacing accounting as a discourse. Component illustrates how, instead, in response to a new discourse of quality, accounting as a discourse can mutate away from that of surveillance to a language game of pseudo-markets. The rolling back of accounting numbers merely *brackets* their importance for a dissemination of accountability. Accounting numbers are the conditional which always accompanies any appearance of decentralized decision-taking. Hence TQM is no mere mask to an accounting regime. Quality not only exists within the fold of pseudo-markets, TQM helps to instantiate the very possibility of pseudo-markets.

In summary, accounting numbers are already in use as an artefact to create 'distance', but top managers in Component seem to be trying to take accounting numbers to their logical conclusion and manage by distance. This is the condition of possibility for middle managers getting the governance of the new province of quality. Under pseudo-markets, the traditional surveillance threat of 'meet the numbers, or we'll want to know why' becomes transposed into *'meet the number'*. Within the language game of 'pseudo-markets', there is a dissemination of accountabilities such that the caveat of *'or else'* can be left unspoken.

## NOTES

1 While we did not study the impact of quality techniques as they affect shifts in accountability on the shop floor, the research discussed below perhaps helps to explain how a subversion of quality can be accomplished. In addition to not exploring an intensification in 'lateral' accountability on the shop floor, our focus differs to some of the labour process literature, where the interest is more directed to continuing debates, such as the deskilling effects of quality.

2 In respect of the practicalities of research, Latour's theory of translation (see also Callon, 1986) suggests that any enactment of quality agendas is likely to leave 'traces' in the accounts members offer each other (see also Garfinkel, 1967). Quality thus becomes a discursive space with traceable power effects. Since shifts in language stand at the heart of moving people about, then the specific power effects which follow from the advent of quality become traceable through members' accounts.

3 Time granted for access did not permit more than a limited amount of participant observation (about three months in all). The greater part of the study therefore relies on interview material and documentation. For our interviews, we developed a very open and 'conversational' instrument. Over the duration of the interview, we introduce a number of relatively bland questions, such as 'Tell me about a typical day', 'Who do you talk to?', 'What influences your priorities?' and 'What problems arise?' The openness and ambiguity of these questions leaves the interviewee to 'create' the agenda. This shift is sustained by specifically avoiding attempts to probe. A specific 'probe' may elicit 'more' information about a specific point, but it gives to the interviewee an impression of what it is that the interview is 'really' about and hence channels their specific performance. By 'biting the tongue till it bleeds', the interviewer leaves the interviewee to shape the interview.

Given our interest in enrolment, we were especially cautious to avoid our research material being unduly affected by interviewees constructing for us potentially spurious 'translations'. First, by covering a number of mundane and wide-ranging matters, we anticipated that it would be difficult for interviewees to enrol material which did not stretch across the everyday issues which engross them. Like ethnographers, we concentrated on getting stories, by calling for examples of the point being made, or asking people to recall a recent occasion to illustrate it. We believe that this 'grounding' of talk in interviews shifts people from 'rehearsed scripts' and gets them away from just recycling the 'party line'. Second, since we were ostensibly concerned with the practical possibilities for implementing an accounting technique, activity-based costing (Cooper and Kaplan, 1988), we anticipated that any re-portrayal of the company would be directed at accounting issues in the hope of enrolling ourselves, wittingly or unwittingly, in agendas. Rather than see a perceived lack of neutrality as a disadvantage, therefore, we saw the prospect of enrolment as a process in which people disclose, often quite transparently, agendas at which we could otherwise only guess. Third, and more usually, we protected ourselves from being beguiled by too specific or eccentric agendas by interviewing in two business areas. This allows features particular to each specific plant to be identified. In addition, by interviewing managers across functions, such as personnel and accounting, some hold on company practices could be established horizontally. Further, by interviewing all the managers in the line, we have been able to cross-check stories vertically. Or, again by cross-checking across the line, we could identify particular or eccentric forms of agendas. For example, many of the statements and claims by the quality manager are 'isolated', in that they do not correspond with those of other managers. In this way, definitions of eccentricity emerge from the site as a recursive effect of our analysis.

4  This naming of strategy by people in Component as a 'drive on production' comes of course partly from hindsight and perhaps should be interpreted as an 'enacted' strategy (Weick, 1977; Smircich and Stubbart, 1985), rather than an 'intended' strategy. However, as will be discussed below, there can be nothing flimsy in agendas which overlap to facilitate production of a million units a day.

5  Supervisors saw themselves as resisting attempts to 'make them into managers'. In discussions, meetings or interviews, they clearly and consistently represented themselves as representing employees. In so far as their acting as 'spokespersons' (Callon, 1986) for employees is traditional, we have not covered our analysis of their interview material in this paper.

6  The proposition here is that much of current 'change agendas', such as direct drilling or delayering, may be aimed at squeezing, or even eliminating, middle managers. The question arises as to why middle managers might go along with, and even enable, things being made difficult for them. We examine possible reasons for this in later sections of the paper.

7  Underpinning this, as will be discussed in the following sections, is certainly something of the nature of an 'examination' (Hoskin, 1990). Note how this 'exposure' could further excite the confessional where the 'over-exposure' instantiates performance *as* failure. However, we found little evidence of either, perhaps for reasons we discuss below.

8  Accounting can effect 'distance' in a number of ways. Discussion in the accounting literature has tended to concentrate on notions of *geographical* space. For example, Robson (1992) and Mouritsen (1991) stress the use of accounting numbers to facilitate evaluation over large

geographical distances. Unfortunately this emphasis can overlook other ways in which distance is important, especially 'social' distance (see also Munro, 1993).

9  The effect of accounting numbers should be seen as enacted through the social (e.g. Dugdale and Jones, 1993). They are integral to the social and do not do anything alone. As Munro (forthcoming) suggests, accounting numbers are best seen as part of the heterogeneous nature of the social (see also Law, 1993).

10  The accountant we spoke to at head office provided a well-rehearsed portrayal of the accounting systems as if all was in good working order. Although this line of enquiry was not explored by us, staff functions do have a vested interest in accounting numbers since, in their surveillance of activities in the line, head office staff 'represent' top managers.

11  The notion of discourse is perhaps the most difficult of all Foucault's (1970) terms to define and yet, with the notion of practice, is his most central term (see also Hoskin, forthcoming). A discourse is more than a set of terms in use, since it has disciplining effects. In that it is related to the notion of expertise, it is necessary to enter a discourse in order to have the authority to say what can be seen. In this sense, as Munro (1993) points out, a discourse governs spaces of representation, more than it dictates representations of space.

12  Connections reflect a distribution of knowledge (Barnes, 1988); a distribution that not only is affected by, but includes the manufacture of truth claims. The connection over expertise described is not therefore to be taken either as valid or invalid in epistemological terms. A connection is robust if it is hard to challenge by others at Component. For example, in other studies we have noted that claims by managers in the computer systems division to have expertise over information systems design is associated with these managers having regular contact with IBM. Of course this effect only works as long as IBM are felt to have the leading reputation for quality in large office systems.

13  As Callon (1986: 216) notes, 'to speak for others is to first silence those in whose name we speak'. Having sole access to Nissan over quality is also to have the strength to exclude what actors in Nissan might say.

14  On the contrary, the specific 'hard' techniques, such as statistical process control, were the least well-embedded aspects of quality. Towards the end of his interview, in response to a question about his 'greatest disappointment', the quality manager talked about 'the slow progress of SPC'. Our experience in other companies suggests this to be typical of manufacturing.

15  The attraction of managing by distance includes dumping the 'burden' of conscience. The appeal for top managers therefore is not directly an economic one, but is centred more on changing accountability in order to free up possibilities for others carrying on more dubious practices (see also Willmott, forthcoming). What top managers don't know about, they can't be held responsible for.

16 It would be inappropriate to attempt to work through all the implications of managing by distance. However, implications for human resource management include a shift by top managers away from a presumed responsibility for managing the organization's culture (Legge, 1989: 28), towards decoupling their ethos from the governance of the new provinces. The benefits of decoupling here suggest a resistance by top managers to taking responsibility for actions conducted in the province. Decoupling offers a brake on accountability going back up the line (see the previous note).

17 Foucault (1970) discusses how key concepts of a discourse are left undefined in the sciences. They are organizing concepts, creating the structure to hold the other terms in place and, equally, being held in place, and hence being defined, by the other terms.

# REFERENCES

Argyris, C. (1952) *The Impact of Budgets on People*, Ithaca: Cornell University Press.

Barnes, B. (1988) *The Nature of Power*, Cambridge: Polity Press.

Blau, P.M. and Scott, W.R. (1963) *Formal Organizations: a Comparative Approach*, London: Routledge.

Callon, M. (1980) 'Struggles and Negotiations to Define What is Problematic and What is Not: The Sociologic of Translation', in K.D. Knorr, R. Krohn and R.D. Whitley (eds) *The Social Processes of Scientific Innovation*, Dordrecht and Boston: Reidel.

Callon, M. (1986) 'Some Elements of a Sociology of Translation: Domestication of the Scallops and the Fisherman of St Brieuc Bay', in J. Law (ed.) *A Sociology of Monsters: Essays on Power, Technology and Domination*, Sociology Review Monograph, 38, 1–23, London: Routledge.

Chua, W.F. (1986) 'Radical Developments in Accounting Thought', *The Accounting Review*, LXI (4), 601–32.

Cooper, R. (1990) 'The Structure and Benefits of Activity-Based Manufacturing Cost Systems', *The Eighth Tom Robertson Memorial Lecture*, University of Edinburgh.

Cooper, R. (1993) 'Technologies of Representation', in P. Ahonen (ed.) *The Semiotic Boundaries of Politics*, Berlin: Mouton de Gruyter.

Cooper, R. and Kaplan, R.S. (1988) 'Measure Costs Right: Make the Right Decisions', *Harvard Business Review*, Sept.–Oct., 96–103.

Covaleski, M. and Dirsmith, M. (1983) 'Budgeting as a Means for Control and Loose Coupling', *Accounting, Organizations and Society*, 8, 323–40.

Covaleski, M. and Dirsmith, M. (1986) 'The Budgetary Process of Power and Politics', *Accounting, Organizations and Society*, 11 193–214.

Covaleski, M. and Dirsmith, M. (1990) 'Dialectic Tension, Double Reflexivity and the Everyday Accounting Researcher: On Using Qualitative Methods', *Accounting, Organizations and Society*, 15, 543–73.

Dearden, J. (1988) *Management Accounting: Text and Cases*, Englewood Cliffs, NJ: Prentice-Hall.

Deetz, S. (1992) 'Disciplinary Power in the Modern Corporation', in M. Alvesson and H. Willmott (eds) *Critical Management Studies*, 21–45, London: Sage.

Dopson, S. and Stewart, R. (1990) 'What *is* Happening to Middle Management?', *British Journal of Management*, 1, 3–16.

Dugdale, D. and Jones, C. (1993) 'Investment Decisions and the Social Construction of Trust', *Interdisciplinary Approaches to Accounting Conference*, January, Manchester Conference Centre.

Ezzamel, M., Hoskin, K. and MacVe, R. (1990) 'Managing it All by Numbers: A Review of Johnson and Kaplan's Relevance Lost', *Accounting and Business Research*, 20, 153–66.

Foucault, M. (1970) *The Order of Things: an Archaeology of the Human Sciences*, London: Tavistock.

Foucault, M. (1972) *The Archaeology of Knowledge* (trans. A.M. Sheridan Smith), London: Tavistock.

Foucault, M. (1973) *The Birth of the Clinic* (trans. A. Sheridan), London: Tavistock.

Foucault, M. (1979) *Discipline and Punish: the Birth of the Prison*, Harmondsworth: Penguin.

Foucault, M. (1991) 'On Governmentality', in G. Burchell, C. Gordon and P. Miller (eds) *The Foucault Effect: Studies in Governmental Rationality*, Hemel Hempstead: Harvester Wheatsheaf.

Gadamer, H-G. (1976) 'The Universality of the Hermeneutical Problem', in *Philosophical Hermeneutics*, trans. by D.E. Linge, 3–17, Berkeley, CA: University of California Press.

Garfinkel, H. (1967) *Studies in Ethnomethodology*, Englewood Cliffs, NJ: Prentice-Hall.

Giddens, A. (1984) *The Constitution of Society*, Cambridge: Polity.

Giddens, A. (1991) *Modernity and Self-Identity: Self and Society in the Late Modern Age*, Cambridge: Polity Press.

Goffman, E. (1955) 'On Face-Work: An Analysis of Ritual Elements in Social Interaction', *Psychiatry*, 18, 213–31.

Goold, M. and Campbell, A. (1987) *Strategies and Styles*, Oxford: Blackwell.

Hicks, J.R. (1946) *Value and Capital: an Inquiry into Some Fundamental Principles of Economic Theory*, (2nd edn), Oxford: Oxford University Press.

Hill, S. (1991) 'Why Quality Circles Failed but Total Quality Management Might Succeed', *British Journal of Industrial Relations*, 29 (4), 541–68.

Hiromoto, T. (1988) 'Another Hidden Edge, Japanese Management Accounting', *Harvard Business Review*, July–August.

Hopwood, A.G. (1987) 'The Archaeology of Accounting Systems', *Accounting, Organizations and Society*, 12, 207–34.

Hopwood, A.G. (1990) 'Accounting and Organization Change', *Accounting, Auditing and Accountability Journal*, 3 (1), 7–17.

Hoskin, K. (1990) 'Foucault under Examination: the Crypto-Educationalist Unmasked', in S. Ball (ed.) *Foucault and Education*, London: Routledge.

Hoskin, K. (forthcoming) 'Boxing Clever: For, Against and Beyond Foucault in the Battle for Accounting Theory', *Critical Perspectives on Accounting*.

Hoskin, K. and MacVe, R. (1986) 'Accounting and the Examination: a Genealogy of Disciplinary Power', *Accounting, Organizations and Society*, 11, 105–36.

Johnson, H.T. and Kaplan, R.S. (1987) *Relevance Lost: the Rise and Fall of Management Accounting*, Boston MA: Harvard Business School Press.

Kaplan, R. (1983) 'Measuring Manufacturing Performance: a New Challenge for Management Accounting Research', *The Accounting Review*, LVIII (4), 686–705.

Latour, B. (1987) *Science in Action: How to Follow Scientists and Engineers Through Society*, Milton Keynes: Open University Press.

Laughlin, R. (1991) 'Environmental Disturbances and Organizational Transitions and Transformations: Some Alternative Models', *Organization Studies*, 12 (2), 209–32.

Law, J. (1991) 'Introduction: Monsters, Machines and Sociotechnical Relations', in. J. Law (ed.) *A Sociology of Monsters: Essays on Power, Technology and Domination*, Sociology Review Monograph 38, 1–23, London: Routledge.

Law, J. (1993) *Modernity, Myth and Materialism*, Oxford: Blackwell.

Legge, K. (1989) 'Human Resource Management: a Critical Analysis', in J. Storey (ed.) *New Perspectives in Human Resource Management*, London: Routledge.

Macintosh, N. and Hopper, T. (1991) 'Management Accounting as a Disciplinary Practice: Theory, Case Analysis, and Implications', *Proceedings of the Third Interdisciplinary Approaches to Accounting Conference*, Manchester: University of Manchester.

Macintosh, N.B. and Scapens, R.W. (1990) 'Structuration Theory in Management Accounting', *Accounting, Organizations and Society*, 15, 455–77.

Miller, P. (forthcoming) 'Accounting and Objectivity: The Invention of Calculating Selves and Calculable Spaces', *Annals of Scholarship*.

Miller, P. and O'Leary, T. (1987) 'Accounting and the Construction of the Governable Person', *Accounting, Organizations and Society*, 12, 235–65.

Miller, P. and O'Leary, T. (1993) 'Accounting Expertise and the Politics of the Product: Economic Citizenship and Modes of Corporate Governance', *Accounting, Organizations and Society*, 18 (2/3), 187–206.

Mintzberg, H. (1973) *The Nature of Managerial Work*, New York: Harper & Row.

Mouritsen, J. (1991) 'Accounting in Time-Space Settings: The Institutionalisation of Organisational Practices through Informational Facilities', *Proceedings of the 8th International Standing Conference on Organizational Symbolism*, Copenhagen: Copenhagen Business School.

Munro, R. (1987) 'From Just-in-Case to Just-in-Time', *The Accountant's Magazine*, August, 52–4.

Munro, R. (1991) 'Enabling Participative Change: the Impact of a Strategic Value', *International Studies in Management and Organization*, 21 (4), 52–65.

Munro, R. (1993) 'Just When you Thought it Safe to Enter the Water: Multiple Control Technologies', *Accounting, Management and Information Technologies*, 3 (4), 249–71.

Munro, R. (forthcoming) 'Managing By Ambiguity: An Archaeology of the Social in the Absence of Control Technologies', *Critical Perspectives on Accounting.*

Munro, R. and Hatherly, D. (1993) 'Accountability and the New Commercial Agenda', *Critical Perspectives on Accounting,* 4 (4), 369–95.

Peters, T.J. and Waterman, R.H. (1983) *In Search of Excellence: Lessons from America's Best Run Companies,* New York: Harper & Row.

Roberts, J. (1990) 'Strategy and Accounting in a UK Conglomerate', *Accounting, Organizations and Society,* 15, 107–26.

Roberts, J. (1991) 'The Possibilities of Accountability', *Accounting, Organizations and Society,* 16, 355–68.

Roberts, J. and Scapens, R.W. (1985) 'Accounting Systems and Systems of Accountability – Understanding Accounting Practices in their Organizational Contexts', *Accounting, Organizations and Society,* 10, 443–56.

Roberts, J. and Scapens, R.W. (1990) 'Accounting as Discipline', in D.J. Cooper and T.M. Hopper (eds) *Critical Accounts: Reorientating Accounting Research,* Basingstoke: Macmillan.

Robson, K. (1992) 'Accounting numbers as 'Inscription': Action at a Distance and the Development of Accounting', *Accounting, Organization and Society,* 17, 685–708.

Rose, N. and Miller, P. (1992) 'Political Power Beyond the State: Problematics of Government', *British Journal of Sociology,* 43 (2), 173–205.

Samuels, J.M. and Wilkes, F.M. (1971) *Management of Company Finance,* London: Nelson.

Selznick, P. (1948) 'Foundations of the Theory of Organization', *American Sociological Review,* 13.

Sewell, G. and Wilkinson, B. (1992) 'Empowerment or Emasculation? A Tale of Workplace Surveillance in a Total Quality Organization', in P. Blyton and P. Turnbull (eds) *Human Resource Management: Conflicts and Contradictions,* London: Sage.

Smircich, L. and Stubbart, C. (1985) 'Strategic Management in an Enacted World', *Academy of Management Review,* 724–36.

Tinker, T. and Neimark, M., (1988) 'The Struggle over Meaning in Accounting and Corporate Research: a Comparative Evaluation of Conservative and Critical Historiography', *Accounting, Auditing and Accountability* 1 (1), 55–74.

Van Horne, J. (1968) *Financial Management and Policy,* Englewood Cliffs, NJ: Prentice-Hall.

Vollman, T. (1990) 'Changing Manufacturing Performance Measures', in P.B.B. Turney (ed.) *Performance Excellence in Manufacturing and Service Organizations,* Proceedings of the Third Annual Management Accounting Symposium, Sarasota, FL: AAA.

Weick, K. (1977) 'Enactment Processes in Organizations', in B. Staw and G. Salancik (eds) *New Directions in Organizational Behavior,* Chicago, IL: St. Clair.

Wildavsky, A. (1992) Seminar Paper on Self-Interest, Department of Accounting and Business Method, University of Edinburgh.

Wilkinson, A., Snape, E. and Allen, P. (1990) 'TQM and the Management of Labour', *8th Annual Organization and Control of the Labour Process Conference*.

Willmott, H. (forthcoming) 'Strength is Ignorance; Slavery is Freedom: Managing Culture in Modern Organizations', *Journal of Management Studies*.

# 6

# TOTAL QUALITY MANAGEMENT AND PARTICIPATION

## Employee empowerment, or the enhancement of exploitation?

*Louise McArdle, Michael Rowlinson, Stephen Procter, John Hassard and Paul Forrester*

The overriding emphasis being placed upon quality in manufacturing and service industries has resulted in a growing debate surrounding total quality management (see Hill, Tuckman, this volume). TQM has been singled out as the innovation in management which is increasingly being regarded as the route to competitive success.

Recently there has been an attempt to draw distinctions between the approaches taken by TQM writers. The British Quality Association (BQA) has made the distinction between 'hard' and 'soft' approaches to quality, where the hard definition places an emphasis upon the systematic measuring and control of work by means of statistical processes (Wilkinson *et al.*, 1992). The soft version places an emphasis upon the more qualitative aspects of quality, stressing customer orientation, employee involvement, teamworking and the culture of the organization. This emphasis upon employee involvement and teamworking within the distinctions of the BQA is significant in a number of ways. While ultimate responsibility for quality lies with senior management within an organization, the introduction of TQM results in the onus for quality being shifted away from particular functional departments and towards each individual employee.

The involvement of each employee in the quality process has been advocated to the extent that it has been argued that all employees should be incorporated into the decision-making process within the organization (Oakland, 1989). This has been

156

endorsed by Hill (1991a: 541), who argues that TQM 'looks likely to institutionalise participation on a permanent basis and managerial employees as well as office and shop floor staff now have more opportunity to participate in decisions'. However, this participation must be accompanied by the appropriate developments in the structure of the organization. The institutionalization of participation can only be achieved if cross-functional management takes place. This cross-functional working allows involvement across departments and work units as the means of satisfying internal and external customer demands. Wilkinson *et al.* (1992) have reinforced this by stressing the need for 'quality of infrastructure', where quality and the associated processes of continuous improvement are built into the everyday activities of the organization. The cross-functional links between departments become an important aspect of TQM. These developments in the infrastructure, it is claimed, will put in place the mechanics of TQM – such as statistical process control, teamworking and quality circles – and thus allow a greater degree of input into decision-making (Hill, 1991a).

## TQM AND EMPLOYEE PARTICIPATION

While Hill (1991a, 1991b) and Oakland (1989) argue that TQM should involve every member of the organization in the decision-making process, the emphasis upon pushing the responsibility for quality to the shop floor has implications for employee participation. Hill (1991a) has further argued that, because of the associated changes in infrastructure, TQM will not suffer the same fate as the quality circle movement of the 1980s, where a lack of institutional and managerial support resulted in a very small take-up and success rate. The focus on managerial support, teamworking, etc. is believed to be the route to success for TQM.

The similarities between the 'soft' side of TQM and the quality of working life movement of the 1960s and 1970s have been noted elsewhere. For example, in their discussion of the 'Japanization' of British industry, Oliver and Wilkinson (1992) have argued that many of the Japanese practices now being adopted by British organizations – such as autonomous working, job enlargement through flexibility and job redesign – are the same developments which were introduced in the 1960s and 1970s as a response to absenteeism, high labour turnover and, more significantly, growing trade union strength in the economy.

The attempts at work humanization which the QWL initiatives represented, however, were essentially a response by capital to its lack of control over the labour process. The fundamental difference is that the current initiatives are not a response to labour pressure but are initiatives taken by management in an attempt to become more competitive. Indeed, Ackers *et al.* (1992) argue that new developments in employee involvement depart from Ramsay's cycles of control thesis, in that the catalysts for increased employee involvement and, in particular, the initiatives associated with TQM, are product market competition and a perceived need to respond to external pressures. It is this difference which Hill (1991a) argues will determine the success of TQM.

New forms of involvement and participation should not be divorced from changes in production technology such as just-in-time (JIT) or flexible manufacturing systems (Thompson and McHugh, 1990). In this context it can be seen that the introduction of involvement and participation schemes is not a defensive human relations exercise:

> improved manufacturing performance is to be achieved by introducing flexible work practices and by pushing responsibilities that were previously the preserve of specialist indirect staffs onto production workers, thereby assisting in the elimination of waste – where waste is defined as any activity that adds cost, but not value, to a product.
>
> (Oliver and Wilkinson, 1992: 325)

The motives for the introduction of TQM within organizations are obviously tied up with the increasing competitive pressures on organizations. This can be seen if one considers the origins of TQM. Wilkinson *et al.* (1992) argue that the key proponents of TQM in Britain are from the operations management field. They advocate the hard or mixed approach to TQM and emphasize the quality of design and the quality of conformance to customer specification. Although the involvement of employees is something advocated by these writers, it is seen as a largely unproblematic process. Where consideration is given to the human side of TQM, it is simply assumed that changes in the management of the labour process are determined by changes in production processes and management systems (cf. Dale and Plunkett, 1990; Giles, 1991).

# TQM AND EMPLOYEE EMPOWERMENT

It would appear from the above that employees are now being given the opportunity to exercise greater influence over decisions within the organization. Moreover, it is argued, this participation is likely to be more enduring than previous attempts, since it is introduced with appropriate changes in organizational design and with necessary management support.

However, the debates over or perceptions of employee participation bear little resemblance to those of the 1970s. Ramsay (1991: 2) points to the need for employers to gain more cooperation for changes in technology. Further, he argues that the need for new standards of quality has required employers actively to seek the acquiescence of employees and to generate commitment to changes in the organization of work around new production systems (Ramsay, 1992: 2).

These attempts to generate commitment have prompted a different focus for the debates surrounding employee participation:

> Recent years have seen the growth of participatory formats that proclaim an organic unity of interests within enterprises. Under this model the aim is submersion of identity and other interests to a large corporate goal, with participation taking place through workgroups and structures that attempt to improve aspects of corporate performance.
>
> (Eldridge *et al.*, 1991: 146)

This unitarist definition of participatory formats assumes that individual values and interests can be subordinated to the goals of the organization. In order to 'incorporate' employees and their representatives, this perspective only allows participation in the decision-making to the extent that such participation enhances the effectiveness of the organization, and is therefore seen as a means to an end of enhanced profitability (Cressey and MacInnes, 1980).

This approach, in effect, divorces the issue of employee participation from wider issues concerning real power within the workplace. Employee participation under these terms restricts any definition to being company- or plant-specific, any increase in the power of employees to influence the decision-making process being tied up with the fulfilment of company goals.

Underlying the attempts by organizations to increase the level of

159

participation in decision-making is the concept of 'empowerment' (Juran, 1979). Employee empowerment can be regarded as the process by which responsibility for quality is pushed down the organization to the point of production (Sewell and Wilkinson, 1992). Those who actually carry out the work become responsible and accountable for the quality of the product or service. Empowerment has become the key concept in organizations such as Rank Xerox (Giles, 1991; Mercer and Judkins, 1990).

An important aspect of this process of empowerment has been the commercialization of the organization. Employees become accountable for quality to their 'customers', with employees having both internal and external customers to satisfy. The concept of empowerment implies a shift in power from one group to another within an organization. Workers become empowered as they are given the resources such as training and equipment to be able to take on the extra responsibility (Sewell and Wilkinson, 1992: 102).

This shift in power away from the centre is a necessary precursor for genuine employee empowerment. As Lammers (1991: 6) points out, 'If the total amount of power of an organizational entity can or must be seen as a zero sum game, a "power raise" for the not so powerful must be at the expense of those who have more power.' Among advocates of TQM, the political and organizational implications of this process of 'disempowerment' are often simply not considered (Wilkinson *et al.*, 1992). In particular, the disempowerment of supervisors and line managers is often seen as unproblematic, as the TQM literature regards managers as resources upon which to draw, rather than as a set of political actors (ibid.).

The vehicles for empowerment within organizations are normally quality circles or other problem-solving teams, autonomous work groups and other team approaches to working. The TQM organization is therefore characterized by delegation and a removal of bureaucratic control procedures (Sewell and Wilkinson, 1992: 102; Wilkinson *et al.*, 1992: 4). Underlying this is a move away from Taylorist control procedures, towards control based on responsible autonomy (Friedman, 1977). The ability to take on responsibility for quality and to become involved in the decision-making procedure is believed to enhance the job satisfaction of employees and therefore to eliminate the need for direct control over their work.

However, against this background of enhanced involvement in decision-making and a greater degree of autonomy, there is a growing literature which has presented a critical perspective of TQM. The simple dichotomy between hard and soft becomes inadequate, and complex issues where the two approaches are inextricably linked become significant. It is argued that the pushing down of responsibility to shop floor level is an extension of managerial control (Sewell and Wilkinson, 1992; Delbridge and Turnbull, 1992; Delbridge *et al.*, 1992). Any moves towards enhanced employee participation are seen as being purely functional in nature (Lammers, 1991): 'empowerment' results not in a power shift in the organization, but in employees becoming morally bound to a system of management which enhances their own exploitation.

The following is a case study of PCB Electronics (pseudonym), an electronics plant in the north-west of England. TQM is well established in the plant and has precipitated some fundamental changes in the organization of work. An analysis of the TQM mechanics supports the critical perspective of TQM and shows how employees are tied into ways of working where empowerment and involvement are loose rhetoric and the reality is a greater degree of control over work.

## TQM at PCB Electronics

PCB is one of two manufacturing plants owned by its parent company. It is responsible for the sub-assembly and final assembly of electronic products. After a radical rationalization programme in the early 1980s which included closing several plants in the UK and making approximately 20,000 people redundant throughout the organization, the company has reorganized its production process around flexible manufacturing systems (FMSs) and cellular working.

The first FMS was installed in the plant in 1985. This was followed in 1986 by the introduction of TQM, based on the philosophy and advice of Philip Crosby Associates. Philip Crosby's approach to TQM is based on the movement within the organization towards 'zero defects', i.e. away from a tolerance for substandard performance towards an elimination of waste caused by a reduction in quality.

Initially the concept of TQM was introduced at the most senior levels within the organization, but after the introduction of flexible manufacturing at PCB it was 'cascaded' down to operator level and introduced with the changes in working practices which accompanied the FMS, such as job enlargement and redesign. The TQM programme was launched in a blaze of publicity. An open day was held, and employees put their names to a public commitment to the goal of zero defects. An extensive training programme was introduced for all employees so that the importance of quality could be conveyed throughout the whole organization.

The TQM programme meant that employees on the shop floor received training in basic statistical analysis so that they could use statistical process control and Pareto measurement to chart their own progress towards zero defects. Essentially, as part of the original Crosby (1979) methodology, work and performance have to become measurable to enable individuals and teams within the plant to monitor the level of defects within the production process. This reminds employees that as part of TQM they are obliged to try and develop ways not only of solving problems as they occur, but also of eliminating persistent substandard performance through the operation of such things as quality circles. The overall effect of this system of performance measurement is that the walls of the plant are covered in graphs and charts which illustrate quality levels, individual progress towards zero defects, and the outcomes of quality circle discussions. The quality circle programme is accompanied by bronze, silver and gold 'gong' awards which are awarded on a national basis throughout the company for the best outcomes of the quality circles, with 'best' being defined as the innovation which results in the biggest elimination of waste and therefore the most cost-effective solution.

Although membership of the quality circles is voluntary, employees at PCB are encouraged overtly and covertly to participate. Since 1988 and the introduction of harmonized terms and conditions within the plant, wage increases for shop floor staff are entirely performance-based. The performance assessment which determines the eventual wage rise is based on both a quantitative assessment – for example, the ability to reach both team and individual targets – and, more importantly, a qualitative assessment of behavioural characteristics which are seen as favourable by management. Being a member of a quality circle and taking an active part in the quality process is seen as desirable behaviour, which will be rewarded accordingly.

At operator level the main changes which were introduced into the operation were as much a part of the changes in the manufacturing systems as to do with the TQM system. However, various

162

procedures were introduced which management believed allowed a greater degree of involvement within the quality process. As part of this, management within the plant has, according to one senior manager, been influenced by

> the movement towards industrial democracy which has taken place . . . within society generally and the electronics industry in particular. [PCB] has sought to increase levels of co-determination for all its employees and is seeking to develop a single status organization through harmonization.

Research to test this statement revealed that any attempted moves towards democracy through co-determination within PCB were limited to the problem-solving techniques which had been established through the TQM system. These involved the setting up of Corrective Action Teams (CATs), and Error Cause Removal (ECR) teams which were essentially an elaborate system advocated by Crosby in order that problems which did occur in the production process could be reported to management who would then take action in solving them. As stated above, however, the company has developed the Crosby methodology to put in place many developments in TQM which have been devised to fit the circumstances in which the company now finds itself.

Part of this development has been the setting up of a continuous development programme for individuals within the organization, termed Quality Improvement for the Individual (QIFTI). This involves training when an employee joins the organization and a series of review sessions in order to make sure that the quality message is constantly reinforced.

From management's point of view the quality programme can be deemed to have been successful. Some of the improvements recorded by the company show savings in production costs and increases in the quality of the finished products in the years 1987 to 1990. For instance, the percentage of products delivered at the appropriate quality standard increased from 97 per cent in 1987 to 99 per cent in 1990; the time taken to assemble the final product was reduced from twenty-one days to three days in the same period; while the cost of non-conformance to customer requirements was reduced from £1,800,000 to £900,000.

These figures, however, do not reveal the extent to which the work has changed within the plant and how workers have entered into the process of TQM at PCB.

163

## QWL, TQM and employee involvement in PCB

It would be tempting to dismiss moves towards employee involvement under TQM as just another ruse constructed by management to encourage workers to engage more freely in their own exploitation. Ramsay (1985) regarded participation as merely a device to serve the interests of management. Indeed the introduction of TQM initiatives, as seen earlier, is an attempt to further the profitability of the organization. However, to dismiss TQM participatory formats, as this approach does, ignores how employees perceive TQM and how they regard the extent of empowerment which they perceive themselves as obtaining through TQM.

The differences in the reasons for the introduction of QWL initiatives and for the adoption of TQM have been discussed above. However, there are more significant differences in how the changes in job design and how the changes in working methods have been greeted by the workforces involved. Nichols and Beynon's (1977) study of the new work agreement at the ChemCo plant illustrated the effect that QWL initiatives had on employees after management introduced job enrichment. As one worker put it:

> 'You move from one boring, dirty, monotonous job to another boring, dirty, monotonous job. And then to another boring, dirty, monotonous job. And somehow you're supposed to come out of it all "enriched". But I never feel "enriched" – I just feel knackered.'

This comment can be compared with those of workers from PCB after TQM had been in place for approximately four years:

> 'I'm forty-six and I've been doing this new job for nearly two years and I've been completely turned around. It has given me a new lease of life. I'd rather work this way. It's hard work with more responsibility and more worry, but there is a lot more job satisfaction.'

These attitudes are not isolated. Another employee argued:

> 'TQM works because the shop floor operators believe that is the way to run a factory – they get satisfaction out of the job and keep the factory running . . . there is more commitment among the workers than among the management.'

There was a general feeling among those interviewed that the change in the way people had worked since the introduction of TQM, although a lot harder, was a better way of working than previously. In essence, workers were required to take on more responsibility for a number of different tasks as the factory was reorganized around the flexible manufacturing systems. Employees regard TQM and its associated techniques as a way of enhancing their own position. The acknowledgement that the work is harder reveals that they are aware of the increased work intensification, but do not see it as something to resist. Unlike the human relations attempts at work humanization such as those experienced by the workers at ChemCo, TQM at PCB enlarges tasks to such an extent that employees have to think more about the work which they carry out and therefore, in human relations terms, are enriched by the work.

With this attitude among the workers at PCB, the impression may be given that management has at last been able to organize the labour process in such a way that the opportunity to resist the intensification has been reduced, and with it the desire for workers to resist their own exploitation (Edwards, 1979). Indeed, TQM does seem to have allowed management to introduce more intensified ways of working, which the employees and the trade union representatives have so far been unwilling to resist.

The appeal of TQM is that it has given workers something to think about and within PCB they see it as a way of alleviating the tedium of work. It could be argued that by giving workers something to think about, management is taking away their freedom of thought and subordinating their subjectivity (Gramsci, 1971; see Tuckman, this volume, for discussion). The employees at PCB have been empowered to make decisions about the quality of work and in doing so they have become even more embroiled in the production system. However, to argue that this is the result of TQM and the internalization of the so-called logics of the market into the workplace does not contextualize the situation at PCB. Workers are impressed upon to regard the factory as a system of internal markets. The next person in the production process is regarded as a worker's customer. This results in their having to produce subassembled parts in line with internal customer requirements, or 'fitness for use'. Faults or defects with work received from workers within the factory are recorded, and persistent faults reported to supervisors or line managers.

This willingness to accept TQM as the only way to work also obscures managerial action, which has thus far prevented a response by the employees.

The shift towards consensual methods of organizing work which TQM dictates does not take into account the drastic rationalization programme carried out throughout the organization prior to the introduction of TQM at the plant. Within the company itself, since the plant's opening in 1979, the workforce has been slimmed by approximately 2,000 and the closure of one of the company's other manufacturing factories in 1989 resulted in production being moved to PCB. There was a distinct feeling among workers within the plant of 'there but for the grace of God . . . ' over the closure, with people being told that PCB could suffer the same fate if quality and production did not meet certain levels.

One worker reinforced this by telling the researchers:

> 'Well you don't feel more secure when every time you kind of stand out for something you think is right you get kind of threatened with the fact that we could be the next ones to go and things like that. It won't be viewed in a favourable light . . . if we are seen to be in disagreement with management. So no one feels secure.'

Tuckman (this volume) argues that such pressure on employees to become involved in the workings of the internal and external market is part of the process of the commodification of internal organizational relations, which results in bringing into the organization perceptions of the pseudo-market. The market and, in particular, the external environment, allow management to shift responsibility for enhanced control and exploitation away from themselves and on to external pressures.

Thus workers are encouraged to identify with the objectives of the organization while the mechanics of TQM represent a more desirable way of working than previously. TQM can therefore be regarded as a form of control over worker subjectivity. Employees become increasingly concerned with the profitability of the organization while they themselves undergo intensified work regimes to enhance profitability. Their willingness to resist increased intensification of work is therefore displaced by a solidarity with the interests of management.

The extent to which the imposition of TQM and the perceived logics of both the internal and external market on to the workforce has allowed management to legitimize their action can be illustrated by the response of one of the shop stewards within the plant to a pay-freeze which was imposed: 'My view is that they [PCB] have done their homework properly and have made the right decision. I don't believe that [PCB] would take advantage of the recession to avoid a pay rise.'

The introduction of internal and external customers and the need to respond to customer requirements which TQM advocates has allowed management the opportunity to eliminate resistance to its decisions through what could best be described as macho management techniques, i.e. the threat of closure of the factory and the constant reminder of the so-called logics of the market. Whether this is a temporary phenomenon is debatable. Workers may be tempted to demand more return from the wage effort bargain should the economic climate favour such a move. However, the company may already have pre-empted such a move by purchasing another production facility in Scandinavia in 1990. While they argue that PCB will still continue to manufacture while there is a demand for the electronic products it produces, the Scandinavian factory offers the facilities to replicate such production.

In expressing the increase in job satisfaction which employees feel in the extension of their tasks, there is a lack of awareness that TQM and its associated forms of work are being used to erode the power-centred base of participation, through such innovations as performance-related pay, self-monitoring and the increased surveillance which comes through quality monitoring (Sewell and Wilkinson, 1992). Management has taken advantage of the weakened state of trade unions within the plant to exclude them from the workings of TQM. This state of affairs is not restricted to PCB. Generally, throughout the 1980s and 1990s, weakened trade unions and the threat of unemployment have meant that at company level there is no longer the feeling that the unions need to be 'incorporated', as they were in the 1970s. Management has the confidence to exclude trade unions from decision-making and to abandon systems for negotiation of changes within organizations. At the level of the labour process this has resulted in a move from placebos, such as QWL initiatives, to initiatives such as TQM which effectively exclude unions.

The lack of desire to resist the intensification of work results in a situation where employees at PCB become morally bound (the use of the logics of the market to legitimize management action) in a production system in which they endorse their own exploitation. TQM may serve their own desire for more job satisfaction; however, the interests which are ultimately served are those of management in the form of greater unit output and the drive for more work and less waste, which are disguised as consensus-based participation provided by the elaborate mechanics of TQM (Thompson and McHugh, 1990). There is in effect no extension of employee rights. TQM has allowed management to extend its hegemonic position over how participation is termed and viewed within the plant.

Furthermore, it is in management's interests to ensure that the move away from power-centred to task-centred participation is never made explicit within PCB. Effectively, the union as the basis of power-centred participation was marginalized in 1988, when terms and conditions were harmonized in the plant and all employees were put on performance-related pay. By removing unions from the wage effort bargain, management effectively paved the way for more involvement at task level, where they can determine the extent of participation and involvement in work. The language of TQM and involvement allows management to talk about worker empowerment. As stated earlier, the introduction of participation and involvement techniques is ultimately tied into the introduction of new production concepts. However, the move towards JIT forms of inventory control within PCB has essentially rendered the production process vulnerable to stoppages or breakdowns in production. This vulnerability is perhaps more acute at PCB, since the aforementioned closure of one of the company's other manufacturing plants has left PCB as the only final assembly plant operating in the UK. The process of empowerment is designed to make employees responsible for correcting any faults in production as quickly as possible. This eliminates time wasted in problem-solving, but also conceals the vulnerability of management and the production system, which employees could exploit to resist the intensification of work.

This pushing of responsibility to shop floor level, however, poses a contradiction for management. The need for tighter control over the production process as advocated by the 'hard' definition of TQM implies more centralized managerial control, but the delegation of responsibility down to the point of production could result in management losing control over production. Sewell and Wilkinson (1992) have argued that management has tried to reconcile this contradiction by moving away from external forms of control such as supervisory and direct forms of control, towards the internalization of control through the quality monitoring system.

Although the appearance of working at PCB seems devoid of direct line manager and supervisory control, other mechanisms for the surveillance of work can be observed. The making visible of the work process through quality and performance measurement provides powerful stimuli for maintaining work standards and quality performance. This process was also noted by Sewell and Wilkinson (1992) in their study of electronics production. They argued that the concept of Foucault's (1977) panopticon could be used to understand the discipline which TQM imposes upon employees through surveillance techniques such as quality monitoring. Within PCB, Zuboff's (1989) adaption of the panopticon as an 'information panopticon' can be used to describe how the monitoring process through the measurement charts is supplemented by the use of information technology in the production process. A bar-coding system is in operation which allows management to trace pieces of work back to the original worker should they prove faulty. This system also allows the use of 'automated guided vehicles' (AGVs) within the plant. These computer-controlled trollies bring work to the operators when they signal, by means of a button on their workbenches, that they have finished the previous task. The AGVs will also remove the completed work. The computer system recognizes each worker when they 'sign on' to the workbench and instructs the AGV only to take work for which the operator is qualified. The use of information technology within the plant can thus tell management where each worker is stationed and the amount of work completed by that person. These overt and more covert methods of surveillance allow management to reconcile the contradiction between the decentralized control of people in the organization which TQM advocates and the more centralized control of the production process.

## CONCLUSIONS

This paper has addressed the concept of employee participation within the context of the debates surrounding TQM. It has argued that management has appropriated the concept of participation and redefined the debate around the task-centred forms of participation as a means of engaging the acquiescence of employees in order to maintain the efficiency of the organization.

Within the case study company, employee involvement and co-determination, according to management, is an integral part of the management of people around flexible manufacturing systems and TQM. However, to argue that TQM has led to a power shift within the organization and an extension of employee rights blurs the reality of what employee participation means in the organization.

Within PCB, power-centred participation has been eroded, while management has promoted task-centred forms of involvement. The concept of empowerment within the plant has resulted in a system which intensifies work but does not allow workers the input into the decision-making process promised by TQM. Although employees at the plant appear to gain more satisfaction from the job enlargement process, there is also the feeling that the so-called logics of the market are used to impose an atmosphere of fear of unemployment as a means of avoiding any resistance from employees.

The TQM process also increases the monitoring of work as employees become bound into a system where they must monitor their own progress through the making visible of work measurement. This is supplemented by the panoptic gaze of the information technology installed into the actual FMS system. Zuboff (1989) has argued that information technology can either automate or informate. Within PCB it has been shown that the informating abilities of information technology allow TQM to become panoptic and therefore can be used as a system to monitor and control employees, as well as a means to enhance production.

Rather than extending the rights of employees in PCB, TQM has introduced management by stress (Delbridge and Turnbull, 1992) into the plant and forced workers to indulge in their own work intensification and exploitation.

## REFERENCES

Ackers, P., Marchington, M., Wilkinson, A. and Goodman, J. (1992) 'The use of cycles? Explaining employee involvement in the 1990s', *Industrial Relations Journal*, 23 (4), 268–83.

Cressey, P. and MacInnes, J. (1980) 'Voting for Ford: Industrial Democracy and the Control of Labour', *Capital and Class*, 11, 34–43.

Crosby, P. (1979) *Quality is Free*, New York: McGraw-Hill.

Dale, B.G. and Plunkett, J.J. (eds) (1990) *Managing Quality*, Hemel Hempstead: Philip Allan.

Delbridge, R. and Turnbull, P. (1992) 'Human Resource Maximization: The Management of Labour under Just-in-Time Manufacturing Systems' in P. Blyton and P. Turnbull (eds) *Reassessing Human Resource Management*, London: Sage.

Delbridge, R., Turnbull, P. and Wilkinson, B. (1992) 'Pushing Back the Frontiers: Management Control and Work Intensification Under JIT/TQM Regimes', *New Technology, Work and Employment*, 7, 97–106.

Deming, W.E. (1986) *Out of the Crisis*, Cambridge, MA: MIT Press.

Edwards, R. (1979) *Contested Terrain*, London: Heinemann.

Eldridge, J., Cressey, P. and MacInnes, J. (1991) *Industrial Sociology and Economic Crisis*, Hemel Hempstead: Harvester Wheatsheaf.

Friedman, A. (1977) 'Responsible Autonomy versus Direct Control over the Labour Process', *Capital and Class*, 1, 43–57.

Foucault, M. (1977) *Discipline and Punish: The Birth of the Prison*, London: Allen Lane.

Giles, E. (1991) 'Putting the Customer First at Rank Xerox', paper presented to the 10th EGOS Colloquium, Vienna, July.

Gramsci, A. (1971) *Selections from the Prison Notebooks*, Q. Hoare and G. Smith (eds), London: Lawrence and Wishart.

Hill, S. (1991a) 'Why Quality Circles Failed But Total Quality Management Might Succeed', *British Journal of Industrial Relations*, 29 (4), 541–68.

Hill, S. (1991b) 'How Do You Manage the Flexible Firm? The Total Quality Model', *Work, Employment and Society*, 5 (3), 397–415.

Juran, J.M. (1979) *Quality Control Handbook*, New York: McGraw-Hill.

Lammers, C. (1991) 'Organizational and Interorganizational Democracy', paper presented to the 10th EGOS Colloquium, Vienna, July.

Mercer, D.S. and Judkins, P.E. (1990) 'Rank Xerox: A Total Quality Process' in B.G. Dale and J.J. Plunkett (eds) *Managing Quality*, Hemel Hempstead: Philip Allan.

Nichols, T. and Beynon, H. (1977) *Living with Capitalism*, London: Routledge and Kegan Paul.

Oakland, J. (1989) *Total Quality Management*, Oxford: Heinemann.

Oliver, N. and Wilkinson, B. (1992) *The Japanization of British Industry* (2nd edn), Oxford: Blackwell.

Ramsay, H. (1985) 'What is Participation For? A Critical Evaluation of "Labour Process" Analyses of Job Reform' in D. Knights, H. Willmott and P. Collinson (eds) *Job Redesign: Critical Perspectives on the Labour Process*, Aldershot: Gower.

Ramsay, H. (1991) 'Reinventing the wheel? A Review of the Development and Performance of Employee Involvement', *Human Resource Management Journal*, 1 (4), 1–22.

Sewell, G. and Wilkinson, B. (1992) 'Empowerment or Emasculation? Shopfloor Surveillance in a Total Quality Organization', in P. Blyton and P. Turnbull (eds) *Reassessing Human Resource Management*, London: Sage.

Thompson, P. and McHugh, D. (1990) *Work Organizations: A Critical Introduction*, London: Macmillan.

Tuckman, A. (1993) 'Out of the Crisis? Quality, TQM and the Labour Process', paper presented to the 11th Annual Labour Process Conference, Blackpool, April.

Wilkinson, A., Marchington, M., Goodman, J. and Ackers, P. (1992) 'Total Quality Management and Employee Involvement', *Human Resource Management Journal*, 2 (4), 1–20.

Zuboff, S. (1989) *In the Age of the Smart Machine*, London: Heinemann.

# 7

# MANAGING QUALITY IN THE MULTI-CULTURAL WORKPLACE

*Patrick Dawson*

## INTRODUCTION

One of the major tenets of modern total quality management (TQM) programmes centres on the view that maximum participation – both of internal employees and of those representing major customers and suppliers – is the keystone to achieving low-cost quality products and services (see, for example, Albrecht, 1992; Brocka and Brocka, 1992; Tenner and DeToro, 1992). However, in trying to establish a 'total quality organization' – which is characterized by total employee involvement, a non-adversarial system of industrial relations and the development of high-trust relationships – little attention has been given to the constraints and barriers which may prevent full employee participation within the multi-cultural workplace. As Hill (1991) has noted, there has been a tendency for senior management to sidestep the broader cultural change aspects in their uncritical acceptance of the general appropriateness of TQM principles to Western workplace cultures. The commercial enthusiasm behind the implementation of TQM may in part be explained by the 'competitive' push for the uptake of quality initiatives and the persuasiveness of neat prescriptive market-driven consultant packages (Dawson and Palmer, 1993). The absence of critical evaluation, or of a simple assessment of the company requirements of change, has served to downplay the contextual communication issues and cultural dimensions, while simultaneously emphasizing the centrality of total employee involvement to creating and maintaining an organization committed to continuous process innovation. Consequently, the cultural change aspects of TQM remain underexplored within the Western context, with many companies indicating a general reluctance to discuss the problems associated with implementing quality initiatives. In this chapter, the experience of Pirelli Cables is used to describe employee responses to the process of establishing a 'quality culture' and to illustrate how the cultural homogeneity of the prescriptions of TQM currently advocated (which largely reflect minor modifications of a Japanese model) may not be appropriate to Australian organizations which are culturally diverse. However, before detailing this particular case, the following section briefly outlines the emergence of TQM in Australia.

## THE EMERGENCE OF TOTAL QUALITY MANAGEMENT IN AUSTRALIA

The emergence of TQM in Australia followed in the wake of the American and European interest in Japanese manufacturing practices which were proving to be so successful in the world product markets of the 1970s. At this time, quality management was identified as a major contributing factor to Japan's competitive advantage and as a consequence the Japanese model of quality management began to diffuse into Western nations. The original American quality control experts, Juran and Deming, became major agents for the diffusion of quality management to international management audiences and visited Australia several times during the 1980s (Allan, 1991: 31–4). This period also witnessed the emergence of a number of consultancy groups which formed around these 'new' quality management principles (for example, Crosby, Conway, Joiner and Scholtes) and acted as diffusion agents in stimulating interest in quality management programmes. These individual quality leaders and consultant groups became the main vehicles for the diffusion of quality management in Britain, America and Australia.

In the early 1980s, the Australian concern with quality management became the focus of attention at the 53rd Annual Convention of the Federation of Australian Radio Broadcasters (FARB) in Perth, Western Australia. At this conference the Federal President and Director of FARB and Jack Keavney (representing Enterprise Australia) were able to get the support of the delegates to mount an Australia for Quality campaign (Sprouster, 1984: 17–18). The campaign was officially launched by the Australian Prime Minister, Bob Hawke, on 2 April 1984, and was a major vehicle for initiating the introduction of TQM into Australian manufacturing industries (Dawson and Patrickson, 1991: 67). At this stage, Enterprise Australia acted as a catalyst and promoter of quality management and provided free seminars to Australian managers.

On 25 September 1986, the Minister for Industry, Technology and Commerce, Senator John Button, made a news release to announce the formation of a 'Committee of Review of Standards, Accreditation and Quality Control and Assurance in Australian Industry'. The review was conducted over a six-month period, and an advertisement inviting submissions from interested sources was placed in all the major Australian newspapers. In response, a total of 197 submissions were received and in conjunction with information collected from a further 199 organizations the committee prepared a final report. The report was presented to John Button on 26 June 1987, and claimed that there was a plethora of public and private sector organizations with little effective coordination and no national strategy (Foley, 1987). The report recommended that the Government assist the development of quality management in Australia, which was accomplished through using the National Industry Extension Service (NIES) (which had been established in March 1987 as an agency to promote process and product innovations). NIES formed a Quality Forum with representatives from industry, unions, government and academia, and through Aptech (a consulting firm) designed a TQM implementation package (Allan, 1991: 48). A further recommendation of the Foley Report was that an Australian Quality Authority (AQA) should be established to coordinate a national strategy on quality management (Foley, 1987). However, the response and activities of both Enterprise Australia (EA) and the Australian Organization for Quality Control (AOQC) proved instrumental in reshaping the direction of the Australian quality movement in the late 1980s. Today, these two bodies act as the main controllers and founder-member organizations (with the Total Quality Management Institute (TQMI) and the Quality Society of Australasia (QSA)), of the new umbrella organization, the Australian Quality Council (AQC), established in 1990 (Sohal, 1991: 8).

One of the main activities of EA which brought about a shift in emphasis in the quality movement, occurred in the mid-1980s when John Sprouster, managing director of Nashua Australia, and Bruce Irvin, managing director of the Australia for Quality

Campaign (both directors of EA), were successful in developing an Australian Total Quality Management Institute (TQMI). TQMI was launched by the Minister for Industry, Technology and Commerce on 10 April 1987, and was set the objective of promoting the diffusion of TQM in Australia (Allan, 1991: 39). In 1988, an annual Australian quality award for outstanding achievement in TQM was established and awarded to organizations which could prove that the principles and practices of TQM had been incorporated into daily operations (Sohal, 1991: 7). Over the past few years, EA and TQMI have continued to work closely together and by the early 1990s were promoting a TQM perspective which emphasized cultural change and the importance of senior management commitment.

In the case of AOQC, which had its roots in quality assurance and which espoused an engineering model of quality management, attempts to influence federal government were largely unsuccessful until the mid-1980s. At this time, the public inability to differentiate between QA and TQM, combined with a growing national awareness of quality as a world manufacturing issue (in part, a result of the 'success' of the Australia for Quality campaign), led to the growing success of AOQC as a diffusion agency.

In 1990, AOQC set up the Quality Society of Australasia (QSA) with the aim of providing recognition and professional status for quality practitioners. Among others, this organization is supported by Standards Australia, the Institute of Quality Assurance and the National Association of Testing Authorities (Sohal, 1991: 7). Thus, the new peak body for quality in Australia, the Australian Quality Council, has incorporated AOQC/QSA and EA/TQMI into its new offices at St Leonards in Sydney, and represents an attempt to unify the two major components in the diffusion of quality management in Australia. It is within this historical context that the quality movement has developed within Australia and particular models of TQM implementation have been taken up by industry and commerce.

## CULTURAL PLURALISM AND THE ADOPTION OF TQM AT PIRELLI CABLES

The decision to adopt TQM throughout the Pirelli Group's worldwide operations was made at corporate headquarters in Milan. In the case of Pirelli Cables Australia Limited (PCAL), the identification of a number of operational problems which required action, in conjunction with the publicity given to TQM by the media and Australian government, all acted to promote the value of TQM to the senior executive. Although there was no formal cost–benefit analysis, the managing director was attracted to the practical problem-solving approach of TQM, and set a limit of A\$200,000 on accumulated expenses and external costs.

The main benefits were seen to centre on the potential for reducing material wastage (labour accounted for only 10–15 per cent of total operating costs) and at this stage, the cultural change dimension was not fully recognized. However, as the programme developed, it became clear that a shift in employee attitudes and behaviours was central to the attainment of greater employee participation in problem-solving teams. In this way, TQM became redefined as a programme of culture change aimed at securing greater employee involvement through the formation of TQM groups versed in the use of statistics. Worker harmony and the development of high-trust relationships were identified as possible outcomes of developing a common set of behaviours around TQM activities.

As a strategy for cultural change, TQM raises a number of questions about existing organizational values and belief systems. A central assumption of many of the existing schemes is that the development of a single dominant organizational culture will improve the participation rates and commitment of employees and ultimately enable the company to become more competitive. It is argued here, that while it may prove possible to identify a unitary organizational value and belief system within Japanese organizations, this is not the case in many Australia-based organizations. Cultural pluralism is a key element of Australian society and is reflected in the deeper, as opposed to surface-level, elements of organizational culture. For example, following Schein (1985), the surface-level elements of culture can be taken to refer to those things in an organization which are readily accessible and which we can observe directly, such as espoused values articulated in company documents, office layout and dress codes. In contrast, the deeper aspects of culture can be taken to refer to those underlying assumptions and beliefs which evolve as groups attempt to make sense of their collective experience within the work environment. The continuity of Japanese society and the high level of internal solidarity (Moore, 1967: 228–313) contrast with the historical development of Australian society, which has sought to absorb a diverse range of cultures. The significance of these differences has been shown by Hofstede's (1990) study of national cultures across fifty countries. He illustrates how questions on the transferability of new technologies and management techniques would be answered differently according to the national cultures and types of organization under scrutiny, and comments that: 'many US managers and politicians have great problems with recognizing that their type of capitalism is culturally unsuitable for a more collectivist society' (1990: 405).

Unlike Japanese organizations, where it is not uncommon to find the combination of a compliant workforce with parternalistic management (Marsh and Munnari, 1976), the Anglo–American organizations studied placed a higher premium on individualism. It therefore follows that cross-cultural comparisons between Australia and Japan (Iida, 1983) are likely to shed very different results to cross-cultural studies of management systems and practices in Australia and the United States. Furthermore, many Australian companies are characterized by the existence of separate subcultures (which may also take the form of professional cultures) comprising enhancing subcultures which support the status quo; dissenting subcultures which advocate alternative methods and work practices to achieve the core values of an organization (in contrast, counter-culture may be defined as a culture which rejects core organizational values and thereby conflicts with the primary cultural system); orthogonal subcultures which while containing unique beliefs also support the existing organizational culture; and deferential subcultures which defer to and yet are remote from the dominant professional group (for a discussion, see Bloor and Dawson, 1994). These various subcultures may shape the dominant organizational culture in a number of different ways and reflect the strategic positioning and political standing of particular group alliances. Consequently, although many TQM programmes set out to establish cultural homogeneity in the workplace (a dominant and common belief system), these changes are often taking place within organizations which are both ethnically diverse and composed of a range of occupational subcultures. Given the multi-cultural composition of the Australian workforce, the adoption of a unitary model of organizational culture (as espoused in many TQM blueprints) is, at best, problematic. The argument forwarded in this chapter is that some of the core assumptions which pervade TQM schemes are highly inappropriate to the Australian context and may even prove divisive within the multi-cultural workplace. Moreover, while TQM training programmes may secure surface-level cultural transitions and present an image of conformity to newly prescribed values, in practice the shop floor experience of TQM is likely to vary enormously both across and within different companies and industries.

In the case of PCAL, these differences were highlighted between two separate plants, namely a cable manufacturing plant and a cable processing plant, operating within a single manufacturing complex located in South Australia. The former factory comprises comparatively complex equipment for the manufacture of single and multi-core flexible cables. The extrusion equipment is old and therefore requires routine maintenance, the operators are pre-dominantly male (forty-six of the forty-seven employees) and the equipment is operated on a three-shift basis. In contrast, the cable processing plant is predominantly female (ninety of the 106 employees) and is based largely around labour-intensive, repetitive manual processing operations. This plant processes cable manufac-tured by the cable plant in order to service customer requirements (for example, in the type of plug and length of cable).

The empirical material collected on the very different experi-ences and responses to TQM at these two plants was gathered as part of a national programme of case-study research on the introduction and effects of TQM in Australian and New Zealand companies (see Dawson and Palmer, 1993). In the case of PCAL, discussions with the factory manager and familiarization with the manufacturing operations at the Adelaide site have been ongoing since the beginning of 1990. Final agreement on the nature and scale of the case was reached in December 1990 and this was endorsed by the executive management group in February 1991. Data collection is due to be completed in 1994 and to date, four main interview programmes have been conducted, comprising the senior executive group in New South Wales (NSW), the local management team at Pirelli Adelaide, and shop floor and super-visory employees at the cable processing and manufacturing plants in South Australia (SA). Local management data and the human resource management issues are discussed in Storey (1994), and the strategic management of change and the implementation of TQM at Pirelli's Minto site in NSW have been documented else-where (Dawson, 1994). The sections which follow draw mainly from shop floor data collected from Pirelli operations in South Australia (henceforth referred to as Pirelli Adelaide).

## The shop floor experience of TQM in cable processing

The introduction of TQM in the cable processing plant (CPP) was met with a certain degree of scepticism by employees. They were uncertain as to the nature of the programme, concerned about the potential effects on the work process, and doubtful about claims for greater employee involvement. Local management advocated that TQM would enable shop floor personnel to get involved in operational decision-making through group problem-solving meetings. The intention was to get employees with detailed knowledge of shop floor operations to contribute to, and be part of, employee teams which would tackle shop floor problems in order to improve the work process and increase the efficiency of shop floor production.

One of the biggest changes to shop floor operations has been the increase in daily interaction between all employees, which has been supported by TQM activities. TQM is seen to have facilitated greater communication between shop floor personnel and improved employee understanding of the processes involved in manufacturing. For example, there is now a greater willingness among operators to help each other out if there are problems in particular areas. Another change which has stimulated a move towards greater teamwork is the use of feedback statistics based on areas of operation rather than individual achievements. As one interviewee explained:

'Every day our figures are done as a whole, not individually. Total scrap and downtime. Now they are telling people if it is ARTOS's [cutting and stripping machine] fault or moulding fault. Now they are telling us to be careful of certain things in case length is different. It is much better now although it took a while to change people's attitudes. Now they have to sit down and talk as a team. Instead of thinking as individuals they are exchanging views. We have a chart that shows how ARTOS is going and not the individual operators.'

(Shop floor interviews, 1991)

On the question of teamwork and shop floor surveillance, the case data contrast with other empirical findings (Sewell, 1992; Sewell and Wilkinson, 1992). For example, Graham Sewell in a study of K-Electric found that management used TQM and accompanying electronic devices first to identify the work performance of individuals and then to display these performance measures publicly throughout the factory (1992: 26). Within Pirelli, the use of TQM statistics were based on areas of operation, rather than being focused on the acquisition of individual performance measures. According to CPP employees, this promoted greater communication and interaction among staff, and highlighted the importance of the work group. Furthermore, while CPP employees supported the move towards teamwork, the labour process was still structured around one operator per machine, and hence, teamwork activities centred on TQM groups rather than modular work arrangements. Again this contrasts with Sewell's account of Kay, who argued that 'Improvements and innovations in production organisation like task-recombination can only be implemented so long as there is parallel means to managerial control – in this case self-management supported by the electronic Panopticon' (Sewell, 1992: 26).

In other words, although there has been a movement towards self-management on the shop floor – in the sense of employees regulating activities between themselves through monitoring operations and correcting faults – the organization of work remains largely as it was prior to TQM. What has changed is the nature of shop floor control, through the development of high-trust relationships between operators, union representatives and supervisors. Collaboration between employees is now an integral part of newly established routines and a more harmonious system of industrial relations is currently in operation.

In part, the acceptance of TQM in CPP can be explained by the success of the original TQM team, which looked at the problem of downtime with the cable cutting and stripping machines (known as the ARTOS TQM). This team has been held up by local management to demonstrate the success of TQM in Pirelli Cables Adelaide, and to illustrate what can be achieved with the right team tackling the right problem. In practice, however, it has not been easy trying to predict what the potential problems may be within teams (such as interpersonal conflicts), nor whether the areas chosen to tackle are going to lend themselves to group problem-solving techniques. In the view of those interviewed, the ARTOS TQM was instrumental in winning over shop floor employees to the benefits of TQM. For example, a piece of internal correspondence from the production manager to all TQM teams in December 1990 was used to highlight the success of the ARTOS TQM. The document outlined the paid efficiencies for the last eighteen weeks (which averaged out at 103 per cent, compared with 65 per cent for the first ten weeks of TQM) and then set about thanking individual team members for the various contributions, concluding: 'Thanks to all the team, your efforts and ideas is what TQM is all about.' This support and attention from management has further served to boost the morale in CPP and in particular the benefits of TQM to the team members. These individuals in turn influence the views of other operators on the shop floor:

> 'People communicate. Before, they didn't say what was going wrong and you would look at their sheets and ask them what happened, and they wouldn't really say what was wrong. They thought it would reflect on them if they had a problem, rather than complain or say anything, they would put up with it. Everything is a lot more open than it was before.'
>
> (Shop floor interviews, 1991)

Although there is now greater interaction among employees and more open discussions on the daily work problems they encounter, as already indicated, work is still organized largely on a one operator per machine basis. There is also a rate set for each machine which operators are expected to meet and thus the individual monitoring and evaluation of employee performance is still an integral part of the managerial control mechanisms which are in place on the shop floor. Moreover, while teamwork remains largely a function of the group problem-solving activities associated with TQM, interviewees argued that improved interpersonal communication on the shop floor, and the greater collaboration between employees in helping each other out, does signify the movement away from individual-based machine-oriented work regimes, to a work process based on more open communication and greater group effort. In short, the evaluation of TQM by supervisors, operators and union representatives were all favourable and supportive of the more general move towards greater teamwork and collaboration on the shop floor. In the words of one shop floor operator:

'Before, you would do things and you weren't listened to. Usually, you do things and you aren't listened to. Now they write things down, and follow things up. The next week we will ask why something hasn't been done, and there is usually a good reason. You can say things objectively. If you aren't happy with something, they will take note. Before we would say something and you would have to chase it up. Now things are done for us, somebody always follows things up. Before it was just, "OK, we'll look into it", and three weeks later nothing was done. That has changed now.'

(Shop floor interviews, 1991)

## The shop floor experience of TQM in cable manufacturing

The experience of TQM in the cable manufacturing plant (CMP) contrasts in a number of significant ways with that of the cable processing plant. First, while there was general support for the philosophy of TQM, criticisms were levelled at the way in which it was being used and 'abused' within CMP. Second, sectional and interpersonal conflicts were identified as major obstacles to collaborative teamwork and the development of less adversarial systems of operation. Third, the local management team and line supervisors were viewed as a major problem impeding the successful introduction of TQM. Finally, the industry was experiencing a major recession and a number of employees had recently been retrenched. Thus, while issues of employment and job security were a major operator concern, many of them spoke at length about a general failure of management to act upon workers' recommendations:

'Total quality management – it doesn't exist here. You have people here who really have no idea what is going on. They are going along for the ride. A lot of those involved in management are in charge of the meetings and they go on their merry way giving the operators a little bit of paperwork. Their workload doesn't increase but those on the floor have increased their workloads. They want information and the guys on the floor treat it as a joke . . . I dropped out of one [TQM team] because they listen to you, but nothing is done. You can only bang your head on a brick wall for so long before it starts to hurt. Like I

183

said, we started out with two pieces of paperwork and now it is eight pieces of paperwork, all through TQM.'

(Shop floor interviews, 1991)

There was a general feeling among shop floor employees that action should be taken to make Pirelli Adelaide more profitable so that customers could be retained and the further retrenchment of staff would not be necessary. On this count, the operators described the frustration which they felt through working within a system (with TQM) which had improved the communication between management and the shop floor, but which had not changed management's willingness to act upon the recommendations made by operators. TQM was seen to have created more work for operators and yet had failed to deliver on the promise of employee involvement in management decision-making. While it was recognized that TQM had facilitated greater liaison between various occupational groups and hierarchical levels within the plant, it was claimed that management action remained the preserve of 'management'. In practice, this meant that if a TQM team suggestion was made by a manager or supervisor, then there was a good chance that it would be acted upon immediately; whereas if a suggestion was made by operators, it would take a considerable time before any action was taken, and then only if continual support for the suggestion had been made by employees and the recommendation had been restated over a number of months. In short, the communication channels had been opened with TQM, but the monopoly on ideas for decision-making had remained in the hands of management. This 'split' between management and the workers was also seen to be reflected in the management of the TQM teams, which were largely structured on a hierarchical basis. As one operator recalled:

'At the TQM meetings, I will say as much as I want to say, but I have to work here still. We had a meeting last Tuesday. They asked us to try things different ways, and we do, but the moment we ask them to do something, they say "No, we can't do that." They expect us to give, but they won't do anything for us.'

(Shop floor interviews, 1991)

Many of the employees interviewed commented that operators should be given the chance to run TQM meetings. They claimed that the majority of supervisors did not have a detailed knowledge of the machines being operated on the shop floor and hence were not able to decide the best course of action. The lack of knowledge about shop floor operations among line supervisors created an additional antagonism among shop floor personnel; namely, that their supervisors did not have an adequate knowledge base form from which to 'trouble shoot' in the case of machine breakdowns or operator difficulties. As a result, operators felt unable to go to the supervisor for help: 'If my machine went wrong, I couldn't go to a supervisor because they don't know a thing about it.' In short, one of the biggest failings of local management was seen to stem from their inability to relate to shop floor workers.

The shop floor perceptions and attitudes of management in CMP contrast with those in CPP, highlighting how similar implementation strategies may not have the same effects between plants located on the same manufacturing complex. They also indicate the importance of TQM team formation, and the early 'success' of TQM groups in stimulating further enthusiasm and support from the shop floor. In the case of CMP, both the supervisors and operators agree that when TQM was first introduced they tried to achieve too much too soon, and consequently achieved very little. Operators also indicated that they felt that TQM was a 'dead loss' when it was first introduced into the plant, and that within a couple of months they had developed a far more positive attitude towards TQM. After a further twelve months the employees interviewed indicated that they had returned to their original view. They advocated that TQM was a 'waste of time' the way it was being practised in the cable manufacturing plant.

In evaluating the effects of TQM on shop floor operations, interviewees claimed that many of the problems experienced on the shop floor were the result of management incompetence and their failure to ensure that trained operators were working reliable machines. They claimed that poorly trained, ill-equipped operators will produce scrap no matter how many TQM teams management initiate. From a shop floor perspective, training was therefore identified as a major issue which wasn't being tackled adequately by management. The common view on the shop floor was that employees should have comprehensive training provided for the machines which they were expected to operate. In addition, interviewees argued that the machines provided should be able to operate at the set standards. From an operator perspective, working conditions had deteriorated, morale had plummeted and the solution to the problem, while obvious, was overlooked by management and the blame was laid to rest on the workers.

The worsening of employee relations and a heightening of conflict between local management and shop floor personnel highlights how the introduction of TQM has not facilitated the replacement of compliance through an employment contract with active employee cooperation (Wilkinson *et al.*, 1991: 24). Conversely, the cultural change programme has clarified the conflict of interest between various occupational groups and the existence of overlapping and competing value and belief systems. Management have been criticized for appearing to use their positions of power and influence to replace disruptive staff and reward those who conform to the newly prescribed set of TQM values. In this way, the introduction of TQM is seen to represent an attempt by management to establish cultural homogeneity (a dominant and common belief system) through the use of cultural change training programmes. However, the long-standing male-engineering sub-culture of manufacturing employees has clashed with the surface-level cultural changes promoted by TQM. These workers oppose the establishment of quality programmes, through questioning the competency of management to tackle the 'real' issues on the shop floor. In the words of one operator:

> 'It has got worse. To try and save money and cut down on the scrap, they are pushing sick machines as hard as they can. They are running shorter jobs, they are keeping levels up but the scrap isn't really coming down. . . . If the machine breaks down it is a relief. You don't see anyone unhappy when the machine breaks down. It is not just because of the time off, it is just relief. One broke down for four or five days, and the operator was over the moon.'
>
> (Shop floor interviews, 1991)

## COMPARATIVE SHOPFLOOR ISSUES AND COMMON CULTURAL THEMES

The two cases illustrate how the shop floor experience of TQM can vary enormously, both across and within different companies and industries. In the case of PCAL, these differences are highlighted between two separate plants operating within a single

186

manufacturing complex located in South Australia. For example, within the cable processing plant, TQM was generally seen as a positive development which had improved the work environment of supervisors and shop floor employees; whereas, within the cable manufacturing plant, TQM was criticized heavily by shop floor staff. The context of the plant, the local experience of TQM and the gender composition of the factory have all influenced employee perceptions and attitudes towards TQM. For example, opportunities for greater communication and interaction were viewed as a positive and non-threatening development by many of the female operators working at CPP and contrasted with CMP, where the male definition of 'worker value' was far more rooted in the technical and engineering elements of the labour process. In addition, the turnover of employees with CPP was greater than CMP; with the latter workforce, the job was seen as a mark of social standing outside as well as within the work environment. In other words, the male operators tended to define themselves by their job, in contrast to the female operators, who viewed their work as one element within a matrix of roles. In CMP, the downturn in the market for manufactured products posed major problems for employees who had spent a working lifetime within the company and were being threatened with compulsory redundancies. In this plant, the fear of unemployment significantly reduced the morale of staff and heightened their resistance to TQM, which was perceived as a new management technique for reducing staff requirements through making operations more efficient. In contrast, redundancies were not imposed on permanent full-time operators in CPP, as the plant was largely able to absorb the downturn through the non-replacement of staff (natural wastage). Whether female operators would have been so accommodating to change if their jobs had also been threatened remains questionable, although the contrasting values placed on the job as defining social status would also seem to have influenced the response of employees to the change process.

Apart from the differences between the two plants, there were also a number of similarities – in particular, on the question of English-language fluency and ethnic origin as a factor facilitating and inhibiting employee involvement in TQM, and the problems of interpersonal conflict and poor communication between the different shift operators:

'We have problems with nationalities. We have got Portuguese, Yugoslavs, Maltese, Australians, English – that causes problems. There is not much trust in our section between the three different shifts. If you think someone has done you a dirty, it is very easy to get them back. But you may be only imagining it. We have two operators who haven't spoken in the last three years. They don't even acknowledge each other. Personality clashes . . . it is pathetic and I don't believe it is as bad as some of the operators think it is, but there are definite problems.'

(Shop floor interviews, 1991)

Within both plants, it was claimed that the majority of staff who were not involved (apart from the nightshift) were Asians and did not understand English that well. As one interviewee commented:

'Sometimes the language barrier is too much of a problem. We can't explain everything that is going on that clearly in the meetings. I think it is also their culture that they don't bring up trouble. They just do their job and then they go home.'

(Shop floor interviews, 1991)

There are a number of people employed at PCAL who are not fluent in the English language. This raises the problem of communication between employees – who are now expected to work together as a team rather than as individual machine operators – and within the TQM teams themselves. For the most part, there has been a general reluctance for those who speak English as a foreign language to get involved in the TQM groups. Although attempts to integrate these employees into TQM initiatives have been made, there remain a number of problems to full involvement:

'The language barrier is a problem. It puts TQM out of its momentum if you have to talk really slowly. It embarrasses them, too, if they have to sit in front of ten guys. We now have English lessons to try and better them as operators. This one guy panics, he goes too fast for himself. We try to slow him down, but he goes too fast.'

(Shop floor interviews, 1991)

English classes for non-English-speaking employees are provided by the company. These classes are scheduled twice a week for two hours (one hour company time and one hour private time). Although this programme is serving to improve the situation, the capacity for TQM to involve non-English-speaking personnel remains severely constrained by the language difficulties these people encounter. Furthermore, the attitudinal differences expressed within the dominant Anglo-Australian culture compared with the other ethnic groups also serves to impede multi-cultural integration within the workplace. As a shop floor supervisor commented:

'When they [the different ethnic groups] first came they stayed together a lot of the time. Some of them just didn't speak because they have been used to not being able to. Some will always put their eyes down and not look at you when they speak, not because they are afraid, but because that is the way they have been brought up. But lately I have noticed that the Australian girls have been sitting with the others. It is a lot better than it used to be. They seem happy, which is good.'

(Supervisor, 1991)

From the experience of introducing TQM at PCAL, language and ethnicity are therefore key factors which may act to constrain severely the degree of employee involvement among non-English-speaking employees. While this point may appear obvious, its significance should not be under-estimated, given the decision-making authority being invested in the TQM teams. Moreover, in contrast to the work of Wilkinson *et al.* (1992: 4–5), TQM was not a compulsory activity within PCAL, but rather was introduced as a voluntary programme. However, access to the programme was severely constrained and the problems of culture and language tend to be overlooked when discussing employees' reluctance to be involved with TQM. The general assumption is that the option is there for any who wish to take it, as one operator commented in criticizing people who didn't want to be involved in TQM:

'Well, they still have to change as they go. If they don't like the changes, bad luck, they are introduced anyway. They have to accept the fact that the changes are happening. If they are not involved, then they are stuck with the fact that they are changing. I don't see why anyone wouldn't want to be in on it.'

(Shop floor interviews, 1991)

This in turn raises the question of the voluntary nature of TQM. On the one hand, it is argued that people do not have to get involved in TQM, and on the other hand, it is argued that those who do not wish to be involved must nevertheless accept and live by the decisions of the TQM group. In this sense, TQM is not compulsory, freely open to all employees (in not being able to accommodate non-English speaking employees adequately) or a non-threatening voluntary activity (in that decisions made within TQM groups could have significant consequences for the reorganization of work of those not involved). In short, TQM is a philosophy of change based upon open communication and employee involvement in the organization and control of work. The main thrust of these changes is towards collaborative teamwork, multi-skilling and cultural commitment. In practice, however, there are a number of contextual and cultural factors which can influence the speed, direction and shape of change, and these have been illustrated in discussing the different shop floor experiences of the cable processing and cable manufacturing plants at Pirelli Cables Adelaide.

## CONCLUSION

One of the main strategic objectives behind introducing TQM into Australian organizations has been to promote employee commitment and participation in continuous process innovation for the purpose of improving operational efficiencies and gaining a competitive edge. Although TQM has many of its roots in the principles of total quality control, the main objective of current programmes centres on revising existing organizational attitudes and belief systems. Attempts to manage organizational culture towards some questionable common features within multi-cultural workplaces are at odds with the reality of Australian management practice. It should be remembered that Japanese management arose in the context of an extraordinarily homogeneous society, thereby setting the context within which cultural pluralism was deemed unacceptable. In contrast, the continual redefinition of cultural norms within Australian society reflect not only the changing ethnic composition of the workforce, but also attempts to accommodate multi-culturalism and the diverse range of interest groups with different allegiances, expectations and values. In this sense, there is the added dimension of changing ethnic composition linked with the pre-existing cultural pluralism, which highlights the importance of contextualizing change initiatives which

190

seek to 'manage' value and beliefs systems of employees working within organizations.

In the case of PCAL, employee participation in TQM teams was a voluntary activity. Union representatives did not view TQM as a threat, and supported employee involvement. The main potential benefits for employees centred on removing irritating and some-times regular problems in their daily work tasks, being able to express concerns and frustrations openly to management, and being able to withdraw from the shop floor for scheduled TQM team meetings. From a company perspective, the potential for improved communication and employee morale, combined with the possibility of improvements in efficiency rates and reductions in scrap, acted as a major financial incentive to continue with the TQM scheme. However, one of the hidden inequalities of TQM was that while all employees were expected to abide by the decisions made by the TQM teams, employees did not have equal opportunity to participate. The TQM scheme was based on a unitary notion of culture and was ill-suited to the development of total employee involvement in a multi-cultural workplace.

In the example of Pirelli Adelaide, English-language fluency and ethnic origin were major constraining forces in the proposed move towards a total quality organization. Communication is at the heart of TQM, and an inability to communicate effectively (in cases where English is a second, third or even fourth language) is a significant obstacle to employee involvement in group problem-solving teams. Moreover, the views and beliefs of employees who did not form part of the dominant Anglo-Australian culture were largely down-played or ignored in group decision-making activities. Consequently, some ethnic minority groups and non-fluent English-speaking employees remain outside of TQM, not because of an unwillingness to be involved, but because of an inability for employee involvement programmes to accommodate these groups and/or individuals adequately. Thus, TQM in Australia is neither voluntary nor freely open to all employees regardless of English-language difficulties or ethnicity; but rather, it may be seen as an adaptation of a Japanese management technique for securing employee commitment within organizations which are not com-posed of multi-ethnic groups. The emphasis placed on employee participation rather than compliance, group performance rather than individual performance, and change rather than stability, assumes the existence of a homogeneous workforce and fails to tackle some of the major problems associated with the introduction of TQM in multi-cultural societies. While TQM may be described as a management strategy for cultural change, ironically it fails to accommodate or account for the possibility of cultural heterogeneity. Within such organizational contexts, TQM can never fully achieve its aim of total employee involvement, and in some cases may even serve to sustain and create ethnic divisions within the workplace.

# REFERENCES

Albrecht, K. (1992) *The Only Thing That Matters: Bringing the Power of the Customer into the Centre of your Business* New York: Harper Business.

Allan, C. (1991) 'The Role of Diffusion Agents in the Transfer of Quality Management in Australia', unpublished honours thesis, Brisbane: University of Griffith.

Bloor, G. and Dawson, P. (1994) 'Understanding Professional Culture in Organizational Context', *Organization Studies*, 15 (2), 279–99.

Brocka, B. and Brocka, M. (1992) *Quality Management: Implementing the Best Ideas of the Masters,* Chicago, IL: Business One Irwin.

Dawson, P. (1994) *Organizational Change: A Processual Approach,* London: Paul Chapman Publishing.

Dawson, P. and Palmer, G. (1993) 'Total Quality Management in Australian and New Zealand Companies: Some Emerging Themes and Issues', *International Journal of Employment Studies*, 1 (1), 115–36.

Dawson, P. and Patrickson, M. (1991) 'Total Quality Management in the Australian Banking Industry', *International Journal of Quality and Reliability Management*, 8 (5), 66–76.

Foley, K. (1987) *Report of the Committee of Review of Standards, Accreditation and Quality Control and Assurance*, Canberra: Australian Government Publishing Service.

Hill, S. (1991) 'Why Quality Circles Failed but Total Quality Management Might Succeed', *British Journal of Industrial Relations*, 29 (4), 541–68.

Hofstede, G. (1990) 'The Cultural Relativity of Organizational Practices and Theories', in D. Wilson and R. Rosenfeld (eds) *Managing Organizations: Text, Readings and Case*, London: McGraw-Hill.

Iida, T. (1983) 'Transferability of Japanese Managerial Systems and Practices into Australian Companies', *Human Resources Management Australia*, August, 23–7.

Marsh, R.M. and Munnari, H. (1976) *Modernization and the Japanese Factor*, Princeton, NJ: Princeton University Press.

Moore, B. (1967) *Social Origins of Dictatorship and Democracy*, Harmondsworth: Penguin.

Schein, E. (1985) *Organizational Culture and Leadership*, San Francisco, CA: Jossey-Bass.

Sewell, G. (1992) '"Someone to Watch Over Me": A Tale of Shop Floor

Surveillance in a Total Quality Organisation', paper prepared for the ISA's Joint Symposium on Comparative Sociology and the Sociology of Organisations, Tokyo and Kurashiki, Japan, 3–7 July.

Sewell, G. and Wilkinson, B. (1992) 'Personnel Management in Surveillance Companies', paper prepared for the Workshop on Personnel Management and Technical Change, Industrial Relations Research Unit, University of Warwick, 29 September.

Sohal, A. (1991) 'Editorial', *International Journal of Quality and Reliability Management*, 8 (5), 7–8.

Sprouster, J. (1984) *Total Quality Control: The Australian Experience*, Cammeray: Horwitz Grahame.

Storey, J. (ed.) (1994) *New Wave Manufacturing Strategies*, London: Paul Chapman Publishing.

Tenner, A. and DeToro, I. (1992) *Total Quality Management: Three Steps to Continuous Improvement*, Reading, MA: Addison-Wesley.

Wilkinson, A., Allen, P. and Snape, E. (1991) 'TQM and the Management of Labour', *Employee Relations*, 13 (1), 24–31.

Wilkinson, A., Marchington, M., Goodman, J. and Ackers, P. (1992) 'Total Quality Management and Employee Involvement', *Human Resource Management Journal*, 2 (4), 1–20.

# 8

# TQM, THE NEW TRAINING AND INDUSTRIAL RELATIONS*

*Ken Roberts and Yvonne Corcoran-Nantes*

## THE NEW TRAINING

This is not the first occasion where an enquiry's aims changed during an investigation. The research was originally planned in 1989, at a time when Britain had experienced eight years of continuous economic growth, when full employment had returned to some parts of the country, and when there were widespread reports of skill shortages, which were expected to intensify as technological and occupational change made increasingly high demands. The 'demographic timebomb' was widely publicized; beginning workers were to become scarce and it was argued that employers would need to train other groups, such as adult women and the unemployed (Payne, 1991). An under-qualified and under-skilled workforce was said to be a major barrier to Britain's economic ascent (Cassels, 1990; Layard, 1992). Such was the thinking behind the numerous government programmes to encourage employers to undertake more training, and to encourage young and older workers to seek more qualifications and skills (Employment Department, 1992).

This was the context in which we embarked upon case studies in nine large establishments. The initial aim was to discover how these businesses were addressing their skill problems. Two of the establishments were oil refineries, two were car assembly plants, and

---

* The research on which this paper is based was funded by the Employment Department, but the views expressed are solely those of the authors.

194

another two were sites of a leading manufacturer of telecommunications products. In addition, we studied two regional divisions of a recently privatized service industry, and the sole UK site of a motor vehicle component manufacturer. We make no claims that these establishments were representative British businesses. However, their sheer size meant that even if they were grossly untypical, trends in their workforces would still have been of national importance. The research was basically qualitative, though much quantitative information was collected about each establishment. During 1991, 269 interviews were conducted with the site managers and within specimen sections of the workforces to obtain the various groups' experiences and views on how the organizations had changed in recent years, together with their assessments of the costs and benefits. The specimen workforce sections were always selected so that they illustrated the application of the sites' general human resource strategies, and they were invariably of strategic importance in the businesses. In the car plants, we interviewed staff in final trim and assembly, and on the catalytic convertors in the oil refineries. We deliberately avoided peripheral units. Section heads, personnel and training officers, and any workforce representatives were always interviewed together with members of the grades that predominated in the units. Our questions were mostly about the individuals' experiences of recent changes in their jobs, their opportunities to acquire skills and qualifications and thereby progress in the workplaces.

We learnt very quickly that none of the establishments had skill shortages or deficits at any level. Nor were any future difficulties anticipated in recruiting, training and retaining the quantities and types of labour required. Were the businesses untypical in these respects? A careful scrutiny of the evidence which had led to forecasts of skill gaps showed that at the height of the 1980s boom, the majority of firms reported no such problems, the proportion reporting any difficulties was no higher than in the 1970s, and in the majority of cases where problems were reported these proved short-lived and did not interfere with production (Confederation of British Industry/Manpower Services Commission, 1987; IFF Research, 1990, 1991, 1992). During the course of our research we developed an alternative set of more plausible hypotheses; that the qualifications and skills of Britain's workforce have pulled well ahead of demand, that workers are facing increasing difficulties in obtaining employment commensurate with their skills and qualifications, that there is a growing problem of employees' vocational aspirations being frustrated, and that increasing numbers are having to reconcile themselves to jobs which make little use of their known abilities, not to mention latent talents.

The weight of the evidence suggests that the businesses that we studied were typical of large UK companies, though not of small firms (see Vickerstaff, 1991), in feeling able to hire and train up to their skill requirements. They were also typical, with the exception of the former nationalized industry, in having increased their training during the 1980s (Training Agency, 1990; Employment Department, 1992). Seven out of the nine establishments were spending more on training, employed more training staff, and were providing more days of training per employee. The former nationalized industry differed not so much in the type of training regime that was emerging, as in its point of departure. In the past it had invested heavily in training, and since privatization was seeking to restructure the outlay so as to obtain better value.

There have been numerous studies which claim to document British industry's historic failure to undertake enough high-quality training, and a variety of proposed remedies (see Ainley and Corney, 1990; Senker, 1992; Sheldrake and Vickerstaff, 1987), but no prior forecasts that training would take off in the late 1980s. The following passages use our case study evidence to discuss the significance of this growth of training which, in the firms that we studied, was best understood as part of a broader set of interrelated changes which were generally referred to, by the site managers, as a movement towards total quality management (TQM).

## TQM IN CONTEXT

During the 1980s TQM became a worldwide management fashion. In the early 1990s a survey of British Institute of Management members found that 71 per cent of the respondents' organizations had implemented formal quality campaigns (Wilkinson *et al.*, 1993). By then, however, social science had learnt to be sceptical about such movements. It was known, firstly, that talk of 'job enrichment' and suchlike sometimes concealed an underlying degradation of labour. It was also known that previous fashions had proved short-lived. There had been quality circles and many other previous attempts to strengthen employee motivation, thereby improving corporate effectiveness, leading to more successful firms and satisfied workforces. It has been argued, however, most persistently and persuasively by Stephen Hill (this volume), that TQM may prove different in so far as previous movements sought only limited change, without tampering with the basic organizational contexts. TQM seeks total change, excellence at all levels and in all quarters of an organization. It seeks to involve all employees, from shopfloor to senior management, in a quality improvement culture. It is not just tacked on, so this argument runs, but promises a fundamental overhaul of the labour process (Hill, 1991).

However, such fundamental changes as were underway in the firms that we studied were not the straightforward result of the top managers reading TQM manuals. The changes were certainly influenced by, but were not really driven by, the TQM philosophy. Our case study firms were probably typical British businesses in this respect; in the British Institute of Management survey, quality campaigns were reported as being primarily market-driven (Wilkinson *et al.*, 1993). The changes that had been implemented in the companies that we studied were really the only responses compatible with survival, given the firms' market situations in the 1980s. All the companies had reduced their workforces during this period. Some of the contractions had been dramatic – from over 13,000 to under 4,000 at one of the telecommunications sites, for example. This was one reason why none of the firms faced skill shortages. Dispensing with rather than hiring labour had been firms' major personnel problem in the recent past; their demands on the labour market had been modest. All the companies had introduced severance schemes. Early retirement had been available to older employees, and all the companies had made some staff redundant. When redundancies had been voluntary, they had also been selective and targeted. The terms were not offered to all staff, while the managements had been proactive in letting dispensable staff know that they had no future on the sites.

Loss of business was never a reason for the contractions. Business had increased everywhere; the sites had become leaner and more efficient. The site managements had been given no alternative. They were typically competing not only against other firms, but against other sites within the same companies. Site managements normally had considerably latitude on personnel matters such as pay, hiring, training and staff deployment, whereas the company headquarters always made the big investment decisions. In order to obtain life-giving investment, the site managements knew that they had to look attractive in terms of unit costs.

New technology was always implicated in the job losses, but changed work practices had typically been a condition for as well as a consequence of the advent of new technology. There had been major changes in the organization of work on all the sites, which invariably amounted to virtually everyone doing more. The sheer amount of work required of each employee had increased, and so had the range of tasks. All the organizations had become flatter – entire levels had been eliminated from the management hierarchies and responsibilities had been pushed downwards. In some way or another, individuals and work groups had been made responsible for guaranteeing the quantity and quality of their work. So in addition to work becoming more intense, employees' responsibilities had become heavier, and there had been a parallel trend towards multi-skilling. The number of separate recognized crafts had been reduced and operatives had been made responsible for routine maintenance. All the firms were seeking functional flexibility within their core workforces. On the shop floors the aim was to have every employee capable of performing every task within a team or section, so that staff could cover for each other's absences during holidays, illnesses and off-the-job training. There is evidence that trends towards job expansion and work intensification were occurring throughout the UK economy in the 1980s (see Gallie and White, 1993; O'Reilly, 1993). On some of the sites that we studied there had been a simultaneous trend towards numerical flexibility, which had been achieved, in most cases, by making more use of subcontractors to cope with peaks in the workflow and occasional skill requirements (see Harrison and Kelley, 1993). In some respects the drive for quality was laying a benign veneer over work regimes which required everyone to do more and bear heavier responsibilities. While on one level TQM was an organizational choice, most of the underlying changes were really survival imperatives, given the firms' market situations.

Training was being developed to produce 'quality' workforces that could cope with the new job specifications, and recruitment had also been overhauled to ensure that only quality applicants survived the sifting. Training had not been developed to enable the sites to cope with recruits with wider ranges of ability, qualifications or prior experience than in the past. Rather, the trend had been to recruit only applicants who corresponded closely to the ideal specification. When recruiting graduates, the companies had begun restricting their searches to those with good degrees in the right subjects. When recruiting apprentices the firms had begun insisting on ABCs in GCSE. When hiring operatives the firms looked for applicants with good work records in similar businesses. Even recruitment for the operator grades had often become an extended process lasting several days and involving tests of ability and aptitude, in addition to the customary interviews and medicals.

Attracting the right types and number of applicants was never a serious problem. When they advertised operative vacancies, all the sites were inundated. Their scope for choice when recruiting to more specialized posts was simply less overwhelming. All the sites were attractive places to work for people in the local labour markets – the companies were household names, they were able to offer at least modest careers in the internal labour markets to all grades, and their rates of pay, for manual employees, were always well above the local labour market averages. On all the sites, the lowest-paid operatives earned in excess of £15,000 in 1991. This was not because the managements were soft on wage issues – good pay had never been conceded voluntarily, but had always been negotiated by the trade unions, and on all the sites labour costs per unit of output had declined. The sites were willing to pay in excess of the local labour market norms, provided this enabled them to attract and retain high-quality, highly productive work-forces. Staff retention was never considered a problem, except among young graduates. Among all other groups, turnover was extremely low on all the sites. The managements knew that the offer of a job could be the equivalent of a pools win, and that dismissal or enforced redundancy could be a socio-economic death sentence.

Training was a key factor in the packages of changes that were in process. This was perhaps to be expected, given the emphasis on training in certain sections of the quality movement: 'training is the single most important factor in actually improving quality' (Oakland, 1989: 263). In the firms that we studied, training was being developed so as to produce quality employees and continuously improve them so that they would do quality work, satisfy customers and keep the firms successful, thereby enabling the staff to be well rewarded, which would motivate them to seek further training, thus continuing the virtuous spiral. Unlike some of the enterprises in previous case studies (Wilkinson *et al.*, 1992; Wilkinson, 1994), the firms that we investigated were not neglecting the 'soft' human resource factors in their drives for quality. Personnel and training specialists were not marginal, but were expected to operate as crucial change agents. Training was to ensure that the structural changes that were being introduced were reinforced by cultural change, and there were some theoretical grounds for anticipating success. The meaning of skill is a matter for debate. Is it an objective property of a task or set of tasks, or of an employee, or is skill simply subjectively attributed or claimed? Whatever the underlying reality, there is plenty of evidence to show that workers who are treated as skilled, and who regard themselves as skilled, tend to be willing to consent, or at least to comply, with managements' goals and methods, and regulate their own work accordingly (Sturdy *et al.*, 1993). It has been argued that lean production is destined to take over throughout the world because it is efficient for organizations and challenging for skilled employees (Womack *et al.*, 1990). Furthermore, there is some case study evidence which indicates that TQM is well received on shop floors and that workers can be persuaded to identify with quality improvement programmes (see Hill, this volume). Would training operate within TQM in the way that the managements intended in our case study firms?

Senior managers in all the companies offered optimistic accounts of the changes that were under way. They argued that all employees, at least those who remained on the payrolls, were benefiting from jobs that were better paid, more interesting and more challenging than in the past. They spoke of the emergence of training cultures in which employees would identify and then act upon their own training needs, thereby harmonizing personal and corporate development and eroding collective conflict. However, we shall explain that lower-level employees in all the companies knew that the changes were not automatically delivering any benefits to them. They may have been acquiring new skills, but they were simultaneously being subjected to tighter control (see also Webster and Robins, 1993). Their work may have become more challenging, but it was also harder and more relentless, and there were clear signs that, if and when they could mobilize sufficient power, employees were prepared to resist these regimes (see also Berggren, 1993). In so far as they were deriving any benefits from TQM, shopfloor employees knew that such gains had to be won through bargaining. And they knew that the benefits of the changes were unequally distributed. In particular, they knew that they could expect little career progression from their new training opportunities. Their new training was not leading to upgraded, higher-level jobs. Nor was it all really new. Our evidence suggests that much of the growth in training that was recorded throughout British industry in the 1980s, and which held up during the recession of the early 1990s, was not creating a better-equipped, higher-grade workforce, but was simply the result of formally organizing and recognizing what had previously been accomplished informally.

## THE TRADITIONAL AND THE NEW

In all the companies that we studied, the trends in skill formation were evolutionary rather than revolutionary. What we describe as 'new training' was basically a bureaucratization of what had previously been a less formal process. The new training, mostly composed of short modules, in which specific skills were taught, then sometimes tested and certified, was not entirely new in any of the companies. However, it was expanding rapidly in all but the recently privatized business. New training was being created by bureaucratizing informal skill acquisition, whereby techniques had once been learnt and know-how passed on between colleagues and from foremen while everyone did their normal jobs, and informal recognition of an individual's skills could lead eventually to promotion to a key job, usually better paid than others, and eventually into a supervisory position. Informal skill acquisition was being reinforced in training periods, which were organized by designated training staff, and at the end of these periods the employees' skills could be systematically tested then certified.

One outcome of this new training was a proliferation of staff with training in their job titles. This was largely a result of formally recognizing a set of tasks once implicit in supervisory roles, though it also indicated a change in supervisory style towards leading and facilitating, rather than just instructing, rewarding and punishing. Foremen had always been expected to show their men how to use new tools and how to tackle particularly complicated jobs. They had also been expected to ensure that their men performed properly. Teaching and quality control had always been implicit in the responsibility of running a unit, though most of the instruction, guidance and appraisal had occurred incidentally, embedded in broader day-to-day interaction. Jobs with training in the title were being designated through rendering these responsibilities explicit, thereby creating roles bearing some resemblance to the German *meister*.

The new training and its certificates were not replacing but coexisting alongside 'traditional' academic and vocational qualifications, and the courses through which these were obtained. In traditional vocational qualifications we include City and Guilds intermediate and final certificates, ONCs, HNCs and their BTEC equivalents, HNDs, professional institute membership, post-qualifying and postgraduate certificates and diplomas. Labelling these qualifications as traditional is not meant to imply that they were necessarily outdated. Some such syllabuses that our respondents were following were only recently introduced. Moreover, the 'traditional' label does not indicate that the qualifications were in decline. Indeed, on the sites that we investigated, the numbers of employees who were pursuing and obtaining such qualifications were usually increasing. This was particularly true of management and supervisory qualifications. Ambitious shop-floor workers and professionally qualified staff in engineering, for example, were enrolling for certificates and diplomas in management studies. However, this *type* of qualification was traditional in the sense of being long established, and the recent growth of new training had been much more dramatic. The main differences between the new and the traditional are most easily described in ideal types which intentionally exaggerate the dominant tendencies within each and ignore the deviations and exceptions, of which, needless to say, we encountered many. Table 8.1 summarizes the main differences.

### Length

Courses leading to intermediate and final City and Guilds certificates, and BTECs, all lasted for a year or longer, and usually much longer on a part-time basis. Also, the courses and qualifications in this traditional sector had always been cumulative. Students were able to continue progressively for many years, up to the end of their working lives in some cases, always 'moving up' as well as

*Table 8.1* Traditional and new qualifications

|  | *New* | *Traditional* |
| --- | --- | --- |
| Length of courses | Short | Long |
| Provider | Employer | College |
| Primary validation | Employer | Education/profession |
| Funder | Employer | Student/public |
| Motivation | Compulsory part of job | Student initiative |
| Prime beneficiary | Employer | Student |
| Career role | Horizontal expansion or keep up-to-date | Vertical progress |

moving 'on'. The courses and qualifications were arranged in a sequential hierarchy. It was necessary, for example, to hold the ONC or the academic equivalent before proceeding to HNC, which could then be followed by an HND. A student following these traditional courses rarely back-tracked. It was assumed, for example, that a professional engineer would have the generic knowledge to move laterally into an adjacent field, such as from hardware into software. It was not just the length of specific courses, but this sequential organization, that meant that progressive careers as a traditional student could be extremely long running.

The new training in the companies that we studied was organized differently. Modules would be completed in hours, days, or weeks at the outside. At the end of a module the trainee's skills would be tested and certified. At some later date the individual might receive more training to refresh and update, or to add new skills. This further training would sometimes, but not necessarily, build directly upon the previous training, and in this sense lead to a higher level of skill and knowledge than earlier. This meant that, however much new training was accomplished, there would not be the same vertical distance between the starting and finishing points as within the traditional system.

Some traditional courses leading to diplomas and certificates were quite short, but these were fairly exclusive to the postgraduate and post-experience levels for employees who were already fully qualified professionals. Conversely, new training was sometimes of extended duration, typically initial post-entry training which combined the old and the new, and could last for up to four years in the case of apprenticeships. However, adult recruits were always given quicker inductions. Prolonged training of the new type was a once-and-for-all-time privilege for some, but certainly not all employees, at the beginning of their working lives.

## Providers

New training was normally provided by the employers. The internal–external contrast was among the clearest distinctions between the new and the traditional. The firms typically provided the space, materials, equipment and – normally the most expensive item of all – the trainers' and the trainees' time. New training often occurred in the employees' normal workplaces and was given by everyday supervisors. Alternatively it could be delivered in training centres by specialist training officers. In contrast, traditional courses were normally taken off-site, typically in colleges, and delivered by teachers who were employed by these establishments.

## Validation

Traditional courses had always been designed and approved, and the eventual qualifications awarded by educational or professional groups. Employers were often, indeed normally, represented on these bodies, but it was never possible for firms to manipulate the courses and certification processes entirely in their own particular interests. Once a qualification became available, it was then up to firms to decide whether to recognize it in their recruitment and promotion, and whether to encourage employees to study for it.

In contrast, the new training was being developed and initially recognized by specific employers. If they bought in existing packages, these were normally adapted to the firm's own needs. Any testing following the training was normally by the firm's own supervisors and training staff. Subsequently, and in addition, a firm might seek external validation. At the time of our research, some of the firms had already submitted, or were considering submitting, their training for recognition in the NVQ framework. The oil refineries were involved in trade associations through which NVQs covering their industry's specific needs were being developed. However, this was always secondary, temporally and normatively, to the training matching the firms' own requirements.

*Funding*

The new training was typically wholly employer-funded. It was usually impossible to recoup any of the costs of equipment, materials or the training staff's or trainees' time from any other party. The provision of this training was occasionally supported by, but was rarely dependent on, grants from training boards, the Employment Department, or any other outside organization. Nor were trainees normally expected to contribute. Employees normally saw no reason to contribute even their own time to be trained on their employers' premises, doing courses recommended by their firms, which were intended to improve their job performance. Sometimes they were rewarded with higher pay, but never sufficiently high to break down the feeling that the employer should meet the full costs of training. If they attended courses outside normal working hours, they expected time off in lieu or overtime rates.

Traditional vocational education, in contrast, usually required the students to invest some of their own time, and often also their cash for course fees, books and examinations. Such courses were invariably heavily subsidized through public educational expenditure, so traditional vocational education was typically receiving dual funding – from the students and from the public in general. The firms that we studied sometimes allowed time off, and often paid for books as well as course and examination fees. However, the firms never contributed all the costs. Even sponsored block- and day-release students were invariably expected to contribute some of their own time, for night school and private study, for example. Perhaps most important of all, none of this support was automatically available. All the managements explained that to qualify, a proposition normally had to be job-relevant and potentially useful to the company. Here they meant not only that the course should be related to the employee's occupation, but that the student's age, existing qualifications, current position and job performance should be such as to make success probable, and the qualification useful within the firm. So, for example, none of the companies could see any advantage to themselves, except possibly in terms of goodwill and industrial relations, in sponsoring fifty-year-old production workers through Open University degree courses: 'I look to see if he's going to be something of an investment, whether he can succeed, and whether he has any potential to grow within the company.' Criteria for obtaining company sponsorship were typically vague. This was sometimes a deliberate policy; among other things, it acted as an additional motivation test.

### Motivation

This was another particularly stark contrast between the traditional and the new. Traditional qualifications were normally pursued on students' own initiative. The education would only happen if the students themselves were sufficiently motivated. The new training was different in this respect – it was normally provided and paid for by the employers and was prescribed as a compulsory part of the trainees' jobs. The firms had taken the initiative in generating this training. The essential condition for the training to happen, therefore, was that the employer should be sufficiently motivated.

### Prime beneficiary

The standard management answer to questions about who benefited from any form of training or further education was 'everyone'. The new training was said to give firms employees who were more productive and reliable, who would provide customers with better goods and services, which would expand the firms' markets, leading to higher profits, and better pay and security for all employees. However, the trainees nearly always felt that the firms were the main beneficiaries, which was why they believed that it was up to the companies to provide all the time and other essentials for the training. Pay increments following the successful completion of new training modules, when awarded, had always been negotiated by the trade unions. They were not freely offered by the company managements – rather, they were an outcome of trade union pressure to secure at least some of the benefits of a more effective workforce for the workers themselves, and a more acceptable concession for the employers than all-round pay increases.

Employees and their managers both viewed traditional courses rather differently. The general view here was that the student was the prime beneficiary. The personal benefits could be in the form of self-development and pride in becoming better qualified. However, employees who were pursuing traditional qualifications usually hoped that their efforts would lead to better jobs either within or outside their present companies. It could be argued that everyone stood to benefit from traditional education and qualifications, because employers gained more knowledgeable and better-qualified workforces, from which customers could expect some spin-off, and, at the end of the sequence, all the firms' employees should be benefiting. Nevertheless, the main drive to earn traditional qualifications was from employees who expected benefits, most of which would not be shared by less industrious or less able colleagues.

### Career role

A final contrast was between the roles of the two kinds of education and training in employees' career development. Traditional qualifications were typically a condition for, even if they did not automatically lead to, promotion. This was the benefit that employees normally expected or hoped for, and the reason why they were willing to invest their own time. The new training was different in this respect; it did not normally lead upwards. It typically increased employees' skills horizontally rather than vertically and kept them up-to-date, abreast of changes, and in these senses qualified for their current occupations rather than higher-level posts.

The students' benefits from traditional courses could be substantial. These qualifications could govern the grades at which they entered, or to which they rose within their companies, though such benefits were not guaranteed. Academic qualifications have never conferred a 'right' to a commensurate job, and likewise with traditional vocational credentials. It was well understood by all the groups that we interviewed, from senior managers to the hourly paid, that benefiting from traditional qualifications depended on having them at the right time and being in the right place. School qualifications were useful only if held at the time of school-leaving. None of the managers or other employees that we interviewed could see any point in established staff seeking more GCSEs or A-levels for career reasons. Other qualifications were best earned when young, in time to join the career streams. So some employees in their mid-twenties saw no point in enrolling for courses leading to HNCs or degrees; their time had gone. 'Even the young lads who're going to night school won't catch the grads up. . . . Further education isn't for run-of-the-mill craftsmen.

There's no gain in it for most people. There's no guarantee that you'll be made up, so there's no incentive.'

## CONFLICTING MOTIVATIONS

At the time of our fieldwork, traditional and new vocational qualifications were being situated within a common framework by the National Council for Vocational Qualifications. This framework suggested that certificated in-service training composed partly or even wholly of on-the-job learning might eventually make an employee as well qualified as the holder of a BTEC level 3 or even level 5. However, whether the new training could really function to this effect was always going to depend less on the intentions of the National Council that accredited the awards than their uses in work situations, especially in hiring and promotion. Our evidence suggests that new training would not necessarily become a functional equivalent to traditional courses and qualifications in the establishments that we studied, even when it led to NVQs. This was partly because new training was not normally cumulative in the same sense as traditional courses. Equally fundamentally, traditional and new qualifications were serving different purposes. New training was intended to make individuals flexible, up-to-date, effective and efficient primarily within their current occupations, whereas traditional qualifications helped to determine the levels of employment to which their holders had access. New qualifications could be rendered irrelevant and useless by technological or organizational change, whereupon the employees needed more training simply to keep abreast. Traditional qualifications were different; they lasted for life. New training made employees more useful and valuable to their present employers, whereas traditional qualifications were more widely recognized. None of the firms that we studied selected employees on the basis of qualifications earned through new types of training in other companies. If they joined the firms that we investigated, employees were expected to begin again in acquiring certificated, job-relevant skills.

The principal purpose of the growth or development of the new training within these firms was to extend the employers' control so as to obtain more effective use of the labour that they hired (see also Mehaut, 1988). As explained earlier, the training had been introduced or reformed at the managements' initiative, not in isolation, but alongside broader changes in work practices.

'Quality' was the stated goal, but the underlying reality was that the pace of technological change required workers to change more rapidly than in the past, just to keep abreast. Simultaneously, the firms wanted fewer staff to do more and to be flexible, so that they could cover for one another and be transferred between jobs. The employers also wanted employees to work quickly, reliably and without close supervision. This was what lay behind the TQM philosophy. Was the strategy succeeding?

None of our firms claimed to have already tuned its skill formation to perfection. They were not complacent – a common disposition towards training not many years ago (Coopers and Lybrand, 1985). Nevertheless, they all felt that they were winning. The firms were all in transition, as they saw it, from being highly manned and low-skilled to high-technology, high-productivity organizations with quality workforces. This transition was seen as incomplete, and running-in difficulties were acknowledged everywhere, but our evidence suggests that some of the problems were unlikely to prove transitional. The managers tended to be 'unitarists' (see also Wilkinson *et al.*, 1991). They believed, or spoke and acted as if they believed, that the changes that had been introduced would benefit all grades of staff. They assumed that once training enabled all staff to recognize the market pressures to which the business had to respond, and once staff realized how their own performances could contribute to total quality, thereby leading to benefits for each firm as a whole and all its grades of employees, compliance would be more or less automatic. However, our evidence suggests that such outcomes were in fact highly problematic.

The fact that training had recently been radically overhauled, and usually enlarged, was probably helping to expose differences between the managements' and workforces' experiences and views of the changes. The managements were correct in believing that their workforces were pro-training. So in promoting and providing training the companies were not encountering deeply rooted workforce resistance. As Hill found in his case studies (this volume), on the surface there was a harmony of interests. The firms wanted more skilled workforces and all the managements had discovered that their employees wanted to be trained: 'They're looking for opportunities. . . . Requests for training exceed what we can offer at present.' However, much of this harmony was superficial.

In every company there was a fundamental difference between

the management's and the workers' aims. The former wanted to develop training, especially new forms of training, to enhance the skill levels and quality of labour within all grades, whereas the normal hope and expectation of employees was that their training and additional qualifications would lead to higher-grade jobs. It was always managers who stressed the value of training for self-development, the intrinsic satisfaction to be derived from doing a better job, the personal fulfilment to be gained from feeling more proficient, how training made employees feel more valued, and the joys of acquiring knowledge for its own sake. The workforces were certainly aware of these benefits. Over and above the temporary release from work, most employees enjoyed the actual process of being trained and appreciated the feelings of enhanced competence. At the same time, they invariably wanted training to lead to promotion and career openings. These benefits had normally been delivered by traditional education and training. They did not want training merely to perform better in their current grades, but to qualify themselves for better jobs. Operatives wanted to move 'off the line' into team leader and other supervisory positions. Skilled workers wanted to progress 'upstairs', into the management grades, 'where you wear a suit and get a company car'. Graduates hoped to fly high quickly. So they wanted the practical experience and time off to take courses and examinations which would lead to full professional status. They also wanted the breadth and depth of experience in critical areas that would put them in line for promotion inside or beyond their present companies.

On balance, most of the workers who were interviewed believed that their jobs were better as a result of the changes that they had experienced. Perhaps most decisively, they still had jobs and, for the time being at any rate, they felt that their employment had become more secure. They invariably appreciated any higher pay. The jobs themselves were different and, overall, were considered better. The employees knew that they were working harder than before, and typically felt that their jobs had become more complicated. They believed that the demands made upon them had increased, particularly the mental demands. At the same time, the jobs had usually become cleaner and less arduous physically. Also, most of the employees appreciated being able to make more use of their brains, and felt that they were in greater control. However, the majority of longer-serving hourly paid workers who were interviewed did not feel that they had become more *highly* skilled.

They were aware that they had acquired new skills, and most realized that they were using more skills than in the past, but this, in their view, was not the same as becoming more highly skilled. Some were acutely aware that they had been deskilled – that their crafts had been outdated and that their experience, judgement, tacit and generic skills which had been so important in the past had been devalued. Also, majorities at all levels, salaried and hourly paid, did not feel that their own promotion prospects had increased. Many were convinced that their opportunities had narrowed, firstly because their firms had contracted:

'It's become more difficult. Rather than creating new positions they're taking things out. . . . We've had no promotion boards for ages. People have resigned themselves to retiring in their present positions. Men who are qualified for the next grade have no chance of getting it. . . . Skills and qualifications are no longer tickets to higher grades.'

Moreover, staff at all levels on most of the sites were conscious that the number of grades through which they could move had been reduced, which meant that promotion opportunities occurred less frequently.

Taking everything into account, the general feeling was that the changes had been beneficial. Yet there was also a prevalent feeling, especially within the hourly paid grades, that managements had derived the greatest benefits (see also Fielder *et al.*, 1991; Stewart and Garrahan, 1992). Our distinction between traditional and new types of training and qualifications helps to explain this disillusion. Employees who received 'new' forms of training were not deriving the benefits associated with traditional qualifications. The employees were aware that their firms were obtaining higher output from fewer staff, and the majority did not believe that their own benefits were of the same order. This is why the managements' satisfaction with their higher-quality workforces was not matched by employee feelings of being better able to fulfil their own aspirations. Our evidence suggests that TQM was less likely to change than ultimately to be thwarted by workforce subcultures.

## INDUSTRIAL RELATIONS AND WORKPLACE CULTURES

When managements believed in a harmony of interests over training and skill acquisition, they were incorrect. They were certainly unduly optimistic when they spoke of training cultures eroding collective conflict. The so-called training culture was patchy and fragile in every company. The changed work practices, and particularly the reduced staffing levels within which the new training had typically developed, had not been embraced enthusiastically by most workers. They had accepted the changes only because they had realized that otherwise the futures of their plants and jobs would be in jeopardy. The trade unions had not welcomed the changes but had acquiesced in their inevitability. The motor company had taken its shop stewards to one of the company's continental plants; 'then they realized that they'd be unable to resist the changes'. Some of the shop stewards concurred. They had been to Spain, Germany, the USA and Japan, and had recognized that, 'If we hadn't accepted change we wouldn't be here today. Everyone grasped this in the nick of time.' However, other shop stewards had drawn different lessons from their overseas trips. They had concluded that even the most efficient plants remained vulnerable to corporate strategy and market downturns. So why should they accept changes in work practices which demanded greater effort when their members' jobs would still be at risk?

Even if, on balance, work had changed for the better, the staple shopfloor view was that, 'At the end of the day you're still putting parts on cars. . . . Your average guy still comes in at 7.30 a.m. and looks forward to 4.30 p.m.' Work was still experienced basically as time sold for money. In all the companies, the main change during the 1980s, as experienced at shopfloor level, had not been the development of training but the advent of new technology and staff cutbacks. Off-the-job training remained a very occasional experience, amounting to less than a week per year. The most common 'new' training experience, as before all the changes, was one-to-one instruction by supervisors.

Labour relations were still seen in conflict terms: managements wanted as much labour for as little reward as possible, and such pressure had to be resisted without self-inflicted damage. All the workers who were interviewed acknowledged that the balance of power had shifted.

'When I came here in 1977 there was so much demarcation that we did practically next to nothing. That was weak management. Now you can say that the pendulum has swung the other way. They keep moving the goal posts. They're going to push people too far.'

Opportunities to beat management were still being taken:

'There's still a lot of wasted time on the shop floor. We used to work three days on and two days off for five days' pay. Now it's called teamwork and it's official. They have a suggestion scheme. You can get up to £12,000 if your idea is good enough, but your suggestion could be used against the men. One guy from another section had worked out how to do his job in six minutes instead of eight. There were ructions from his mates.'

Shop stewards and their members agreed that the unions' influence was much diminished and that managements had successfully asserted their right to manage – to set staffing levels, dictate technology and the pace of work. In the 1980s the managements had had no real alternative but to become assertive, because they realized that the plants and their own jobs were at risk. In turn, the trade unions had recognized that they had no option but acquiescence. When they had opposed severance schemes, members had grasped the terms. While negotiators were refusing to accept reduced staffing levels, their members had been changing to the new work practices. So the unions in all the plants had accommodated: 'The attitude now is let's see how it works, rather than go on strike.' Most of the managements felt that they had gained the upper hand. 'The trial of strength over who runs the place is over. It's neither personnel nor the trade unions, but the division managers. Management is now more relaxed and more confident.'

But even if the unions' influence was diminished, their structures were still intact, and the trade unions in all the plants remained bargaining organizations. Their relationships with plant managements could not be described as partnerships. The managements recognized that 'the unions still put all their efforts into conflict situations'. The unions were still negotiating and reaching collective agreements on pay and job grading. In three of the plants that we studied, industrial action was threatened during the fieldwork. Training was being drawn into collective bargaining. Here the unions' interest was always to negotiate training that would entitle members to higher-graded jobs and rates of pay. As far as union representatives were concerned, the so-called right to manage had been conceded only temporarily, against a background of high unemployment and a hostile government. At the time of our fieldwork the trade unions had little control over job content, grading or training. Workers seeking access to, or support for, own-initiative education and training were approaching line managers or training staff, not union representatives. The point still held that if and when the trade unions became able, once again, to assert their prerogatives, training was likely to be shaped through collective bargaining.

In one sense training was already constrained by collective bargaining, because even if the trade unions were not seeking to negotiate the content of courses or access, they were bargaining about the grades and pay entitlements of members who acquired new skills. Managements were seeking to introduce pay and grade systems that gave workers incentives to learn skills that the firms needed. The unions were always seeking to derive any possible advantage from these changes. They could bargain over the grading of particular jobs or negotiate pay commensurate with members' new skills, even when commensurate jobs were not immediately available. Or they could bargain for automatic promotion up the grades with length of service, and leave it to managements to ensure that training was delivered and work practices introduced to enable the firms to benefit from the senior staff's experience.

## DIVISIONS OF INTEREST

It will be many years before it is possible to establish conclusively whether in the long term, TQM can deliver benefits in the form of enhanced employee motivation, quality work and corporate effectiveness throughout the economy. The current evidence is inconclusive. Most large organizations in Britain seem to have been sufficiently impressed by the TQM philosophy and results to date to institute quality campaigns, and in general, employees seem receptive to the quality message. Firms that operate TQM mostly report fewer defects and customer complaints, yet few report bottom-line gains in sales and profitability, and only 8 per cent of the respondents in the British Institute of Management survey referred to earlier rated their own firms' quality campaigns as 'very successful' (Wilkinson *et al.*, 1993). Would the firms experience greater success if they persisted with TQM for long enough? Or is initial employee enthusiasm liable to evaporate, when TQM fails to deliver tangible benefits?

Our fresh case study evidence is not encouraging on the long-term potential of TQM. The pioneers may have reaped advantages that all employees in the firms were able to share, but this becomes impossible when most enterprises adopt TQM; they cannot all become market-leaders. Equally to the point, the benefits of TQM are invariably distributed unevenly within organizations, and all grades of employees, but particularly those least privileged, are invariably sensitive to these inequalities.

We began our research wondering whether traditional divisions between skilled and non-skilled grades would be weakening in the face of the employers' new skill-formation strategies. Alternatively, we wondered whether the divisions would persist as obstacles. In the event, neither of these scenarios was encountered – all the companies were able to meet their skill requirements without challenging the divisions in question. Indeed, in some cases the firms were taking advantage of the divisions in their new skill-formation processes. The hierarchical division between skilled and other grades remained intact and unchallenged everywhere except in the oil refineries, and almost impossible to penetrate in an upward direction. All the managements were keen on multi-skilling and breaking down divisions between former crafts. In addition, they were all keen to redraw the line between craft and process work so that, for example, operatives performed some routine repairs and machine-setting. However, except at one of the oil refineries, it was serving the managements' purposes to maintain a clear division between the recruitment, training and grading of operatives and the usually higher-skilled craft grades who installed, maintained and programmed the machines. Operatives had less spent on their initial training and were not eligible for 'skilled' rates of pay. Previous researchers have noted that in Britain the distinction between craft and other manual occupations is now traditional and firmly entrenched (Penn, 1990; Whittaker, 1990). In contrast, in each firm that we studied, the division between craft and technical skills was being obliterated by new technology.

There were always some opportunities for both skilled and process workers to earn promotion to management. However, these opportunities were restricted by the shape of the workforces – the management grades were always less heavily populated than those beneath – and because of the recruitment of graduates directly into management occupations. There was no trend or management pressure towards exactly the same staff status for everyone. The division between the salaried and hourly paid, or staff and works, was always maintained in some way or another. Individuals who crossed this line knew that they had changed sides, between those who managed and those who were managed. Obliterating this divide was an objective of neither managements nor trade unions. Rather, the division was always acknowledged as a real and inevitable split of function and interest.

All sections of the firms' workforces were able to define, and act to further their own particular interests. Their aims, whether pursued individually or collectively, were invariably limited to improving their positions within the existing organizations. The changes of the 1980s may have been opposed at the time, but subsequently had been accepted pragmatically. There were no grounds for attributing deeper political objectives to the examples of resistance that we encountered (see Tanner *et al.*, 1992). As has always applied under capitalism, the balance of costs and likely benefits was encouraging the various sections of the firms' workforces to seek betterment *vis-à-vis* other groups within the same companies, and all workers in other enterprises (Coram, 1992). However, everyone knew that some groups within their firms were more powerful than others – this was why there was a top and bottom in every organization. And everyone knew that capital's requirements had to be satisfied, otherwise it would move elsewhere, and all sections of the workforces would lose.

Much was changing in the firms that we studied. Technological change was constant. Old jobs were disappearing and new occupations were being created. The numbers employed, and the proportions at different levels, were also changing. Managements were enthusiastic about TQM and appeared to believe that all sections of the workforces could become equally keen to acquire skills and make themselves into quality employees. Yet within all this flux, certain divisions were surviving; those between management and labour, skilled and other occupations, well-qualified and less qualified employees. This meant that the workplaces were destined to remain sites of struggle and conflict between different interest groups. During the years immediately preceding our research all the managements felt that they had progressed towards solving their sites' labour and skill problems. In contrast, even when on balance employees who had kept their jobs believed that their own terms and conditions of employment had improved, they did not necessarily feel that changes were giving them access to the skills, qualifications and occupations that they really wanted. There was still intense competition for such qualifications, skills and occupations, and the tendency everywhere was for traditionally privileged groups – those well equipped with traditional academic and vocational qualifications, and those who were trained for highly skilled jobs early in their working lives – to be deriving the greatest benefits from the changes. The implementation of TQM was not dissolving these divisions, but was being structured by them.

## REFERENCES

Ainley, P. and Corney, M. (1990) *Training for the Future*, London: Cassell.

Berggren, C. (1993) 'Lean production – the end of history?', *Work, Employment and Society*, 7, 163–88.

Cassels, J. (1990) *Britain's Real Skill Shortage*, London: Policy Studies Institute.

Coopers and Lybrand Associates (1985) *A Challenge to Complacency*, Sheffield: Manpower Services Commission.

Confederation of British Industry/Manpower Services Commission (1987) *Special Survey: Skill Shortages*, London: Confederation of British Industry.

Coram, B.T. (1992) 'Spoiling the Class Divide: Struggles Within the Working Class over Distribution', *British Journal of Sociology*, 43, 393–420.

Employment Department (1992) *Labour Market and Skill Trends, 1993/94*, London: Employment Department.

Fielder, S., Rees, G. and Rees, T. (1991) *Employers' Recruitment and Training Strategies*, project paper 4, Social Research Unit, University of Wales, College of Cardiff.

Gallie, D. and White, M. (1993) *Employee Commitment and the Skills Revolution*, London: Policy Studies Institute.

Harrison, B. and Kelley, M.R. (1993) 'Outsourcing and the Search for Flexibility', *Work, Employment and Society*, 7, 213–35.

Hill, S. (1991) 'Why Quality Circles Failed but Total Quality Management Might Succeed', *British Journal of Industrial Relations*, 29, 541–68.

IFF Research (1990) *Skill Needs in Britain*, London: Employment Department.

IFF Research (1991) *Skill Needs in Britain 1991*, London: Employment Department.

IFF Research (1992) *Skill Needs in Britain 1992*, London: Employment Department.

Layard, R. (1992) *The Training Reform Act of 1994*, Swindon: Economic and Social Research Council, Annual lecture.

Mehaut, P. (1988) 'New Firms' Training Policies and Changes in the Wage-Earning Relationship', *Labour and Society*, 13, 443–56.

Oakland, J.S. (1989) *Total Quality Management*, Oxford: Heinemann.

O'Reilly, J. (1993) 'Functional Flexibility, Training and Skill in Britain and France', London: Employment Department, paper presented to seminar on Employers' Labour Market Behaviour.

Payne, J. (1991) *Women, Training and the Skills Shortage*, London: Policy Studies Institute.

Penn, R. (1990) *Class, Power and Technology*, Oxford: Polity Press.

Senker, R. (1992) *Industrial Training in a Cold Climate*, London: Avebury.

Sheldrake, J. and Vickerstaff, S.A. (1987) *History of Industrial Training in Britain*, Aldershot: Gower.

Stewart, P. and Garrahan, P. (1992) *The Nissan Enigma*, London: Manssell.

Sturdy, A., Knights, D. and Willmott, H. (1993) 'Skill and Consent in the Labour Process', in A. Sturdy, D. Knights and H. Willmott (eds) *Skill and Consent*, London: Routledge.

Tanner, J., Davies, S. and O'Grady, B. (1992) 'Immanence Changes Everything: a Critical Comment on the Labour Process and Class Consciousness', *Sociology*, 26, 439–53.

Training Agency (1990) *Training in Britain*, London: HMSO.

Vickerstaff, S. (1991) 'Training and the Small Business', paper presented at seminar on Employers' Labour Market Behaviour, London: Department of Employment.

Webster, F. and Robins, K. (1993) 'I'll be Watching You', *Sociology*, 27, 243–52.

Whittaker, D.H. (1990) *Managing Innovation*, Cambridge: Cambridge University Press.

Wilkinson, A. (1994) 'Managing Human Resources for Quality', in B.G. Dale (ed.) *Managing Quality* (2nd edn), Hemel Hempstead: Prentice-Hall.

Wilkinson, A., Allen, P. and Snape, E. (1991) 'TQM and the Management of Labour', *Employee Relations*, 13 (1), 24–31.

Wilkinson, A., Marchington, M., Goodman, J. and Ackers, P. (1992) 'Total Quality Management and Employee Involvement', *Human Resources Management Journal*, 2 (4), 1–20.

Wilkinson, A., Redman, T. and Snape, E. (1993) *Quality and the Manager*, Corby: The Institute of Management.

Womack, J.P., Jones, D.T. and Roos, D. (1990) *The Machine that Changed the World*, New York: Macmillan.

# 9

# EMPOWERING THE 'QUALITY' WORKER?

## The seduction and contradiction of the total quality phenomenon*

*Deborah Kerfoot and David Knights*

### INTRODUCTION

Organizations are increasingly turning to 'quality' in order to enhance their market-place profile, improve competitive performance, and maximize the potential for expansion and intensification of sales within their existing customer base. In order to complement their overall marketing strategy, several companies in the financial sector have embraced the 'quality' philosophy, adopting a systematic approach to improving both products and service delivery by the inclusion of a formal total quality management (TQM) programme in their business plan.

Such a programme involves systematic attempts to generate organizational conformance to the requirements of both internal and external customers of the company. It seeks to do this by using a variety of techniques or procedures drawn from the prescriptive models of particular managerial gurus (e.g., Juran, Deming, Crosby). Typical of these procedures are the development of quality improvement teams, methods of statistical process control, quantifying the cost of non-conformance to customer

---

* We thank the TSB-funded Financial Services Research Centre for a grant that enabled this chapter to be written and the ESRC whose funding has ensured a continuing interest in this field of study. We also acknowledge the helpful comments of several colleagues and participants at the eleventh international labour process conference in 1993, and especially Hugh Willmott for his suggestions to an earlier draft of the chapter.

requirements, eradicating defects, and generating a commitment to continuous improvement.

This chapter is concerned to examine the discourse or 'rhetoric' of 'quality' in terms of the conditions that render it plausible to practitioners, and the effects that it has as a practice on organizations and their employees. A major objective of our analysis is to provide a critical understanding of the development of quality as a contemporary managerial and organizational phenomenon. Through a theoretical analysis of quality management, we seek to explore the seductive nature of quality programmes and their relationship to the labour process, drawing on a few illustrations from our research in financial services. More specifically, we suggest that while seeming to 'flatten' the hierarchy, the effect of quality management is to renew the legitimacy of large bureau-corporate capitalist organizations. Following this theme, but focusing also on certain tensions and contradictions within quality programmes, we examine conceptions of empowerment and the linkages between quality and human resource management.

We do not see our task as one of producing 'blueprints' or additional 'tools' that can be readily appropriated to enhance managerial 'expertise' and sustain an effective control over labour, but nor are we concerned to condemn quality programmes as nothing more than yet another manifestation of managerial totalitarianism designed to sustain worker subjugation and exploitation. On the contrary, it is our concern to be critical both of the prescriptive nature of much of the literature in the quality field and of its antithesis within what may be seen as a purist academic Marxist tradition.

What we do focus on, however, are some of the contradictions that arise in the implementation of quality management programmes. These contradictions may be seen to derive from the crude and mechanistic 'engineering-like' model of organizations and the equally simplistic understandings of human behaviour that inform TQM. Our research in the financial services encourages us to question the potential for quality management to work if it continues to subscribe to such limited and misleading models of the 'reality' which it seeks to change.

The chapter is divided into three sections, the first of which considers how the discourse of quality is appealing to practising managers and their corporations as they seek to become more responsive to a world of diverse and discontinuous demands.

The second section of the chapter provides an outline and critical examination of the concept of empowerment, suggesting that at best it is built upon simplistic assumptions about human nature that leave its prescriptions contradictory. The final section follows on from this by noting how the tensions and contradictions within and between quality and human resource management limit the degree of convergence between them. The conclusion draws these arguments together and, from the perspective we have developed, identifies some issues for empirical field research.

## THE SEDUCTIVE QUALITY OF QUALITY PROGRAMMES

As we have already suggested, we want to contribute neither to the evangelical optimism nor to the totalitarian pessimism of the literature that examines quality management initiatives and, more particularly, TQM. Rather, our concern is to understand, on the one hand, the conditions that have led to quality management programmes being widely adopted, and, on the other, critically to evaluate their impact on the labour process and the organization of work. In this section we concentrate on the former concern – that is, with the conditions under which quality programmes have assumed an overwhelming significance in contemporary management within Britain.

In contrast to those who dismiss quality management as no more than a repressive doctrine aimed at reinforcing existing patterns of labour intensification and control, we regard the management control of employees as an unintended consequence of the development of quality programmes, rather than their direct objective. Where quality programmes 'fit' with the labour process then, is less to do with controlling labour directly than with assisting in the management of certain problems pertaining to competitive capitalism. In its unadulterated or 'perfect' form, competition between corporations would lead to their demise, as each sought to undercut another on price in search of the largest market share (see Deming, 1982). As is well known, however, free market competition does not function in this manner. Its self-destructive rapacity is managed by a whole series of demand and supply-side mechanisms and techniques, which overall amount to a refusal to compete on price. This avoidance of price wars takes the form, for example, of cartel agreements, both official and unofficial, product differentiation, advertising, and 'added value' campaigns based on product and service quality. The competitive urge is also deflected into ceaseless strivings for change and innovation in processes of organizational self-renewal, of which TQM is a recent complement. This revolutionary impetus within capitalism has intensified during the 1980s and 1990s as a result of the entrepreneurial and competitive pressures stemming from New Right policies (Lash and Urry, 1987; Keat and Abercrombie, 1991) and what may be seen as the globalization of corporate business. Underpinned by what is arguably an idealized and idealistic model of free competition, neo-rightist initiatives have established wholesale economic deregulation of markets and specific industries, of which financial services have been but one instance.

Similarly, labour markets have been subjected to successive waves of regulatory legislation which have eroded the potential for collective organization within and between workforces, and reshaped the scope of effectiveness for organized struggle. As the management of labour through collective bargaining methods and procedures has been undermined, increasingly individualistic determinations of wage rates, supported by merit and performance pay, have created a cultural and managerial vacuum awaiting the arrival of new coordinating mechanisms of collective and productive power. From corporate culture (Deal and Kennedy, 1982; Peters and Waterman, 1982; Goldsmith and Clutterbuck, 1985) through human resource management (Fombrun *et al.*, 1984; Peters, 1987; Armstrong, 1988), TQM may be seen as one of the most recent in a long line of managerial discourses that have professed to fill the gap left open by the decline of earlier forms of collectivism. Quality management, or more accurately its managerial plausibility, is at least in part a reflection of the necessity for large corporations to find new and innovative ways of competing constructively, and of managing fragmented workforces.[1]

Yet another condition giving impetus to this mechanism of organizational self-renewal is the transitory, shifting and proliferating demands of consumers (Du Gay and Salaman, 1992) in what is increasingly being described as a 'post-modern' society (Harvey, 1989; Lash, 1990). In this context, quality management might be seen as a corporate alternative to the strategy of 'flexible specialization' (Piore and Sabel, 1984; Atkinson, 1984) where the 'demassification' of consumption is managed through the establishment of industrial networks of small-scale, subcontracted production units, flexibly capable of switching product lines at a moment's notice. While decentralization is an option for the large corporation seeking to meet new demands for flexibility, controlling and coordinating the separate units becomes increasingly difficult in the absence of some over-arching philosophy or set of standards, as represented by managerial programmes such as TQM. By stimulating workforce and organizational flexibility, quality management aims to provide 'fitness for purpose' with 'error-free' products and services that not only lock customers into patterns of consumer loyalty, but which ensure cost-effective – and thereby profitable – mechanisms of provision. Within financial services, the difficulty of competing on product innovation because of the ease of imitation, and on price for fear of destructive competition, has resulted in a concentration on service quality.

Quality management is also one of the latest weapons in the battle for corporate image and high-street reputation, where every company seeks to become the corporate leader in their sector. For just as product differentiation can facilitate competitive advantage despite high prices, 'correct' corporate image accommodates this across the full range of products or services on offer. In financial services, the growth of bancassurance networks has made this strategy particularly appealing, and it is the case that at least one of the leading banks has in its mission statement the objective of becoming the 'Marks and Spencer' of their industry.

It may, then, be argued that quality management 'breathes new life into' the large corporation, facilitating its survival in the threatening circumstances of intensified competition in destabilized consumer markets. As a sympathetic and complementary managerial and organizational response to wider social change, quality management encapsulates the contemporary pressure to devolve responsibility to the individual. This classical liberal ethos has been reinvigorated by New Right political philosophies and economic policies that seek to stimulate a greater degree of financial and other forms of self-reliance, away from what is held to be the 'stranglehold' of the 'nanny state'. In turn, underpinned by current debates over rights and citizenship, the concept of individual autonomy finds a residual legacy within an ideology of privatization, strategic cutbacks in welfare, and a policy of *laissez-faire* non-interventionism. Within employment, this is echoed in a preoccupation with the individualized, self-regulated and autonomous worker, of which quality management may be seen to represent its timely apotheosis.

However, while at this level quality management reflects a concern to collapse or 'flatten' organizational hierarchies, it is also a motive force in their reconstitution and retrenchment. This occurs through processes or claims to empower workers, which we discuss in more detail below. Suffice to say here that worker empowerment and autonomy under quality programmes is heavily circumscribed by the demands for continuous improvement and error-free standardization of products. Through a range of what are themselves perhaps bureaucratic procedures for identifying obstacles to efficient production and quality service, norms of quality are established and internalized. Partly out of a fear of the consequences of non-conformance and partly because of reward incentives, these procedures generate the kind of self-discipline that 'secures as it obscures' (Burawoy, 1979) hierarchical forms, thus giving a renewed legitimacy to the authority of bureaucratic structures. In developing this theme of self-discipline, we now turn to a discussion of the concept of empowerment.

## EMPOWERING THE QUALITY WORKER?

A large tranche[2] of the literature on quality, and more especially on TQM, revolves around the potential and importance for employers to delegate responsibilities down the hierarchy, thus involving employees in decision-making activities (Oakland, 1989; Dale and Plunkett, 1990: 5–6). This derives partly at least from a belief that bureaucratic forms of organization relieve employees of responsibility for the consequences of their actions by virtue of systems whereby senior members of the hierarchy are ultimately accountable for decisions and, more importantly, their effect on productive performance.

In order to ameliorate the worst excesses of bureaucratic hierarchy, quality management has stimulated a process of 'making' employees responsible and accountable for the content and quality of their own jobs. In one of our research sites, the TQM programme imposes the obligation on all bank staff to reflect on difficulties that obstruct the smooth running of their work and, if they are not able to resolve these locally, to pass them on to a Quality Action Team (QAT) so that corrective action might be implemented. Recognition in the form of an acknowledgement or even a company reward from the Quality Improvement Team (QIT) coordinator, whose job it is to promote QATs to resolve 'snags' or demands for corrective action, is used to encourage this kind of responsibility. Similarly, employees are held accountable to self- and managerially defined objectives by means of the 'team report-back' meeting; to quality team leaders; and thence ultimately, although informally, through their annual appraisal.

As Wilkinson *et al.* (1992: 6) express it, 'if TQM is applied as its proponents suggest, the focus for responsibility for quality is in the hands of those who do the work'. This is then defined as employee empowerment (see, for example, Juran, 1979) echoed in the thrust for workers to define, correct, but most notably, to anticipate problems, referred to as continuous improvement, or *kaizen* (see, for example, Imai, 1986) in the total quality organization. Here empowerment is concerned with increasing employee decision-making participation in relation to everyday workplace tasks, through the vehicles of, for example, quality circles and most notably teamworking (see McArdle, this volume, for discussion). Through the latter, in particular, workers are deemed to develop an identification with the aims of the corporation that employs them, commitments beyond the line of duty, and a general desire to cooperate with colleagues both within and across functional areas (Oakland, 1989: 236; Wilkinson *et al.*, 1992: 5–6).

Although employee participation is seen predominantly as a condition of building quality through cooperation (Hill, 1991; Wilkinson *et al.*, 1991), one of the attractions of delegation is that it helps to bypass the problems of 'communicative distortion' (Habermas, 1975) that are an inescapable feature of bureau-corporate hierarchical relations. For where, because of career concerns or employment security, subordinates 'feed' their managers information they think will be found palatable, policies based upon such information are likely to be unreliable, if not wholly misguided. Under regimes of hierarchical command, worker autonomy and empowerment offer a potential to overcome these difficulties deriving from the physical and social distance between senior managers and the immediate demands of day-to-day work on the office or factory floor.

Quality circles are a particular device for seeking to remove the conventional barriers of hierarchy or inter-divisional tensions. In another of our research sites, a quality circle was established to discuss and seek to resolve problems that bank business units felt they experienced with the mortgage division. Frequently they had suffered loss of business to competitors, either because of slow processing or what they considered inappropriate rejections of mortgage applications. The problem for the business unit was that they had mortgage targets to meet. Under the quality programme, however, this dissatisfaction was never expressed as business units dared not be critical of the mortgage division in the latter's questionnaires to assess the quality of their service. This was because to do so could result in discrimination and therefore an even worse service.

Once the quality circle met, everyone was informed by the quality facilitator that participation would be equal and that rank would not count. However, the very membership of the quality circle was itself 'rigged' in favour of the business units (see below). The only women in the meeting represented the mortgage division and they appeared somewhat overwhelmed, finding it difficult to express any opinions at all in the early stages of the meeting. Although we have not yet had time to check out the views of each of the participants, it is our view that the outcome has favoured the business concerns, which, given the circumstances, is not surprising. The three areas of importance for improvement that were eventually agreed upon were:

1 **Decisions on mortgage applications**: the concern of the business people was that these were sometimes arbitrary or certainly not sensible in terms of the current competitive market for loans. For this reason, the second area of importance was:
2 **Appeals**: here, business people felt that anomalies that were occurring did not secure adequate treatment in appeals.
3 **Telephone communication**: with the stress that this is a two-way process where Homeloans could get information that was required speedily and business staff could secure information and advice on the progress of applications.

Each of these related to the business concern; only the third issue, telephone communication, was seen of some importance to Homeloans, in terms of their concerns to prevent branches breaching the rule about not letting customers have the telephone number of the mortgage division. Business staff could determine the parameters of the discussions not only because the meeting was instigated by them, but by virtue of its 'rigged' nature in terms of numbers (three business and two Homeloans), seniority (area director and his PA, branch manager on the business side against a team leader and a QIT coordinator on the Homeloans side), and gender (two women from Homeloans, the rest men including the two facilitators).

In these circumstances, all talk of equality of participation and the irrelevance of rank is largely rhetorical. Indeed, getting the two (more junior) women to participate at all was quite difficult and only occurred with any degree of spontaneity when the mechanical (and one might add masculine) framework of the meeting was abandoned. Yet after this had happened, it was undermined by the facilitator, who summed up the diversion as reflecting a lot of 'emotion' in the issues that needed to be taken out so that they could become objective about them. Although it was never expressed directly in the meeting, the QIT coordinator in Homeloans declared during the coffee break that both sides had different motivations. Of course the TQM stock answer to this would be that they should all have the same motivation to serve both internal and external customer needs. However, this is entirely unrealistic when the business units want mortgage acceptances to meet their targets and the mortgage division seeks to process business with the least risk of default. These are mutually incompatible objectives, as are those of the mortgage division and customers whose credit rating may in any way be viewed suspiciously.

This short vignette raises some difficulties with two of the central features of quality. First, that employees are to become empowered and autonomous; and second, that bureaucratic managerial controls are to be rescinded. Clearly neither set of employees had become more empowered or autonomous. If anything, the quality programme had provided the mortgage division with ammunition (i.e., the service questionnaire to branches) to deny power and autonomy to the business units, and bureaucratic rules relating to mortgage acceptances continued to dominate the process.

Nonetheless, the principle of quality management is concerned with the business of devolving decision-making authority down organizational hierarchies, so that the ultimate responsibility for quality is to be ceded to employees. It is here that the trend to 'de-layer' managements and remove or reduce whole categories of managers has found an impetus. This creates the semblance of a new era of trust between managements and workforces, and what is ostensibly a wholesale transformation in the nature of

227

supervision and control under cultures of equality as opposed to coercion.

Clearly, at the level of quality as a rhetorical device, it should come as no surprise that one of the attractions of quality for managements, not least in its guise as TQM, is that employee autonomy and empowerment create the conditions under which workforces may become more flexible and adaptable. In either the context of working practices or customer service, this demand for flexibility has increased as markets and hierarchies have entered an era of instability. In banking, for example, counter staff have had to become flexible enough to be able to switch from money transmission processes to prospecting for life insurance customers or even selling certain insurance products. Furthermore, the career system has been reconstructed to reward the selling activities so as to encourage this flexibility.

While the demand for flexibility has given renewed impetus to policies of delegation, anxieties within a hierarchically coordinated organization remain, because of the question of ultimate responsibility resting with senior management. For passing responsibility down the hierarchy is no guarantee that it will stay there. The attraction of TQM is that it adds another dimension – that of the internal market – for all employees are persuaded to treat their colleagues as customers. Through the device of the 'internal customer' (Ishikawa, quoted in Brown *et al.*, 1991), individual commitment arising from delegation and worker autonomy can be readily transformed into a more reliable form of collective self-discipline. Work group members in the quality company are not only responsible to themselves in accounting for their own performance records and errors, but to other team members by means of the 'consumer' analogy. All social interactions are heralded as potential moments of value added exchange within the 'quality chain', where the bottom line of production, quality, is the espousal and enactment of a service for 'customers', be they in the high street, the next department or the desk opposite.

As suggested in the previous section, this restoration of some form of collective commitment and self-discipline among individualized and often fragmented workforces is an important, if not consciously directed, consequence of quality programmes. What better way to establish it than through performance standards relating to 'conformance to customer requirements', rather than the earlier industrial relations bargains of 'instrumental reciprocity' where employee discipline, cooperation or productivity could only be secured in exchange for explicit wage awards negotiated by the union or local shop/office floor committee. Along with Wilkinson *et al.* (1992: 6), we would also challenge the unproblematic manner in which delegation or employee involvement is conceived within TQM programmes. However, we consider it not to be a question of employees' willingness to participate (ibid.) but the 'quality' of their participation. In earlier industrial relations climates, and perhaps still to a limited degree in the manufacturing sector, a resistance to the 'fads and fashions' of managerial control may well be prevalent. Yet research in financial services (ibid.: 13; Boaden and Dale, 1993; and our own preliminary findings) suggests that TQM is not *openly* resisted, either by employees or unions.

This is not to argue that staff in financial services embrace such programmes with conviction and commitment; they may simply comply unenthusiastically with the demands (e.g., raising snags that prevent smooth working practices, attending quality improvement teams, measuring performance, etc.) of the programme. Indeed, in the language of the quality literature, employees may 'conform to the requirements' of the programme, including the demands of internal or external customers, but only as minimally defined.

The quality literature fails to consider the way that programmes and their content may be differentially defined or interpreted by employees. This is because at the level of application, quality programmes subscribe to a commonsense view of human nature that presupposes all behaviour to be an unproblematic response to simple stimuli. Consequently, quality management presumes an unquestioning subject unproblematically responding to its demands. It could be argued, then, that the quality management literature has difficulty in distinguishing between employee conformity and compliance, on the one hand, and commitment and consent, on the other (Sturdy, 1992). Implicitly, though, it anticipates the development of commitment and consent through quality programmes that are expected to transform workplace cultures, so as to result in employees becoming actively engaged in their work. Holding to a naive belief that shifts in organizational culture can readily be accomplished as an outcome of managerial will (Boaden and Dale, 1993 – in particular, pp. 20–1), the quality literature fails to consider the possibility that quality concepts, prescriptions, or invocations may be subject to a broad range of interpretations and, even within the same interpretation, may produce differential forms of engagement and/or resistance.

So, the literature subscribes to a view of employees as submissive and obedient with respect to the introduction of quality programmes. At one and the same time in relation to the content of quality programmes, through empowerment, individuals are expected to be active and capable of powers of interpretation. These, it might be argued, are two inconsistent assumptions about employee behaviour or human nature that render some of the prescriptions of quality management impoverished, if not contradictory. Paradoxically, then, quality management relies for its success precisely on an active subject with interpretive powers that is denied or discounted at the moment of its introduction in companies. That is to say, employees are neither treated as equals nor even consulted when companies decide to adopt programmes of quality management: they are often merely trained in its practices once the programme has been adopted by the senior management.

## QUALITY AND HUMAN RESOURCE MANAGEMENT

Our earlier discussion of the rise of 'quality' in organizations sought to provide an indication of the politico-economic (and by implication, the social) conditions within which quality and TQM could take hold in the UK context. In this section, we explore further the specific configuration of conditions that facilitated the encroachment of the quality dialogue in financial services companies.

It is generally agreed that quality management has its genesis in operations research and production management, where design specifications of material products and the processes of their production can be readily standardized and subjected to statistical monitoring and tests – for quality assurance and quality control, for example. These discrete manufacturing models of quality are constructed as a 'blueprint' in which the processes of production are reduced to their technical content. Reflecting its early engineering roots, what could be described as the 'hard' aspects of quality management (Hill, 1991) are variously concerned to maintain 'zero defects' (Crosby, 1979) and 'fitness for use' (Feigenbaum, 1972; Juran, 1979) by means of statistical monitoring and control, and performance measurement standards, among a variety of production techniques (see Dale and Plunkett, 1990; MacDonald and Piggott, 1990, for useful summaries). Yet clearly even the most sophisticated techniques of manufacturing, such as those based on computerized technologies (for example, CAM and CAD/CAM), take place within a social context, where the human interpretation of 'input' and 'output' processes remains important.

Partly in recognition of this social context, and especially when seeking to broaden its application to non-manufacturing activities, quality management has developed a 'soft' side (Hill, ibid.) in which there is a need for increased employee involvement, teamwork and group problem-solving. Here, there is an assumption that all employees are at least partially engaged in providing service to the ultimate consumer by means of the 'quality chain' (Smith 1988; Oakland, 1989). This is seen to extend throughout the organization and includes the internal as well as external 'customers' of any transaction in a company. Quality, then, needs to be extended to all aspects of an organization's activities, not just the standards associated with finished products. It is here that the distinction is said to lie between *ad hoc* quality initiatives and total quality management as a way of running a company.

Here we find some similarities between quality management and human resource management (HRM). Traditional personnel policies, so the argument goes, are increasingly being displaced by the strategic management of employees through HRM (Alpander, 1982; Tichy *et al.*, 1982; Beer *et al.*, 1984). In spite of some considerable disagreement about its content (e.g. Legge, 1988; Keenoy, 1988; see also Noon, 1992, for discussion), HRM appears to offer a mode of managing people grounded in a notion of the competitive advantage to be had by identifying, and thence directing, the creative power of labour. Having said that, HRM is neither a coherent nor consistent set of management practices (Legge, 1989; Keenoy, 1988); arguably what makes it distinctive is an attempt to align the methods of managing employees with aspects of the business strategy (see Guest, 1990: 378–9; Storey, 1992: 24–5).

It is on this point that the 'soft' aspects of quality management could be seen as consistent with HRM (also Wilkinson *et al.*, 1991). Both necessitate some integration of policies for managing employees with the business plan of an organization, directed toward the commercial success of the enterprise. Further, employees so managed are to be regarded more as an 'asset' than a cost of production. (See Hendry and Pettigrew, 1990; Keenoy, 1988; Kerfoot and Knights, 1992; also Guest, 1987, for a critical discussion of this issue.) *De facto*, then, some degree of convergence exists between HRM and quality management in the attempt to expose employees to the bottom line of profitability and 'the market', and in the utilization of workforces as a productive commodity.

With respect to financial services, a contradiction of quality management and HRM is that, on the one hand, TQM seeks to stimulate trust and commitment as a way of generating quality, and meeting the strategic goals of the organization. On the other hand, this is against a background of massive rationalization across the industry involving numerous branch closures and changes in traditional hierarchical functions and statuses. Partly this has been an outcome of large-scale mergers, structural reorganization and ostensible 'delayering' of organizational hierarchies. In turn, this has occurred as a response to perceptions of over-supply in financial services, falling rates of profitability, and increasing competition following deregulation of the sector. Together these have resulted in major redundancy programmes, affecting both workforces and managers. Self-evidently, the scale and extent of what is euphemistically described in the sector as 'organizational outplacing' has affected greater numbers of office-floor workers than their management superiors. For example, phased redundancies have seen the numbers of clerk cashier operatives in some companies fall by as much as 20 per cent of total staff.

Yet the point here is that the managerial grades have been no more exempt from recent waves of upheaval and transformation than others elsewhere in organizations. Here the ideology of 'delayering' coincides with the concern of banks to displace the older 'professional' banker with younger (and it might be added cheaper), more sales-oriented, branch managers. Managers, then, are often similarly affected by shifting patterns of sectoral employment and the demands which this places upon organizational members.

This first contradiction thus relates to inconsistencies between 'structural' and 'process' responses to what is perceived to be a more competitive market-place. A second contradiction concerns the problems of organizations bringing in quality programmes having *no* necessary connection to HRM. If HRM were more closely integrated with senior executive decision-making, perhaps the tension of seeking greater employee trust and commitment while, at the same time, handing out redundancy notices, would not be so blatant. It might also facilitate a greater integration of HRM and quality management practices whereby accountability, empowerment and the development of a workforce aware of, and committed to, achieving the strategic goals of the organization could be more readily achieved.

However, our research so far has revealed no examples of this integration. Accordingly, the promotion of quality management and its concerns with trust, commitment and, as one manager expressed it, employees having the 'right attitude', is in direct contradiction with the atmosphere of job insecurity caused by frequent corporate restructuring and associated threats of redundancy. Clearly, then, the introduction of quality and human resource programmes as discrete and stand-alone policies with no direct connection between them leaves organizations vulnerable to the charge that their policies are inconsistent and senior management superficial in their commitment to the transformation of work for which they are designed.

When seeking to apply quality management to their organizations, financial services companies have tended to focus attention on 'back office' support functions, and service quality at the point of distribution (see, for example, Gronroos, 1984; Brown *et al.*, 1991; Howcroft, 1991; also Lewis, 1989 for review). The application of quality management to the back office as a means of reducing processing errors, defects, and improving service to customers, can more readily be based on the manufacturing model. Here quality assurance and control may bring about immediate benefits: all the more so when these back office functions have been moved to a central data processing 'factory', as in many banks and insurance companies. In this sense, financial services corporations have, for some considerable period, been at least partially concerned with quality. The *strategic* management of quality, however, is arguably a more recent phenomenon, finding contemporary resonance with companies concerned to gain greater direction and control both over working practices in their organization, and its customer/company interface, as part of a wider concern with implementing the long-term business plan of the enterprise. In this sense, quality is no longer an option for management but a necessary concern of the business activity.

The pursuit of quality in financial services companies in recent years could be seen essentially as a search for competitive advantage through differentiation strategies (Porter, 1980; 1985). This has occurred largely as a result of a concern among companies to differentiate themselves from their competitors in terms of service, within an industry widely acknowledged to hold minimal differences between products across competitors.

Several conditions have combined to bring some consideration of quality within management's gaze. These include increasing levels of competition following a growing deregulation of the industry since the late 1960s (for example, the events surrounding 'Big Bang', the Building Societies Act, 1986, and the Financial Services Act, 1986), continuing into the 1990s with intensified merger and takeover activity, the breakdown of trade barriers within the Single European Market, and a general expansion of international competition. Together with a number of legislative interventions in social policy in the home market, and the consequent devolution of a greater degree of responsibility for personal welfare to the individual in the 1980s (for example, the Social Security Act, 1986), these factors have served to accelerate and sustain an increasingly competitive market-place both for companies and for personal financial services products.

More specifically, but to varying degrees, financial services companies have come to regard the interaction of employees, both with one another and with external customers, increasingly as a major new source of cost control and profitability. Here we fall in line with the argument of Fuller and Smith (1991) in suggesting that there has arisen a greater dependence on staff to provide what could be described as 'quality service work' (also Austrin, 1991: *passim*). It is here that we see a second point of specific linkage between the quality dialogue and HRM. Our earlier point likened HRM to quality management, where both aim to expose workforces more directly to the language of the market, to improving or sustaining corporate profitability, and in the emphasis on staff as a productive commercial resource. In addition, we regard the language and practices of HRM as especially significant in the 'reliance' on people to implement 'quality' and to deliver a quality service.

At one level, this debate on the links between quality and HRM could be seen as referring purely to the set of interactions between staff and managements, or within and between staff themselves at the customer–company interface in discussions about service quality (see, for example, Lewis, 1989; Sheehy, 1988; Gronroos, 1984), the importance of which for financial services was signalled earlier. But at another level, where quality extends to those relations between staffs throughout the layers in an organizational hierarchy, and where 'customers' are as much internal to the organization as outside of it, then the significance of 'quality service work' is even more central. Quality management implicitly relies on employees to use their skills instrumentally in the service of the organization; to give 'quality labour' and to be able to 'perform' on demand (Fuller and Smith, 1991). Thus an additional linkage between quality management and HRM concerns the degree of engagement of staff, not only with the results of their labour in output terms, but with its content as personally meaningful and significant.

In its treatment of the human resource, on the one hand, as a *human* and, on the other, as a *financial* asset, HRM parallels the contradictory assumption of employees as active in relation to the content and simultaneously passive with respect to the design and adoption of quality programmes that was discussed earlier. As a human resource, employees are seen as valuable for their interpretive powers – precisely the traits that are undermined or made subservient to balance-sheet criteria when the human resource is seen to be a financial asset. Where links between quality and human resource management are evident, this tension further multiplies the difficulties of convergence or integration.

## CONCLUSION

Because of some of the self-contradictory tensions that we have outlined in this chapter, it is our view that quality management may promise more than it can deliver. While these tensions derive largely from a limited conception of social and organizational relations that is evident in the designs of those who advocate quality management, they are exacerbated by the managerialist mode through which quality is implemented in organizations. As we have argued, they are also a reflection of the implicit, yet contradictory, assumptions about human behaviour that underlie quality programmes. For though the employee is expected to submit unquestioningly to quality programmes as management policy, in terms of concepts of empowerment and continuous improvement, the demand is for an actively engaged subject.

Recognizing the need for further empirical fieldwork to shed light on these issues, we question whether 'new' managerial discourses offer deliverance from the mundaneness of routinized work, or further distance employees from it. Moreover, an additional question is the extent to which these philosophies have the effect of sustaining managerial belief in the validity of their own competencies. Far from transforming workplace cultures and employee 'motivation', 'quality' and HRM may be seen to provide management with a range of what are held to be expertises, that not only generate the illusion of controlling uncertainty, but restore legitimacy for managerial privilege and authority.

For those managers who are retained, the rise of such initiatives as quality and HRM creates yet another landmark or watershed for delineating those who will 'succeed', as distinct from those who will not. Given the precariousness of their position, managers are thus as much concerned to sustain the definition of their work as involving expert knowledge, as they are publicly preoccupied with articulating their conversion to the central tenets of the quality and HRM philosophies. Clearly, then, the self-disciplinary effects of 'new' managerial discourses may be more intense for management than the workforce on whom they are often targeted (see also Webb, this volume, for discussion). Because of their visibility, middle managers are particularly vulnerable in the absence of claims to specialist expertise. Fearing to be, so to speak, left behind in a climate where 'quality is all', we may speculate, nonetheless, on the degree to which, although mouthing its incantations, they will respond to the call to think and feel quality in any more engaged a manner than their subordinates.

## NOTES

1 This analysis is peculiarly Anglo-centric, since new managerial initiatives such as TQM did seem to follow the period when management through collective bargaining had begun to diminish partly as a result of the declining power of unions and the rise of unemployment. In other countries where union power had never reached the levels prevalent within British industrial relations in the 1960s and had not, thereby, been the subject of government attack, the new management initiatives may have been part of the process of dismantling collective opposition to change and flexibility.

2 Predominantly that part of the literature which the British Quality Association (see Wilkinson *et al.*, 1992: 23) describe as focusing on 'soft' qualitative issues or, at least, on a mixture of 'soft' and 'hard' issues.

# REFERENCES

Alpander, G. (1982) *Human Resources Management Planning*, New York: AMACOM.

Armstrong, M. (1988) *A Handbook of Human Resource Management*, London: Kogan Page.

Atkinson, J. (1984) 'Manpower Strategies for the Flexible Firm', *Personnel Management*, August, 28–31.

Austrin, T. (1991) 'Flexibility, surveillance and hype in New Zealand Financial Retailing', *Work, Employment and Society*, 5 (2), 201–21.

Beer, M., Spector, B., Lawrence, P., Quinn Mills, D. and Walton, R. (1984) *Managing Human Assets*, New York: Free Press.

Boaden, R. and Dale, B. (1993) 'Managing Quality Improvement in Service Industries', unpublished working paper, Manchester: School of Management, UMIST.

Boaden, R.J., Dale, B.G. and Polding, M.E. (1991) 'The Management of Quality within a Major Bank', presented at the Workshop on Quality Management in Services, European Institute for Advanced Studies in Management Conference, Brussels, May.

Brown, S.W., Gummesson, E., Edvardsson, B. and Gustavsson, B. (1991) *Service Quality: Multidisciplinary and Multinational Perspectives*, Lexington MA: Lexington Books.

Burawoy, M. (1979) *Manufacturing Consent*, Chicago, IL: Chicago University Press.

Crosby, P.B. (1979) *Quality is Free*, New York: McGraw-Hill.

Crosby, P.B. (1984) *Quality without Tears*, New York: McGraw-Hill.

Dale, B.G. and Plunkett, J.J. (eds) (1990) *Managing Quality*, Hemel Hempstead: Philip Allan.

Dawson, P. and Patrickson, M. (1991) 'Total Quality Management in the Australian Banking Industry', *International Journal of Quality and Reliability Management*' 8 (5), 66–76.

Deal, T. and Kennedy, A. (1982) *Corporate Culture*, Reading, MA: Addison Wesley.

Deming, W.E. (1982) *Quality, Product and Competitive Position*, Cambridge: Mass: MIT Press.

Du Gay, P. and Salaman, G. (1992) 'The Cult(ure) of the Customer', *Journal of Management Studies*, 29 (5).

Feigenbaum, A.V. (1972) *Total Quality Control*, New York: McGraw-Hill.

Fombrun, C., Tichy, N.M. and Devanna, M.A. (1984) *Strategic Human Resource Management*, New York: Wiley.

Fuller, L. and Smith, V. (1991) 'Consumers Reports: Management by Customers in a Changing Economy', *Work, Employment and Society* 5 (1), 1–16.

Goodstadt, P. and Marti, R. (1990) 'Quality Service at National Westminster Bank – The Continual Striving for Excellence', *International Journal of Quality and Reliability Management*, 7 (4), 19–28.

Goldsmith, W. and Clutterbuck, D. (1985) *The Winning Streak*, London: Penguin Books.

Gronroos, C. (1984) *Strategic Management and Marketing in the Service Sector*, London: Chart Bratwell.

Guest, D. (1987) 'Human Resource Management and Industrial Relations', *Journal of Management Studies*, 24 (5), 503–21.

Guest, D. (1990) 'Human Resource Management and the American Dream', *Journal of Management Studies*, 27 (4), July, 378–97.

Habermas, J. (1975) *Theory and Practice*, London: Heinemann.

Harvey, D. (1989) *The Condition of Postmodernity*, Oxford: Blackwell.

Hendry, C. and Pettigrew, A. (1990) 'Human Resource Management: an Agenda for the Nineties', *International Journal of Human Resource Management*, 1 (1), 17–44.

Hill, S. (1990) 'Why Quality Circles Had to Fail, But TQM Might Succeed', London School of Economics (mimeo).

Hill, S. (1991) 'How Do You Manage the Flexible Firm? The Total Quality Model', *Work, Employment and Society*, 5 (3), 397–415.

Howcroft, J.B. (1991) 'Customer Satisfaction in Retail Banking', *The Service Industries Journal*, 7 (1), 11–17.

Imai, M. (1986) *Kaizen: the key to Japanese competitive success*, New York: Random House Books.

Ishikawa, K., (1985) *What is Total Quality Control? The Japanese Way*, Englewood Cliffs, NJ: Prentice-Hall.

Juran, J.M. (1979) *Quality Control Handbook*, New York: McGraw-Hill.

Juran, J.M. (1981) 'Is Japan Cornering the Market on Product Quality?', *International Banking*, 36, January, 22–5.

Keat, R. and Abercrombie, N. (eds) (1991) *Enterprise Culture*, London: Routledge.

Keenoy, T. (1988) 'HRM: A Case of the Wolf in Sheep's Clothing?', *Personnel Review*, 19 (2), 3–9.

Kerfoot, D. and Knights, D. (1992) 'Planning for Personnel? – Human Resource Management Reconsidered', *Journal of Management Studies*, 29 (5), September.

Lash, S. (1990) *The Sociology of Postmodernism*, London: Routledge.

Lash, S. and Urry, J. (1987) *The Decline of Organised Capitalism*, Oxford: Polity.

Legge, K. (1988) 'Personnel Management in Recession and Recovery: a Comparative Analysis of What the Surveys Say', *Personnel Review*, 17 (2), 1–72.

Legge, K. (1989) 'Human Resource Management: A Critical analysis' in J. Storey (ed.) *New Perspectives on Human Resource Management*, London: Routledge.

Lewis, B. (1989) 'Quality in the Service Sector: A Review', *International Journal of Bank Marketing*, 7 (5), 4–12.

MacDonald, J. and Piggott, J. (1990) *Global Quality: the New Management Culture*, London: Mercury.

Noon, M. (1992) 'HRM: A Map, Model or Theory?' in P. Blyton and P. Turnbull (eds) *Reassessing Human Resource Management*, London: Sage.

Oakland, J.S. (1986) 'Systematic Quality Management in Banking', *The Service Industries Journal*, 6 (4), 193–204.

Oakland, J.S. (1989) *Total Quality Management*, London: Heinemann.

Peters, T. (1987) *Thriving on Chaos*, London: Pan Books.

Peters, T. and Waterman, H. (1982) *In Search of Excellence*, New York: Harper & Row.

Piore, M. and Sabel, C. (1984) *The Second Industrial Divide: Possibilities for Prosperity*, New York: Basic Books.

Porter, M. (1980) *Competitive Strategy: Techniques for Analysing Industries and Competitors*, London: Free Press.

Porter, M. (1985) *Competitive Advantage*, London: Collier Macmillan.

Sheehy, B. (1988) 'The Changing Face of the Quality Debate: Balancing Product and Service Quality', *National Productivity Review*, 7 (2), 169–72.

Smith, S. (1988) 'Ten Compelling Reasons for TQM', *The TQM Magazine*, October, 291–4.

Storey, J. (ed.) (1989) 'Introduction: from Personnel Management to Human Resource Management', *New Perspectives on Human Resource Management*, London: Routledge.

Storey, J. (ed.) (1992) *Developments in the Management of Human Resources*, Oxford: Blackwell.

Sturdy, A. (1992) 'Clerical Consent: Shifting Work in the Insurance Office', in A. Sturdy, D. Knights and H. Willmott (eds) *Skill and Consent*, London: Routledge.

Tichy, N., Fombrun, C. and Devenna, M.A. (1982) 'Strategic Human Resource Management', *Sloane Management Review*, 23 (2), 47–61.

Wilkinson, A., Allen, P. and Snape, E. (1991) 'TQM and the Management of Labour', *Employee Relations*, 13 (2), 24–31.

Wilkinson, A., Marchington, M., Goodman, J. and Ackers, P. (1992) Total Quality Management and Employee Involvement', *Human Resource Management Journal*, 2 (4), 1–20.

# INDEX

*Note*: Abbreviations are used as in the text. Page numbers in **bold** type refer to **figures**. Page numbers in *italic* type refer refer to *tables*.

accountability 17, 24, 92, 129, 134, 144–5, 147; *see also* lateral accountability
accounting 25, 138; numbers, 129, 135, 136–7, 142–3, 146–7, 149–50; systems 128–9, 135–6, 140, 150; *see also* surveillance
Ackers, P.: *et al.* 158; (Wilkinson, A. *et al.*) 11, 109, 157, 158, 225, 229
Albion Spirits (AS) 109, 110, 119–22, 123
Allen, P. (Wilkinson, A. *et al.*) 15, 50
Allen Wallis W. 61
Armstrong P. 13, 100–1
ARTOS TQM 181–2
assessment 45
audit 23, 91–2, 102
Audit Commission 91, 92, 96, 97
Australia 26–7, 174–5; *see also* Pirelli Cables
Australia for Quality Campaign 26, 174
Australian Organization for Quality Control (AOQC) 175, 176
Australian Quality Council (AQC) 175, 176
Australian Total Quality Institute (TQMI) 175–6

automated guided vehicles (AGVs) 169
automotive components 24–5, 41–7, 70, 78–9; *see also* Component
autonomy 24, 124, 128–9, 135, 160, 223–4
awards: quality 38–9, 61, 176

backsliding 49
bancassurance networks 223
bank business units 225–6
Bank, J. 107, 108
bargaining systems 100
Beynon, H.: and Nichols, T. 164
Binns, D. 6, 17
bonus systems 91
Boynton *et al.* 6
Bradley, K.: and Hill, S. 68
British Institute of Management 196, 197, 214
British Quality Association 38, 156, 237
British Telecom 73
BS 5750 71, 92
BSI (British Standards Institute) 71
budgets and budgeting 128, 135–7, 143; devolved 90
bureaucracy 9, 28, 55, 224
Business Process Re-engineering (BPR) 9–10, 29

Button, Senator John 175
buyers 119

Callon M., 150
capitalism 13–14, 21, 221–2
car components *see* automotive
    components
car plants *see* motor industry
career role 207–8
central government 92
chemical industry 79
choice 93
Citizen's Charter 77, 82, 87, **93**, 93
citizenship concept 83–4, 93
Civil Service 89, 90, 91, 95
co-determination 163
Cochrane, A. 100
commitment 8–9, 40, 49, 159
communication 180, 181, 184, 187
community care 100
*Competing for Quality* (1991) 76
competition 69, 73, 76, 95, 158,
    197, 221
complaints procedures 88
Component 131–45
components *see* automotive
    components; precision
    engineering components
    manufacturer
computer systems industry 24,
    109–22, 122–5
conflict 13, 74, 75, 183–6, 212–13
Conservative Party Manifesto
    (1992) 77
consultancy groups 174
consumer demand *see* customer:
    demands
continuous improvement *see*
    improvement: continuous
contracting out 22, 88, 91
contracts 87, 88, 96, 99–100, 102
control 34, 35, 87–8, 100–1, 102,
    181
Cooper, R. 138, 142
Corrective Action Teams (CATs)
    163
cost centre managers 95
costs 63, 96, 138, 147, 234; *see also*
    standard costing

Cressey, P. (Eldridge, J. *et al.*) 159
crises 34
Crosby, P. 3, 57, 63, 66, 161, 162
cross-functional management
    9–10, 157
cultural change 21, 39; and TQM,
    36, 38, 40, 49–50, 65, 66, 177
cultural pluralism 26–7, 176–86,
    190
customer: demands 72–3, 114,
    141, 222; feedback 116; public
    services 92–3, 102;
    representation 139–41;
    responsiveness 105, 109–22;
    service 67; 'sovereign', 105;
    Telewave Electronics 113–15; *see
    also* internal customer
customer care 38, 97, 98, 105
customer–supplier chain 15, 21,
    24, 56, 58–9, 61, 77, 123
'cycles of control' (Ramsey) 34,
    35

Dale, B.: and Cooper, C. 1; and
    Lascelles, D. 72; and Plunkett, J.J.
    7–8, 16
Dawson, P.: and Webb, J. 11
decentralization 44, 52, 94, 98, 128,
    223
decision-making 43–4, 51, 52,
    156–7, 165; financial sector 224,
    227–8; PCAL 180, 184
decoupling 151
delayering ideology 52, 95, 149,
    232
Delbridge, R. *et al.* 107
delegation 128, 129, 146, 224, 225;
    Component 133, 135
Deming Prizes 61
Deming, W.C. 3, 5, 7, 12, 36, 37,
    56, 174; on cultural change 38;
    Japan lectures 61; on quality
    management 60–1
democracy: industrial 163
denationalization 73
Department of Trade and Industry
    (DTI): British 70, 72
development timetables 116–17

DHSS (Department of Health and Social Security) 92
discourse notion (Foucault) 138, 145, 150
disempowerment 160
distance 133–4, 135, 137
dualism: organizational 23, 34, 35, 36

economies of scale 138
education 86, 87, 90, 95, 102; *see also* qualifications; training
efficiency 46, 94, 96–7
Eldridge, J. *et al.* 159
employee empowerment *see* empowerment: employee
employee involvement/ participation 11–12, 14, 15, 18, 20; financial sector 225; PCB Electronics 164–9, 170; power-centred 26, 170; public services 98–9; task-centred 26, 168, 170; and TQM 8–9, 25–6, 44–5, 51–2, 156, 157–8, 159
employees: as internal customers *see* internal customer
employment *see* work
empowerment 58, 59, 74–7, 83, 93; employee 11–12, 17–18, 28, 66, 99, 130; financial sector 224–30; PCB Electronics 165, 170; and TQM 73–6, 159–69
enrolment 148–9
Enterprise Australia (EA) 175, 176
Enterprise Initiative (1989) 71
enterprise rhetoric 14, 105, 124
Error Cause Removal (ECR) 163
ethnicity 27, 187–8, 190–1
'evaluative state' (Henkel) 101–2
exploitation 21–2, 24, 26

factory closure 166
factory floor *see* shop floor
faith and politics 10–11
Family Health Servive Authorities (Audit Commission 1993) 96
Federation of Australian Radio Broadcasters (FARB) 174
feedback 116, 180

Feigenbaum A. 61
financial sector 28, 72, 219–40
Fisher, J. 78
fitness for the market 73
fixed-term contracts 99–100
flexibility 198, 228
flexible manufacturing systems 158, 161, 165
Foa, P.: and Foa, U. 84–5
fold: quality as 138–9, 141–3, 146, 147
Foley Report (1987) 175
Ford, Henry 5
Fordism 74
Ford 78–9
foremen 62, 201–2
Foucault, M. 150, 151, 169, 170
front-line workers 97–8
Fuller, L.: and Smith, V. 234
funding: education/training 205–6

Gaebler, T.: and Osborne, D. 102
globalization 222
GM (General Motors) 68
Goffee, R.: and Scase, R. 13
Goodman, J.: (Ackers, P. *et al.*) 158; (Wilkinson, A. *et al.*) 11, 109, 157, 158, 225, 229
Gramsci A. 74–5
grant-maintained status (schools) 89

Hamper, B. 68
Haslam, C. (Williams, K. *et al.*) 79
Hatherly, D.: and Munro, R. 129, 139
Hawke, Bob 174
Hawkey, P. 83
health service *see* NHS (National Health Service)
hegemony 74–6, 79, 168
Hewlett-Packard 69
hierarchies 10, 12–13, 20, 66, 89, 183, 215; flattening 198, 220, 224
high-trust relationships 177, 181
Hill, S. 107–9, 122, 127–8, 157, 172, 197; and Bradley, K. 68
Hochschild, A.R. 98

Hofstede, G. 178
Homeloans 226–7
housing provision 90
Huczynski, A. 8
Human Resource Management
  (HRM) 10, 28, 230–35, 236

identity 131, 136, 143–5
improvement 36–7, 45–7, 48–9;
  continuous 3, 6, 8, 9, 39–40, 56
independent status 89
indoctrination 21–2, 50
industrial relations 27, 194–218;
  and workplace cultures 211–14
inefficiency see waste and
  inefficiency
information services 121–3
information technology 85, 169,
  170
infrastructure 157
innovation 13, 47
inspection 91–2, 102
interaction 234
internal customer 4, 6, 14–15, 37,
  73, 106; financial sector 228;
  PCB Electronics 165
internal market 6, 55, 56, 73;
  Albion Spirits 120–2; financial
  sector 228; Midas 116–18; public
  services 82–104; Telewave
  Electronics 112
interviews 148
Investors in People Initiative 97
Irvin, Bruce 175
Ishikawa, K. 35, 36, 37, 62, 127
ISO 9000 71
issue identification 37–8, 43

Japanese industry 35, 178;
  competitive advantage 4–5, 55,
  64–6, 174; firms in Britain 50
Japanese Union of Scientists and
  Engineers (JUSE) 61–2
Japanization 54–5, 157
job: enrichment 164–5, 196;
  redesign 50; satisfaction 164–5,
  167, 170
job losses 22, 95, 121, 123, 166,

197–8; financial sector 232, 233;
  see also unemployment fear
Johansson, H.J. et al. 9–10
Jones, D.T. (Womack, J.P. et al.)
  78–9
Juran, J.M. 5, 36, 37, 38, 61, 174
just-in-time (JIT) 70, 158, 168

K-Electric 181
Kano, N.: and Lillrank, P. 35
knowledge: distribution of 150

Labour Party 79
Lammers, C. 160
language barrier 27, 187–9, 191
Lascelles, D.: and Dale, B. 72
lateral accountability 25, 129, 139,
  141–2, 144, 146, 148
Latour, B. 140, 148
leadership: effective 11–12, 29
Lillrank, P.: and Kano, N. 35
local authorities 89–90, 90–1, 92,
  95
local government 95
local management of schools
  (LMS) 90

macho management techniques
  167
McHugh, P. (Johansson, H.J. et al.)
  9–10
MacInnes, J. (Eldridge, J. et al.) 159
Major, John 77
Majorism 77
management: at a distance 25, 137,
  145–6; by distance 137, 145–6,
  147, 150–1; by fact 38; by fear
  12; by stress 75, 170; cross-
  functional 37, 157; failure
  183–6; macho techniques 167;
  promotion to 210–11, 215–16;
  public services 82–104; see also
  delayering ideology; hierarchies;
  quality management; total quality
  management (TQM)
managers: Component 132–4; cost
  centre 95; TQM role 24, 42, 44,
  107–9, 127–8; see also middle

managers; plant managers; senior managers; top managers
manufacturing industry 55, 76
Marchington, M.: (Ackers, P. *et al.*) 158; (Wilkinson, A. *et al.*) 11, 109, 157, 158, 225, 229
market *see* internal market
market testing 87, 91
market transactions 58
marketing 117
Marsden, D. *et al.* 69–70
mass production 5–6, 55, 57, 59–61, 65
Massey, A. 90
materials quality 70
Midas 109, 110, 115–19, 123
middle managers 37, 142–3, 146, 149; and quality circles 34, 35, 39, 48; and standard costing 139–41, 142, 143; Component 136–7; public services 95; Telewave Electronics 112; and TQM 24–5, 42, 44, 107–9, 127–8
Ministry of International Trade and Industry (MITI): Japan 64
monitoring 170
Morris, T. (Marsden, D. *et al.*) 69–70
mortgages *see* bank business units
motivation 10–11, 206, 208–11
motor cycles 64
motor industry 69–70, 195, 212; *see also* automotive components
multi-cultural workplace 173–93
multi-skilling 198
Munro, R. 150; and Hatherly, D. 129, 139
Murray, R. 62

Nadler, D. 29
National Council for Vocational Qualifications 204, 208
National Industry Extension Service (NIES)(Australia) 175
National Quality Campaign 71, 72
New Right ideology 55, 56, 59, 64, 222

new training 27, 194–218
'Next Step' agencies (Civil Service) 89
NHS (National Health Service) 74, 79, 88–9, 90, 91, 92, 95
NHS trusts 89, 91
Nichols, T.: and Beynon, H. 164
Nissan: access to 140–1, 150
Noon, M. 10
Normann, R. 84
NVQs (National Vocational Qualifications) 204

Oakland, J. 1, 2, 4, 8, 14, 58, 157
*Observer* magazine 106
office automation companies 40–7, 49
oil refineries 195, 204, 215
Oliver, N.: and Wilkinson, B. 157, 158
one-stop shops 98
organizational change 88–90
Osborne, D.: and Gaebler, T. 102

panopticon concept (Foucault) 170, 171
part-time contracts 99–100
participation *see* employee involvement/participation
participatory formats 159
Pascale, R. 2
Patient's Charter 87
pay and conditions 91, 97, 100, 162, 168, 199, 206, 222
PCB Electronics 25–6, 161–9, 170
Pendlebury, A.J. (Johansson, H.J. *et al.*) 9–10
performance 12, 91, 162, 168; indicators 91, 102; measurement 23, 65, 162, 181
Peters, T.J. 107; and Waterman, R.H. 5, 84
Pirelli Cables Australia Limited (PCAL) 26–7, 174; cable manufacturing plant (CMP) 179, 187; cable processing plant (CPP) 179, 180–83, 187; shop floor comparisons 186–90;

TQM and cultural pluralism 26–7, 176–86, 191
plant managers 139–41, 143
Plunkett, J.J.: and Dale, B. 7–8, 16
politics 10–11, 76–7; –management split 92, 102; and faith 10–11; in the making 131, 145; public services debate 85–7
Pollert, A. 94
Pollitt, C. 7, 73–4, 83
post-modern society 222
power 74–7
precision engineering components manufacturer 41–6
pressure 51, 83, 112, 166, 170
price wars avoidance 221–2
problems 13–14; -solving 37–8, 43, 162, 163, 180, 182
procedures 65, 71
producers, 87
product development 111–12, 116–18, 118–19
production 168–9
profits generation 11–12
pseudo-market 25, 73, 137, 147–8, 166
public services sector 21, 22–3, 73–4, 76; management 82–104
purchaser/provider split 88–9

qualifications 201–8, *203*
quality: definition 56; history and significance 4–11, 130–1
Quality Action Team (QAT) 224–5
quality assurance 54–6, 56–7, 71, 73–4, 92
quality chain 56–9, **57**, 231
quality circles 19, 21, 42–3, 48, 52, 67, 68–9; British 39; British–Japanese comparison 35; financial sector 225–6; Japanese 62; limits 33–6; PCB Electronics 162
quality control 55, 59–65; and mass production 59–61; seven tools of 62, 130
Quality Improvement for the Individual (QIFTI) 163

Quality Improvement Team (QIT) 225, 227
quality management 2–4, 11–15, 15–19, 36–7, 231–2
quality programmes: seductive quality of 221–4
quality service work 234–5
Quality Society of Australasia (QSA) 176
quality of working life (QWL) movement 25, 157–8, 164–9
quality-adjusted life years (QALYs) 86
quasi-contracts 88, 102
quasi-markets 6

R. & D. (research and development) 111–12; *see also* product development
Ramsey, H. 34, 158, 159, 164
rationalization 166
recession 67
reconstruction: post-crisis 58
recruitment 199
redundancies *see* job losses
Rees C. 1–2
Rees, J.: and Rigby, P. 67–8
refuse collection 96–7
regulation 91–2
residential care 90
responsibility 4, 17, 66, 133, 164–5; shop floor 157, 159–61, 168–9
responsible autonomy 160
revolution: quality 6–7, 11, 87–94
Rigby, P.: and Rees, J. 67–8
'right first time' 56, 63–4, 65
Roberts, J.: and Scapens, R.W. 146
Roos, D. (Womack, J.P. *et al.*) 78–9

sales reps 114
Sarch, Y. 106
Scapens, R.W.: and Roberts, J. 146
Scase, R.: and Goffee, R. 13
Schein, E. 40, 177
Seifert, R. 99
self-assessment 45
self-control notion (Juran) 37

self-development 210

senior managers 7, 44, 101, 109, 200; and quality circles 34, 35, 48; Component 134 136–7

service industries 72; *see also* public services sector

Sewell, G. 181; and Wilkinson, B. 55–6, 107, 138, 145, 169

Shewhart, W.A. 59

shop floor: PCAL 180–83, 183–6, 186–90; quality responsibility 157, 159–61, 168–9; re-marking of 142, 146; workers training (Japan) 62

shop stewards 212

skills 27, 194–6, 198, 200

Smith, V.: and Fuller, L. 234

Snape, E. (Wilkinson, A. *et al.*) 15, 48, 50, 196, 214

social institutions 11–13

social services 95

'soveriegn customer' 105

space: creation 145

Sprouster, John 175

staffing reductions *see* job losses

standard costing 136, 137, 138, 139–41, 142, 143

standards 23, 71, 87–8, 92, 102, 169

*Standards, Quality and International Competition* (DTI) 70–1

state: and quality 76–7

statistical approaches 60–1

statistical process control 65, 73, 150

*Statistical Quality Control* (JUSE) 61–2

statistical quality control (SQC) 61

Stinchcombe, A. 100

stress 51, 83, 112, 166, 170

subcultures 178

subjectivity 74–6, 77–8

supervisors 149, 185

suppliers 122; *see also* customer–supplier chain

surveillance 128–9, 135, 137, 143–4, 146–7; paths 25, 138–9; PCAL Cable Processing Plant 180–81; PCB Electronics 169

target costing 138

Taylorism 10–11, 52, 74, 77–8, 83

teamwork 17–18, 45, 156, 180–81, 182

technology: information 85, 169, 170; new 198, 215, 216

Telewave Electronics (TE) 109–10, 110–15, 123

tendering 87, 91, 96, 100

tension 51, 83, 112, 166, 170

Thackray, J. 29

Thurley, K: and Wirdenius, H. 10

*Time* 67–8

top management 7; and quality circles 35–6, 39; and TQM 36, 47, 48, 49, 51–2, 108

top managers 25, 95, 127, 140, 146, 150–1

total quality management (TQM) 1–2, 7–11, 19–24, 54–9, 157–8; Australia 173–5; 'buying into' mechanisms 40; case studies 40–7, 48, 49–50, 109–22, 122–5; as class offensive 21–2; as code of conduct 124–5; components 65–6; in context 196–201; definition 106–7; development 66–74; discussion 47–52; employee empowerment 73–6, 158–69; financial sector 219–20, 223, 224, 228–9; 'hard' and 'soft' 38, 156–7; Japan 54–5, 64–5; in operation 109–22; PCAL shop floor 180–83, 183–6; PCB Electronics 161–9; Pirelli Cables 176–86; potential 33–6, 215; in practice 28, 40–7; theory 36–40; *see also* cultural change; employee involvement/participation; middle managers

Toyota 4

trade unions 27, 78, 206, 212; weakened 167, 168, 213–14, 236–7

Trades Union Congress (TUC) 29, 98–9

training 65–6, 73, 97, 144; new 27, 194–218; PCAL 185; PCB

Electronics 162; public services 97–8

translation theory (Latour) 148

Transport and General Workers Union 78

Tritter, J. 82

trust 100–1, 177, 181

Tuckman, A. 83, 166

Turnbull, P. (Delbridge, R. *et al.*) 107

'ulcer syndrome' 132

unemployment fear 20, 166, 167, 168, 170, 187; *see also* job losses

United States 7, 38, 63–4, 178

vocational qualifications 202–8

volume production *see* mass production

wages *see* pay

Waldegrave, William 82

wartime production 60–1

waste and inefficiency 4, 5, 6, 7, 22, 56

Waterman, R.H.: and Peters, T.J. 5, 84

Webb, J.: and Dawson, P. 11

Western Electric Company: Bell Telephone Laboratories 59–60

Wheeler, W.A. (Johansson, H.J. *et al.*) 9–10

Wilkinson, A.: (Ackers, P. *et al.*) 158; *et al.* 11, 15, 50, 109, 157–8, 225, 229

Wilkinson, B.: and Oliver, N. 157, 158; and Sewell, G. 55–6, 107, 138, 145, 168; (Delbridge, R. *et al.*) 107

Williams, J. (Williams, K. *et al.*) 79

Williams, K. *et al.* 79

Willman, I. (Marsden, D. *et al.*) 69–70

Wilson, D. 29

Wirdenius, H.: and Thurley, K. 10

Womack, J.P. *et al.* 78–9

Wood, S. (Marsden, D. *et al.*) 69–70

work: humanization 25, 157; intensification 22, 164–5, 167–8, 170, 198; organization 94–101; practices 3, 46, 198; relations 13–14; restructuring 94

worker harmony 177, 181

workforce reduction *see* job losses

workplace cultures 211–14

Yokawa 69

Young, J. 69

Zuboff, S. 169, 170